AF855931

Remaking Custom

Jeffersonian America

Jan Ellen Lewis, Peter S. Onuf, and Andrew O'Shaughnessy, Editors

Remaking Custom

Law and Identity in the Early American Republic

Ellen Holmes Pearson

University of Virginia Press | Charlottesville and London

University of Virginia Press
© 2011 by the Rector and Visitors of the University of Virginia
All rights reserved
Printed in the United States of America on acid-free paper

First published 2011

9 8 7 6 5 4 3 2 1

LIBRARY OF CONGRESS CATALOGING-IN-PUBLICATION DATA
Pearson, Ellen Holmes, 1962–
Remaking custom : law and identity in the early American Republic / Ellen Holmes Pearson.
p. cm. — (Jeffersonian America)
Includes bibliographical references and index.
ISBN 978-0-8139-3078-7 (cloth : acid-free paper) — ISBN 978-0-8139-3093-0 (e-book)
1. Law—United States—History—18th century. 2. Law—United States—History—19th century. I. Title.
KF366.P43 2011
349.73—dc22 2010025069

For Michael

Contents

Acknowledgments

A dear friend of mine recently told me that writing acknowledgments was like a "gracious victory lap." Many friends, colleagues, and family members deserve to join me on that victory lap, because they gave me so much support while this project evolved from idea to dissertation to book. I was Jack P. Greene's sixty-ninth doctoral student—we Jackobites keep count—but we were never just a number with Jack. He is a remarkably skilled and patient mentor, and I will always be grateful for his wise advice. His unique ability to cultivate an intellectual community among his students sets an example for all of us. Many years ago, Warren M. Billings of the University of New Orleans recognized some trace of scholarly potential in me, and I thank him for his continued guidance and friendship.

Over the years, many scholars have taught me the meaning of collegiality and professionalism. At a crucial time in my graduate career, Mark F. Fernandez peeled me off the ceiling, made me laugh, and has continued to serve as my "intellectual big brother." At the Johns Hopkins University, the members of Jack's Colonial British America Research Seminar offered many useful suggestions. Michael Johnson's lively seminars always gave me food for thought, and he provided valuable criticism at the dissertation stage as well. Good friends and colleagues Brad Wood, Jeff McClurkin, Matthew Paoni, Michelle LeMaster, Catherine Cardno, Craig Yirush, Emma Hart, and Kelly Schrum helped me to endure the rigors of research and writing. Other Hopkins scholars who shared their expertise with me include John Marshall, Richard Kagan, and J. G. A. Pocock. Akhil Reed Amar, Jack Rakove, and the participants in the Supreme Court Historical Society's 2000 Summer Workshop made helpful suggestions. Donald Lutz, Peter Onuf, Ralph Lerner, and participants in the Liberty Fund's second annual "Camp Constitution" provided spirited and thought-provoking debate over American identity and the Founding. Peter Onuf's mentorship has extended far beyond this conference. He is truly a dude above all other dudes. Charles Goetsch, Esq. of New Haven generously shared his own research with me early in the project. My colleagues at the University of North Carolina Asheville have made teaching, research, and writing a joy. Former History Department chair Grant Hardy and current chair Dan Pierce have offered me invaluable advice and have led by their own scholarly examples. I owe a special debt to Alfred Brophy, Eliga Gould, Kevin Gutzman, Sally Hadden, David Konig, and the late Kathryn Preyer, who read and commented on parts of this work along the way. Warren Billings read the entire manuscript, and Mary Sarah Bilder, bless her, read it twice. It is a better product because of their rigorous criticism.

Several grants and fellowships helped to fund my research for this project. The Johns Hopkins University supported me with teaching, tuition, and research fellowships. The American Historical Association provided a Littleton-Griswold Research Grant, and the Virginia Historical Society supplied a Mellon Fellowship that funded my research in their beautiful facilities. I am particularly grateful to Frances Pollard and the staff of the VHS for their hospitality. I also relied on the kind assistance of Margaret Cook and her staff at the Earl Gregg Swem Library at the College of William and Mary and archivists at the Alderman Library Special Collections of the University of Virginia, the Eisenhower Library at Johns Hopkins, the Library of Congress, the Rockefeller Library of the Colonial Williamsburg Foundation, and the South Carolina Historical Society. Catherine Fields and her staff at the Litchfield Historical Society always welcomed me with open arms and made the very best of lunch companions.

Chapter 1 draws on my earlier essay entitled "Revising Custom, Embracing Choice: Early American Legal Scholars and the Republicanization of the Common Law," in *Empire and Nation: The American Revolution in the Atlantic World*, edited by Peter Onuf and Eliga Gould and published by the Johns Hopkins University Press in 2004. I gratefully acknowledge the Press's permission to republish it. Richard Holway and the staff at the University of Virginia Press have been patient and professional throughout the publishing process. I especially want to thank project editor Ruth Steinberg and copy editor Jane Curran, whose careful review of the manuscript caught ever so many rookie mistakes.

Finally, I thank my family for giving me love and support over the years. My late father-in-law, William Pearson, was particularly encouraging. My father, Mickey Holmes, died while this book was in the final stages of production. I wish that I had hurried a little faster, so that they both could have seen this book in print. My sister, Sara J. Holmes, lent her meticulous touch to early chapter drafts and her unique sense of humor throughout. Brother Eric and my mother, Judy Holmes, took my career leap into academia in stride and continue to tolerate my fascination with people long dead. Over the past twenty-five years, my beloved husband Michael Pearson has kept me sane, fed, happy, and humble. I dedicate this book to him.

Remaking Custom

Introduction

In a footnote buried in the third volume of his *Commentaries on American Law*, retired New York chancellor James Kent paused to outline for his readers the duties of a law book author. The first thing that a law book should do, Kent explained, "is to state the law *as it is*, truly and accurately." If the author was a "lecturer or commentator," then he could be "more free in his observations on [the law's] history and character, and he ought to illustrate it by comparison with the institutions of other countries and ages."[1] It was lucky for historians of the law and American culture that Kent and his colleagues held these convictions, and therefore moved beyond mere descriptions of the law to enter into observations on American law's history, character, and distinctiveness. Through these descriptions and comparisons, the reader can learn about much more than merely the law as it was. This book is about the ways in which the United States' first generation of legal scholars used their lectures and writings to explain American law and its history and character.

At the center of this work is a group of prominent judges and attorneys who felt an obligation to share their expertise by teaching the law and publishing their speeches, law texts, and other works.[2] Other early national law experts compiled their states' court decisions into reports, and published technical and procedural manuals to aid local magistrates, but it is the legal scholars addressed in this book who were willing to provide firsthand commentary on the law's English origins and American adaptations. They had participated in the refashioning of their newly independent polities just after the Revolution, and they used that experience to act as intermediaries between the founders and their audience. Sometimes they interpreted the founders' rationale for changes, and at other times they invented the reasons for change. Their objective was to "state the law" as it was, but as they shared their visions for the new nation's evolving laws and societies, they also made original contributions that helped to shape American identities.

One of the key tools that they used to promote American improvements on English law and government was a legal treatise first published in the 1760s by Sir William Blackstone, entitled *Commentaries on the Laws of England.* In his four-volume work, Blackstone, the first Vinerian Professor of the common law at Oxford, synthesized the work of generations of judges, legal treatise writers, and political theorists and made their principles accessible even to those not schooled in the law.[3] American lawyers received the *Commentaries* enthusiastically. It sold at least one thousand copies before an edition was printed in America in 1771–72, and it went through a number of subsequent editions, abridgements, notes, and analyses. In the absence of American legal treatises and home-grown precedent, late eighteenth- and early nineteenth-century American lawyers and law students turned to the *Commentaries* as a general reference on the common law. American law writers used words like "elegant" and "pure" to describe Blackstone's writing style, and they admired his ability to articulate complicated principles and procedures.[4] For those who pursued the law as their vocation, Blackstone's volumes were inspirational and indispensable. New York Chancellor James Kent claimed to have been so taken by Blackstone's clarity and style while a student at Yale, that immediately upon reading the *Commentaries* he resolved to make law his profession.[5] In 1771, newly minted North Carolina lawyer and future U.S. Supreme Court justice James Iredell wrote that Blackstone "not only brought in the clearest manner the general rules of law," but also revealed "the reasons upon which they [were] founded."[6] Because the *Commentaries* was the most accessible model of English common-law principles that they possessed, Revolutionary-era Americans used it as a legal foundation for their new polities.

Blackstone's pervasive influence on American legal scholarship lingered long after the Revolution. American law practitioners relied on other English law texts in addition to Blackstone, but the *Commentaries* emerged as the central reference point with which to measure the general principles of their laws and constitutions against those of England. The first law professors and legal-treatise writers in the new republic used the English jurist's legal and political principles to teach their students about American law's English heritage. Simultaneously, the treatise served as a handy whipping post for all that Americans considered corrupt or unrepublican in England's laws and Constitution. Scholars used the British legal text to show the ways in which American legal and constitutional framers changed the common law to fit their newly formed polities. These alterations of English models went far beyond mere changes in institutional forms for America. The customs and institutions that they adapted to republican use were part of the Anglo-American cultural fabric.

The early republic's law lectures and legal treatises provide a discreet body of literature that is both descriptive in its depictions of the legal attitudes and practices of the era, and prescriptive in the remedies these legists proposed for what they considered to be their polities' most pressing social and legal problems. Legal treatises were designed as instructional manuals to teach aspiring lawyers the technical and theoretical aspects of the law. They also served as reference works for law practitioners and laypersons who sought information about specific legal questions. The first American treatises tended to mimic Blackstone's organization. Some, such as St. George Tucker's *Commentaries*, were multivolume annotated and appended versions of Blackstone's *Commentaries*. In fact, because he added appendixes that dealt with specific differences between English law and American or Virginia law, Tucker's edition of the *Commentaries* ran to five volumes rather than Blackstone's four. American authors followed Blackstone's lead and divided their works into categories such as the nature of law in general; the structure of government and legal institutions; rights of persons; rights of things, meaning property law; "private wrongs," meaning offenses against individual persons; and "public wrongs," or offenses against the community or the state. Within those broad categories, American scholars treated issues such as the place of the common law in their societies, government institutions and responsibilities, property and inheritance, land and territory, among other issues. Of course, they had to put an American stamp on their products; therefore they often emphasized differences, as well as similarities, between English and American law. Exploring what elements of the law these legal scholars considered most important to their republican governments can help us to understand what innovations they thought already set American law apart, what defects they detected in their new institutions, and what improvements they thought were still necessary for their legal systems.

Exploring legal scholars' visions of American identity requires some understanding of how they defined "republican" governments. At bottom, scholars agreed that a republican government operated under the consent of the people, conducting its business through representative institutions in a manner that protected fundamental rights of citizens. However, depending on their local understandings of this term, scholars interpreted the composition and obligations of republican governments in a variety of ways. Many early American legal scholars argued that colonial American governments always exhibited republican characteristics, which from the very first settlements made the American identity fundamentally superior to that of England. How these ideas of representative government, government by consent, and equality before the law played out on the local level differed from place to place.

I use one other term that requires explanation. In order to provide some descriptive variety, and to situate these learned men in their proper positions as esteemed members of their profession, I have borrowed the English term "legist" from other historians of the common law. This moniker, originally used to refer to experts in ancient or civil law, more broadly means "law expert," or one skilled in the law. All of the men treated in this work were among the most highly respected law practitioners in their polities. They were known beyond their own communities, and the term fits them comfortably.

Most of the law experts featured in this book were locally rather than nationally prominent; therefore a brief introduction may be useful. St. George Tucker was one of the more important figures among America's first law professors and legal treatise writers. A native of Bermuda, he moved to Virginia in 1772 to read law under George Wythe. During the Revolution, he served in the Virginia militia. After the war, Tucker resumed his career at the bar and eventually established himself as a reputable lawyer and judge. In 1790, Tucker replaced George Wythe as the College of William and Mary's professor of law and police. He taught there until 1803, when he accepted a seat on the Virginia Court of Appeals.[7] In the same year that he resigned his post at William and Mary, Tucker published an Americanized edition of Blackstone's *Commentaries on the Laws of England*. He based his edition on his law lecture notes, which consisted of Blackstone's *Commentaries* interleaved with his own comments and appendixes addressing Virginia and U.S. law. The Virginia jurist also included several previously published essays in which he suggested such social improvements for Virginia as a plan for public education and a process by which slaves could be emancipated and relocated.[8] His volumes became a staple, not just in Virginia, but also in lawyers' libraries throughout the new nation.

Another key figure in early American law education was James Wilson, a Scottish immigrant who rose to prominence as a lawyer and statesman in Pennsylvania. He signed the Declaration of Independence, represented Pennsylvania at the Constitutional Convention, and later served as associate justice of the U.S. Supreme Court. Wilson was instrumental in promoting several distinctive features of the federal Constitution, most notably the underlying theory of popular sovereignty. In 1789, while Wilson was still serving on the Supreme Court, the College of Philadelphia's board appointed him as the school's first professor of law. He discontinued his lectures after two winters, but he wrote an entire course of lectures with the intention of publishing them. Professional duties and financial problems prevented him from doing so, and they were not published until 1804, six years after his death.[9]

At a time when few colleges boasted law programs, private law schools were important to the growth of law education in America, and many of these proprietors published law treatises and other key tracts. The most successful of these academies was Connecticut Superior Court judge Tapping Reeve's school in Litchfield. Reeve began mentoring prospective lawyers in the traditional manner, in which lawyers would take students into their offices to "read law." Because of his reputation as an attentive teacher, Reeve found himself with more students than he could handle in his law offices. Therefore, he built a separate building in which to hold his formal lectures, his law library, and his students' moot court sessions. Reeve and James Gould, his protégé and successor, taught over eleven hundred students from 1784 until the school closed in 1833. The Litchfield professors never published their lectures, and most of their manuscript lecture notes no longer exist, but dozens of student notebooks remain. Litchfield students' transcribed lecture notes, with corresponding citations to English and American legal authorities, provide evidence of Connecticut and American legal culture from the 1790s through the 1820s, alongside the legal and social philosophies of the school's two proprietors. In addition to the lecture notebooks, Reeve shared his expertise in two published volumes, *The Law of Baron and Femme* (1816) and *A Treatise on the Law of Descents* (1825).[10]

Other law experts followed Reeve's lead and established proprietary law schools and then subsequently published treatises. Prominent Virginia judges such as Creed Taylor, St. George Tucker's son Henry, and Connecticut's Zephaniah Swift ran law schools in which young men pursued courses of intensive reading, oral examinations, and moot court exercises. Henry St. George Tucker regularly lectured at his Winchester, Virginia, school, but most proprietary law schools did not follow a formal course of lectures. The lack of written lectures and extant correspondence or student notes from these later proprietary schools makes it difficult to distinguish between ideas that teachers passed on to their students and concepts that students gleaned from what were essentially independent reading programs. Some of these proprietary law professors also published treatises, such as Henry Tucker's *Commentaries on the Laws of Virginia* (1826) and Zephaniah Swift's *A System of the Laws of the State of Connecticut* (1795).[11]

Several other noted lawyers and judges also wrote key legal treatises and served as mentors to subsequent generations of lawyers. Pennsylvanians Hugh Henry Brackenridge and Peter S. DuPonceau wrote treatises and delivered orations on American law in which they contrasted various aspects of American law and government with those of England.[12] Nathaniel Chipman, a former student of Tapping Reeve and a prominent Vermont lawyer, statesman, and judge, also authored two legal treatises on constitutional and legal theory.[13] South Carolina judge and planter John Faucheraud Grimké contributed a compilation of laws for his home state as well as a manual for executors and administrators of estates.[14] James Sullivan, judge, attorney, and governor of Massachusetts, published his *History of Land Titles in Massachusetts* while serving as attorney general of that state.[15] Although he never held a judgeship, noted attorney David Hoffman contributed to legal education and the growing body of legal literature by starting a law school at the University of Maryland in 1816. By the mid-1820s, he had published his first two lectures, a syllabus, and a course of study.[16]

The men described above are at the center of this work because they incorporated something of their society's history and character into their law books, but their individual works represented only fragments of American law. The scholar who provided a longed-for synthesis of the new nation's legal principles was New York's James Kent. After reading Blackstone's *Commentaries* as a student at Yale, Kent resolved to study law. He read law and then practiced in Poughkeepsie for a few years before moving to New York City in the early 1790s. Through the patronage of several prominent local lawyers, he eventually established himself as a noted legal scholar and practitioner. In 1794 the board of Columbia College appointed him to the school's first professorship of law, but attendance at his lectures waned quickly. After two years, Kent returned to his law practice and public service. He eventually rose to the post of New York's chancellor and held that position until 1823, when he reached the state's mandatory retirement age of sixty. He returned to teaching but again quickly lost interest. This time, however, he transformed his lecture notes into a four-volume synthesis of American law that he published between 1826 and 1830. Kent's *Commentaries on American Law,* a comprehensive distillation of U.S. law, finally provided U.S. legists with an American rival to Blackstone's *Commentaries.*[17] Although Kent's work still responded to Blackstone's assertions about the common law, in the minds of many American jurists Kent's *Commentaries on American Law* signified a watershed in American legal scholarship.

The publication of Kent's American treatise is a logical place to end my examination of early American legal scholars because, with this comprehensive American treatise, the nation's legal culture seemed to have emerged from England's shadow. This progress toward legal independence was gradual, and certainly it did not end with Kent's treatise. But the process was self-conscious, in that the scholars whose works I discuss understood that they helped to create American identities, and that their work in the law reached beyond merely shaping a unique legal culture. I chose these particular figures in American law precisely because they were local leaders who, in the long run, had a national impact. They also embody the idea that the common law was locally driven; therefore when we discuss the evolution of American identity, we must speak in the plural. American legists shared many ideas about what was American. They communicated with one another, and they read and borrowed ideas from one another's work. But there were also local distinctions that these men's works show us. Their first priorities were their own polities, but at the same time they contributed to the formation of a national legal identity.

We can, in part, determine the impact of these legists' treatises on the legal profession by the frequency of reference to the works in other law books and in the presence of citations to these treatises in early national case law. Members of the community of judges and lawyers who occupied prestigious positions in the late eighteenth and early nineteenth centuries knew—or at least knew of—one another. They served on the bench together, they read and cited each other's works, and they sometimes corresponded to share ideas.[18] It was not unusual to see attorneys and judges citing American law treatises as authority in state and federal cases. Swift's treatise on Connecticut law, for example, appeared regularly in Connecticut's law reports, and a bit further afield, the Tennessee Superior Court reports contain at least one brief reference to this Connecticut treatise.[19] Citations to Tucker's edition of Blackstone's *Commentaries* appear in law reports from states such as Virginia, Tennessee, and Missouri, as well as the U.S. Supreme Court reports. The Virginia judge's *Commentaries* were cited as authority on a number of legal and procedural questions, including questions of race and freedom in the early nineteenth century.[20] After 1828, James Kent's American *Commentaries* was cited in many cases, particularly when it came to procedure and English legal history. He was also frequently used as an authority in cases involving commercial and maritime law.[21]

Although it is harder to measure legal scholars' impact on the lay population, American legal treatise writers subscribed to Blackstone's assertion that even those who did not pursue the law as a profession should understand some fundamental legal principles; therefore they pitched their work to a broader audience. In his introductory lecture to the Columbia law class in 1794, James Kent pointed out that the broad accessibility of political office required that the rudiments of the law should be generally accessible as well. Education in the law was necessary to competent law making and to the performance of civic duties.[22] Even if a citizen did not aspire to public service, there were other reasons to learn fundamental legal principles. Particularly in a republic, St. George Tucker asserted, a citizen's knowledge of the law was crucial, for "in a government founded on the basis of equal liberty among all its citizens, to be ignorant of the law and the constitution" was "to be ignorant of the rights of the citizen." Ignorance, after all, was "the most terrible enemy to liberty, except despotism."[23] Finally, on a more practical level, South Carolina judge John F. Grimké suggested that any man who owned property, anyone such as doctors and clergy who might be called upon to execute a will, and even women who were "occasionally called upon to attend and assist the sick" should know the legalities of making a will.[24] It stands to reason that some lay persons took advantage of these works when the need for legal knowledge arose.

In addition to their legal treatises, early national law experts took advantage of other forms of media that appealed to a broader public. Almost every piece of legal literature provided some measure of social commentary. While multivolume treatises such as Tucker's version of Blackstone's *Commentaries* and Kent's American *Commentaries* provided detail on legal procedure and principles, these scholars also took the opportunity to comment on their polities' problems. Introductions to law digests and reports provided another forum for shorter insights into the social and political priorities of these legists. But their commentary was typically from the perspective of scholarly detachment. Charges to grand juries, public orations, and tracts designed for public consumption provided opportunities for broader commentary on the problems that American societies faced. Zephaniah Swift, for example, used his position as a respected judge to speak on behalf of the nascent abolitionist movement. Hugh Henry Brackenridge's dramatic account of Indian conflict and captivity on Pennsylvania's frontier and other publications in which he aired his opinions about Indians are also instructive snapshots into one jurist's reactions to questions of race, territorial expansion, and possession.[25] These publications offer other avenues for examining how legists dealt with the problems presented by America's unique and changing societies.

As law experts dealt with change, they also appreciated the continuity that they found in their law's colonial roots. English settlers in the New World brought their nation's laws with them, and they believed that their colonial charters gave them access to all of the privileges and protections of Englishmen living in England.[26] On the other hand, colonists adapted English common law to local conditions, utilizing only those parts of the common law that they considered to be necessary to their unique social and economic situations. Early national legists drew upon colonial histories in their articulations of the origins and evolution of the common law within their polities. Their own history lessons, however, sometimes moved into the realm of historical myth as they spun tales about autonomous settlers establishing their colonies without English aid. Colonists' ability to select the laws that fit their own polities, as long as the laws were not repugnant to those of England, allowed them to develop regional differences, but sometimes legal scholars exaggerated the autonomy within which colonial polities operated. They glossed over the parts where English settlers received the economic and legal benefits of membership in a powerful empire. Nevertheless, legal scholars recognized that the common law's ability to adapt to local needs helped them to preserve regional differences among the colonies. Even as they helped to cultivate a national identity around pride in American legal innovations, legists continued to characterize their law on local terms. They recognized the importance of maintaining local diversity and in providing mechanisms for improvement in their local legal cultures.[27]

The following chapters explore the political, constitutional, and social problems that American legists confronted in their writings. The first and second chapters examine the debates over political and legal theories surrounding the common law and constitutional forms. Early national legal scholars had to defend their use of the common law while at the same time debating whether that body of customs was best for their governments. They also spent considerable time explaining, defending, criticizing, and suggesting changes to their polities' constitutional forms and practices. The next three chapters deal with law experts' confrontations with specific problems in the reshaping of American legal identities. Characteristics unique to the United States, such as abundance of land for individual ownership, slavery, and territorial expansion presented opportunities for legal innovation. These innovations, however, sometimes required inventive justifications for injustices toward marginalized peoples. Although much of the book treats these legal scholars within one moment in time, the final chapter considers changes in American culture that, by the 1820s, shifted the place of custom in the nation's legal culture. Law books published during this decade had to negotiate new challenges brought about by increased territorial and commercial expansion.

Legal scholars of the new United States shared a desire to show their students and readers that American law had evolved and was continuing to grow away from that of the mother country. On the other hand, they understood that their legal culture's foundations were English. They addressed the central questions of what elements of English law were relevant to the new republican polities of the United States and what changes or improvements in that law were necessary as they defined the nature of those new societies. They created practical law curricula that combined English legal theory with ideas from the constitutions, governments, and laws of the United States. James Wilson, for one, emphasized the innovations brought into being in the former colonies. Because the principles of the states' constitutions, governments, and laws were "materially different" from those of England, Wilson believed that law practitioners had to be aware of the variations in American and English legal history. However, Wilson was also of the conviction that America's constitutions, governments, and laws were "materially *better*" than those of England.[28] It was up to the law educator to show the next generation of practitioners where Americans had improved upon their English legal inheritance and to help shape legal and social institutions that would enhance the American character.

1 America's Common Law

Custom, Choice, and History Lessons

Anglo-American cultural identity, so tied to custom and an immemorial constitution and law, shaped colonial British American society from the first settlements to the establishment of independent governments and legal systems, and beyond. English law was locally variable in nature, a quality that enabled each colony to formulate customs that suited its peculiar social circumstances and, over time, to harden them into law. This provincial autonomy resulted in a wide variety of local legal systems that even the cohesive force of rebellion and a strengthened federal government could not meld into one "American" law. War and confederation instead helped to sanction the diversity of laws among the united American states, much as they helped to delineate the legal differences between England and its former colonies.[1]

Newly independent Americans looked upon their legal and constitutional innovations as some of the principal cultural advantages that they possessed over the parent country. Individual honor and reputation were central to a man's political success in the early republic. This culture of honor extended to Americans' worries about how outsiders perceived their new nation.[2] Despite impressive economic growth, particularly during the middle and later parts of the eighteenth century, and the increased social sophistication that accompanied this growth, Americans never felt that they measured up to metropolitan standards. During the colonial period, settlers had developed an idealized notion of English society that included images of English superiority in cultural pursuits such as art, education, material wealth, and social graces. Their increasing involvement in English economic activities and political interactions with the center made them painfully aware that their social and cultural institutions were anemic in comparison with those of the parent country.[3] Pre-Revolutionary settlers dealt with these tensions between metropolitan ideal and colonial realities awkwardly. They attempted to erect their own cultural institutions based on English models, while they simultaneously tried to portray their own societies as less corrupt, rather than less sophisticated, versions of the parent country's culture. These notions of cultural inferiority continued beyond the Revolution. But after 1776, and even more so after ratification of the Constitution, Americans could hold out their republican governments as the first step in building a society that promised to contain a national character vastly superior to any already in existence, including that of England. They proudly announced to the world that they had removed all of the corrupting, feudal vestiges of the Norman invasion and restored the English common law to its pre-invasion form.

Despite the parts that they perceived as corrupt, however, Americans knew that England's common law offered a fine template for their own legal culture, and they remained indebted to English precedent.[4] Therefore, leaders of the new polities continued to use the familiar, if cumbersome and outmoded, common law, but they longed for a more orderly system than the English model provided. Common law, with its mysterious origins and generations of precedent, ran contrary to the Enlightenment-era impulse to place all aspects of society into rational categories. But as a product of this same Enlightenment quest for order, Sir William Blackstone's *Commentaries on the Laws of England* provided American legal practitioners with a template that allowed them to implement those reforms that their polities needed, while also retaining those elements of English law that they still deemed practical. Blackstone's work provided the central text from which American legal scholars drew applicable law principles, but it also represented, according to James Wilson, a source of "excellent materials of contrast."[5] Therefore, while Blackstone's work had come to represent how Englishmen differed from others, it could also help Americans explain how they differed from the English. In pointing up these divergences, the early republic's legal scholars reinterpreted the law's character. They reframed the meaning of custom in a common-law culture by adding elements of consent and choice. Moreover, they confronted the question of who owned the common law. Along the way, they sculpted a vision of America as a nation of superior laws, a nation that they believed would realize unsurpassed cultural and social achievements.

Neither the English version of the common law nor Blackstone's *Commentaries* offered a perfect fit for the new American polities. Some of the more dissatisfied legists debated whether they should retain a system of law that was so uniquely English or whether they should scrap the common law for the more orderly and scientific mode of codification, after the fashion of the civil law. By the mid-eighteenth century, even many English judges and lawyers were persuaded that their confusing, unwieldy system needed change. Lord Chief Justice William Mansfield led the first wave of reform in England, which included the establishment of a standardized law reporting system and the creation of a commercial law code.[6] Radical English reformists like Jeremy Bentham agitated for a codification of English law, and some Americans agreed that it was time for Englishmen—and Americans—to reduce their law to a scientific, rational code, styled after the continental Europeans' civil codes.[7]

Few Americans could conceive of abandoning English common law in favor of a different system. Each colony had already molded English law to its own purposes, and the legal systems in place at the outbreak of war with England generally served the states' needs. Americans had to grapple with the question of what parts of English law were still useful to their new governments and what could be jettisoned in favor of republican innovations.[8] Although some revolutionaries wanted a large-scale revision of the laws, most balked at such wrenching change, especially in the light of all of the other upheavals of war and governmental restructuring. Moreover, the immediacy of the crisis demanded quick fixes to legal questions. Full-scale revision of state laws was not high on the agenda of Revolutionary legislatures, most of which tabled proposals for extensive revision until after the war. For example, in 1776 the Virginia legislature charged a committee that included Thomas Jefferson and his mentor, George Wythe, with revising Virginia's laws. The group initially entertained the possibility of abolishing the entire system in favor of a new code of law. However, they eventually concluded that to abrogate their entire legal system and to compose a new code of law after Justinian's example would be too bold a measure and, in the words of Thomas Jefferson, "an arduous undertaking, of vast research, of great consideration and judgment." Such a work would, among other disruptions, render all titles to property uncertain until, "like the statutes of old," the courts could sort out and test every component of the new code.[9] The exigencies of war and the time constraints involved in creating new governments left no time for such luxuries as compiling fresh codes of law.

Their own colonial experiences told revolutionaries that abandoning or retaining the common law was not necessarily an all-or-nothing prospect. Instead of introducing such chaos into their new polities, they opted to preserve the common law and make only those modifications necessary to conform the laws to their republics.[10] In fact, Anglo-American law had undergone a slow evolutionary process from the establishment of the first settlements. Although some post-Revolutionary changes could be deemed radical, many of these modifications merely involved official sanction of practices that were in effect before the Revolution.[11]

American professors and legal writers also followed Blackstone's practice of dividing the law into *lex scripta* and *lex non scripta*, or written and unwritten law. The English jurist explained that unwritten law included general customs common to the entire country as well as "*particular* customs" and laws valid only in certain localities within the kingdom. In ancient times, according to Blackstone, all laws were "intirely traditional" and transmitted orally. By the eighteenth century, one could find these laws in the country's court records, but because of the local nature of these oral traditions, variations in custom still existed from place to place.[12] Written law, on the other hand, consisted of the statutes, acts, and edicts enacted by the King-in-Parliament. Although statutes were the explicit work of a legislative body, rather than the product of ancient custom, Blackstone assured his readers that they were not independent of the common law. Instead, they either upheld a portion of the common law or they remedied a defect within the common law. Therefore, the King-in-Parliament saw fit to enact a statute to revive certain customs that had fallen into disuse, to fix a flaw in the common law that resulted from change of time and circumstances, or to remedy the "mistakes and unadvised determinations of unlearned judges."[13]

In the decades before and after the Revolution, Anglo-American legislatures made or modified law only in those cases when the construction of a law was not applicable to the circumstances of a government or people, or if a practice had become absurd or outmoded. According to James Wilson, statutes were only a small proportion of Pennsylvania's laws, and they should be "considered as a supplement" to the "most important part of her system of jurisprudence," the common law.[14] American legists generally subscribed to the idea that the less a legislative assembly interfered in the workings of the common law the better. One Litchfield, Connecticut, Law School student quoted professor James Gould's insistence that "every sovereign state in order to have any national system of jurisprudence must have an unwritten law . . . for the stat[ute] or written law" could not "afford a rule for every action," nor, in Gould's opinion, could any statute "furnish rules sufficient to give notice in one single & the most simple case imaginable." Replacing the common-law form with legal codes would, in Gould's opinion, leave no resources with which to fill in the gaps between statutes, and such a lack would cause "difficulties in infinitum."[15] The flexibility of unwritten law must exist to balance rigid statute law, according to Gould and many of his contemporaries.

Perhaps most importantly, despite their animosity toward the English government, American revolutionaries were convinced that the common-law system was the best in the world, because it had evolved, from time immemorial, into an institution that combined "in the most exalted degree the attainment of human rights with the least possible inconvenience & delay."[16] Much of this unwritten Anglo-American law derived its authority from immemorial usage and long-standing local custom. To overstate the importance of custom to English social and legal cultures is difficult. The idea that the English common law was born out of immemorial custom was deeply ingrained in the English consciousness, and the common law's ability to endure across the ages was a source of great pride for Englishmen. Habitual usage was, to the English mind, the most perfect litmus test of a regulation. If a practice could hold up to years of use without rejection by the governed, it carried considerable legal authority among the English. Americans shared English pride in their common legal tradition, and they too emphasized the importance of custom, particularly in giving substance and strength to a constitution and law seemingly without beginning.[17]

The idea of an ancient, unwritten law was so much a part of Anglo-American culture that it was difficult, if not impossible, for many to imagine living without it. Decades after the Revolution, Americans' attachment to the common law was still strong. In an 1824 address to the incoming law students at the College of Philadelphia, French-born lawyer Peter DuPonceau stated that the common law was "interwoven with the very idiom that we speak . . . we cannot learn another system of laws without learning at the same time another language." He called the common law "a metaphysical being," grown out of feudal customs that had gradually "become incorporated and in a manner identified not only with the national jurisprudence, but, under the name of *Constitution*," with America's government. DuPonceau's inclusion of elements of the common law within "every civil and political institution, and every thing connected with the government of the country," stretched the common law's influence into the daily lives of every American citizen.[18] Pennsylvania jurist and law professor James Wilson conceded that the ancient laws and customs of England were "not only good, but the very best."[19] Therefore, instead of replacing them, the revolutionaries chose to retain the common law's fundamental principles, along with the various modifications they had made over the years to fit the needs of their respective colonies. From this template, they could make further changes to fit their newly independent polities.

The decision to retain common law was a mixed blessing for America's legal scholars. The system was familiar, but English treatises on the common law were inadequate for American use. Blackstone, for example, was accused of providing too general a survey of law to serve as much more than an introduction to the legal profession. St. George Tucker feared that the American law student, instead of diligently studying all other essential books of legal learning, would read the *Commentaries* three or four times and then believe himself "a thorough proficient in the law." Although one of American law's virtues was its simplicity, Tucker believed that as American law rapidly grew more sophisticated, learning it would take considerably more time and effort. Tucker warned that while the *Commentaries* was a "methodical guide . . . in apprizing the student of what the *law had been*," the student had to look elsewhere to find information on what the law had become in England's former colonies.[20] David Hoffman, professor of law at the University of Maryland in the 1820s, referred to Tucker's admonitions about the limitations of the *Commentaries* in his own lectures. He called Blackstone's work "only a bird's eye view of this various, extensive, and complicated science," presenting "nothing beyond the mere rudiments of English law."[21]

Blackstone's work was certainly a valuable source of English contrast as Americans continued to refine workable legal structures for their localities. But America's legal scholars knew they would have to supplement Blackstone with American materials. Therefore, they combined the disciplines of history, law, and politics in their lectures so that they could articulate to their students the origins and evolution of the common law within their states and their nation. Each colonial settlement had adapted English common law independently of the other colonies, resulting in as many different kinds of common law as there were British colonial polities. After Independence, these distinctive versions of common law continued to evolve as each state built its own form of republican government. Once they became an independent confederation of republics, the former colonies had to redefine common law to fit new republican parameters. To complicate matters further, the different manner and pace in which each colonial polity evolved meant that each new state's jurisprudence was to some degree distinctive and peculiar to its jurisdictions. This situation lent itself to innumerable variations in the ways legal scholars in the country's regions presented the common law and its American modifications to their students and readers.

II

Once they had explained to their audience why the founders decided against scrapping the English common-law system in favor of a distinctive American legal system, legists had to defend this choice against arguments that America could not lay claim to the common law. For some leaders on both sides of the Atlantic, America's claims to common-law protections posed problems. Even before their break with England and the decision to keep common-law principles at the center of their law, American legists felt compelled to respond to English critics who raised doubts about the common law's authority in the new nation. The first U.S. law professors and legal treatise writers had participated in the Revolution and in the decision to retain common-law principles in their respective polities. They were determined to assert their nation's right to adapt the common law to their own societies. Ten, even twenty years after Independence, some of them still seemed unduly preoccupied with defending the former colonies' decisions to retain the common law against lingering questions about the common law's authority in America. In lectures, speeches, and treatises, they repeatedly revived these arguments over the legitimacy of American common law. To illustrate their points, legists gave their students and readers lessons in British and Anglo-American colonial history. They replaced English versions of the common law's ancient history with their own interpretations to assert their right to England's legal principles; then they used histories of the common law in Anglo-America to show how it was best applied and administered on the local level, thus making it an ideal set of principles for a socially and economically diverse nation.

On the surface, this persistent compulsion to defend the former colonies' rights to English common law may seem odd, particularly after 1783, when British recognition of American independence effectively ended the possibility that Britain might mount an assault against the former colonists' rights to adopt common law. But upon closer scrutiny, these history lessons were not just about the law. Legal scholars used them for a variety of cultural, political, and practical purposes. First, they used these lessons to reinforce the idea that American law should remain rooted in common-law principles. As practitioners as well as scholars of the law, they understood that maintaining common-law foundations was the most efficient way to allow American law to acquire its own character. Teaching their students about the law's history also helped legal scholars to inculcate professional values in their audience. These historical interpretations served as avenues for legal scholars to lead their audience through the evolution of American common law, while also sharing their visions of America's emerging legal and cultural identities.

Blackstone defined a valid custom as a practice that was of continuous local usage and in existence so long as to make it impossible to remember its beginning. The practice had to be the object of peaceful acquiescence, and it had to bear the qualities of reason, certainty, and consistency. Above all, it had to be compatible with the common law.[22] To some, the notion of an American common law worked against the fundamental principle of the common law's immemorial status. How, critics asked, could places that had been founded within legal memory possess legal systems that were immemorial? To justify America's right to a common law of its own, legal scholars used a variety of creative arguments primarily based on reinterpretations of Blackstone's list of criteria for a legitimate custom.

According to English legal tradition, for a custom to qualify as immemorial it must have existed before the accession of Richard I. Any custom proven not to exist before that period was not truly custom. Under this definition, of course, there could be no custom in the former colonies, because there were no English settlements in those places at the time of Richard I's reign.[23] Litchfield's James Gould dismissed the criterion of "immemorial" existence by responding that, immemorial custom or not, England had no exclusive right to the common-law system. Common sense dictated that a common-law system was the most practical form for colonial British America, and after the Revolution that practical necessity had not changed. He flatly rejected the idea that the American states could have no common law of their own simply because they had no immemorial existence, usage, or custom. This absurd idea, recorded Gould's student Ely Warner, was based on a premise that legists called "*petitio principii*—we cannot because we cannot."[24]

In their lectures Gould and his mentor Tapping Reeve set out to refute the notion that the common law was an exclusive fraternity to which young upstart polities need not apply. They wanted to do away with the idea that a legal system could be secure only if it originated in the mists of time immemorial. To accomplish this objective, Reeve and Gould attempted to dismantle the concept of an immemorial English common law altogether. They argued that if English law really was immemorial, no former British colony could have had a common law of its own but rather was "bound down by the English precedents entirely and indeed to the common Law as it stood before the time of Richard 1st." They called this idea "absurd" because much of the contemporary English common law had, like the American colonies, grown up within the time of legal memory. Law merchant, the law of paraphernalia, and executory devises, for example, all evolved after Richard I had been long dead.[25] Thus, Gould and Reeve asserted that to have valid common law it clearly was not necessary that it should have existed from time immemorial.

Around 1800, upon assuming sole responsibility for the Litchfield Law School's introductory lecture on the American common law, Gould further advanced Reeve's argument that even English common law was not entirely of time immemorial. He taught his students that the rule making the beginning of Richard I's reign the commencement of "immemorial time" had been established only sixty years after Richard's accession. He concluded that because sixty years was sufficient time to establish England's body of fictional, immemorial customs, surely the same amount of time would prove adequate for the establishment of American legal tradition. A Litchfield student paraphrased Gould's lecture in his notebook, stating that "the notion of immemorial usage" was "a mere *fiction*," and that "the common law was built up by *Courts of Justice*."[26] According to Gould, if English law was not truly immemorial, then to require that a distinctive American common law must descend from immemorial usage was "preposterous and absurd."[27]

At the College of William and Mary, St. George Tucker freely admitted that English jurists' narrow definition of "custom" excluded his home state of Virginia from the privilege of owning her own set of customs. But he argued that each Englishman who settled in an American colony brought English legal custom with him to the New World. It was only natural for settlers in need of municipal regulations in their new environment to adopt English law, the system they knew best. Not only did English emigrants import the rights and privileges to which they were entitled as Englishmen, but they also brought with them "that portion of the laws of the mother country, which was necessary to the conservation and protection of those rights." He pointed to the charter of 1584 between Queen Elizabeth and Sir Walter Ralegh in which the monarch promised that every English settler on Ralegh's land, along with their heirs, would enjoy "all the privileges of free denizens, or persons native of England."[28] All subsequent Virginia charters, Tucker claimed, contained the same guarantee, thus making it official both that Virginia settlers came to the New World with their status as Englishmen and full protection of the common law intact, and that they retained by compact with the Crown this protection as their birthright.[29] Tucker's history created a broader definition of Englishness than that of his counterparts across the Atlantic.

One of the more intriguing historical arguments against American possession of any form of English common law was based on the theory of conquest. It boasted an impressive lineage, originating in Sir Edward Coke's reports of *Calvin v. Smith* (1608), also known as *Calvin's Case*. This case involved, among other things, the issue of what parts of the empire were entitled to the protection of English law. In his *Commentaries*, Blackstone used the case to declare that because England gained possession of American colonies by conquest, and English common law had no automatic authority in conquered lands, Americans could not claim the common law's authority. Blackstone included a discussion of the case in all editions of his *Commentaries*, but he expanded on his original treatment in the seventh edition, published in 1775, probably in response to colonial leaders' increasingly strident demands for the rights and legal protections of Englishmen. In the later edition he included more direct references to the American colonies' particular situation, stating that *Calvin's Case* set up two kinds of colonies: those that England claimed through the settlement of a deserted and uncultivated land; and those already-populated lands that England procured through conquest or treaty. If English citizens colonized an uninhabited territory, then all applicable English laws then in being transferred to the colony. If, however, English citizens conquered a land that was already populated and possessed of its own laws, the Crown was entitled to make alterations to existing laws. Until the monarch made these modifications, however, the laws of the conquered country remained intact. Blackstone argued that the English brought America under their rule by conquest of the indigenous people or by treaties, and that English common law, therefore, had "no allowance or authority" in Anglo-America, "they being no part of the mother country, but distinct (though dependent) dominions."[30] This assertion provoked considerable opposition in England's former colonies.

Although Blackstone presented America's acquisition by conquest as a historical fact, the idea was hardly a settled matter when he published his *Commentaries*. Debates over the nature of America's acquisition remained unresolved, and many legal and political theorists on both sides of the Atlantic recognized colonization as a valid mode of acquisition, alongside descent and conquest. Moreover, to suggest origin in conquest was to admit that the United States was, and would always be, under Britain's control and that only Britain's monarch could bestow upon them the right to use the common law. Even after the U.S. status as an independent nation had been determined through a successful revolution, American legists viewed such conquest theories as another way for the English to assert their cultural and political superiority over their former colonies. To maintain their cultural independence, Americans felt compelled to persist in disputing this theory long after the Revolution.

In response to Blackstone's depiction of America as a conquered land, St. George Tucker countered that Virginia, for one, did not come into English possession by conquest. In fact, he argued, the only former colonies fitting the description of a conquered land were New York and New Jersey, which the English took from the Dutch by conquest and subsequent treaty in 1667.[31] The other colonies, however, regardless of mode of acquisition—purchase, conquest, or cession—were not settled by conquered people but rather by "the conquerors themselves, or colonists, settling a vacant territory." Blackstone's claims regarding the status of a conquered territory simply did not apply "to any colony, which was settled by English emigrants, after the Indian natives had ceded, or withdrawn themselves from, the territory."[32] A history lesson that peacefully erased Native Americans from the landscape strengthened the notion that Englishmen had no competition for the land, therefore no conquest was necessary.

Blackstone's discussion of conquest as the mode of acquisition certainly did not sit well with James Wilson. The Pennsylvania jurist asserted that Coke's opinion on *Calvin's Case* did not fit the American colonial situation and therefore that the colonists could legitimately claim all rights and protections of English citizenship. Wilson bristled at the depiction of America as a conquered, and therefore inferior, entity. By whom, he asked, was America conquered? In his version of colonial history, Wilson depicted a confident and independent group of English citizens who, "permitted and commissioned by the crown, . . . undertook, at their own expense, expeditions to this distant country, took possession of it, planted it, and cultivated it." As Englishmen in their own corner of the king's empire, "they grew and multiplied, and diffused British freedom and British spirit, wherever they came." Were these, Wilson asked, countries of conquest?[33] Again, Wilson's story of peacefully settled lands omitted the constant struggles with Native Americans. In light of the conquest theory's assumption that a conquered people accompanied a conquered land, it was in Americans' interest to portray their land as unpopulated or containing an easily removed people.

In their refutations of the conquest theory, Wilson and Tucker used history to defend common law's authority in America on both legal and cultural grounds. American legists viewed conquest theories as another way for England to assert her cultural and political superiority over her former colonies. When they rejected the designation of America as colonies of conquest in favor of a theory of rights by settlement, Tucker and Wilson placed American law on an equal footing with English law.[34] After the Revolution, the notion that Americans had not only adopted but also improved upon English law by taking out the "unrepublican" parts served to diminish lingering feelings of cultural dependence on England. Yet denials of the conquest theory remained in legists' arsenal for future use. Over the next few decades, others took up these arguments to defend the nation's right to common-law protections and to celebrate American common law as an ideal tool for strengthening the authority of local law and thus protecting local interests. It remained important for American legists to communicate to their students that they had fought the Revolution to gain the rights of Englishmen. Once they had made that point, they could begin to show that after Independence, they had improved on the rights of Englishmen and had created distinctive and much broader sets of American rights, privileges, and protections. Legists' discussions of American improvements on English models served to diminish lingering feelings of cultural dependence on England and to strengthen their arguments that American society was superior to that of England.

III

As legal scholars described how American framers improved upon English notions of rights and privileges, they also used Blackstone's interpretation of *Calvin's Case* to re-create a central argument for Independence. They drew a distinction between Blackstonian notions of law as command and American conceptions of law founded on popular consent. Blackstone defined municipal law as a command or "rule of action dictated by some superior being." The language of law was one of obligation, "thou shalt, or shalt not" commit a specific act. Expressing a sentiment that soon became part of the debates over American independence, Blackstone argued that consent of the people did not bind the sovereign originator of the command.[35] While American legists agreed with Blackstone that law was a permanent, universal rule of action obligatory upon the whole community, they disagreed with the English jurist as to the legitimate source of the rule. In contrast to the English monarchical government and hierarchical legal system, Americans rested their governments and laws on the foundation of popular consent. In the words of Zephaniah Swift, law derived its authority from the "universal and immemorial consent of the people."[36]

The importance of consent and choice in America's republics represented key elements in their defenses of common law's local influence and Americans' right to a common law of their own. St. George Tucker illustrated the importance of American law founded on consent with a history lesson on Virginia's seventeenth-century charters. He borrowed the words of other Virginians to assert that when Virginia's first settlers claimed English common law as their natural and conventional right, they "had the authority both of reason and of compact . . . which they had neither forfeited nor waived by emigrating; such emigration being undertaken with the consent and approbation of the parent state."[37] Tucker then turned Blackstone's words of common law and consent to America's favor, quoting from the first volume of the *Commentaries*, in which Blackstone stated that "the common law depends upon custom which carries this internal evidence of freedom along with it, that it probably was introduced by the voluntary consent of the people."[38] In other words, the voluntary consent of the people was all it took for legitimating common-law principles in England. Therefore, even the venerable Blackstone believed that the authority of the English common law in America did not rest on "the ground of an *express adoption* by the *several colonies only*, but upon . . . the mere implied consent and usage of the first settlers."[39] As far as Tucker was concerned, Englishmen boasted no superior right to consent. Certainly Americans possessed an equal right to consent to the common law's authority in America. James Wilson's lectures echoed Tucker's sentiments when he discussed the relationship between custom and consent. The Pennsylvania jurist believed that a long-standing custom carried with it "intrinsick evidence of consent," for long and general custom was founded "on nothing else, but free and voluntary *consent*." To Wilson, consent-based law of such long-standing authority was "a most secure asylum from the operations of absolute, despotick power."[40]

Tapping Reeve and James Gould pushed the idea of America's cultural parity with England another step when they used the history of Connecticut's relationship with the common law to show how the concepts of consent and choice worked together in their republic. They taught that Connecticut's settlers voluntarily imported and adapted the common law from England, and "the concerns of the people were & always [had] been conducted with reference to that law." At the establishment of Independence, however, the common law of England no longer bound Connecticut until the Revolutionary assembly passed a statute making it so. But Connecticut courts adopted only that portion of it that was not "absurd unjust or inapplicable" to local circumstances; therefore, the common law was binding in Connecticut "only so far as it [had] been adopted," and only so far as it fit local needs.[41] Here, Reeve asserted local rights to determine which parts of the common law were best applied to their unique social circumstances.

American legists, however, were not content to rest their adaptations of the common law merely on popular consent. The key to their ability to incorporate English common law into a republican legal system and then to adapt that law to their distinctive republics lay in how they used the concept of choice. Pennsylvania judge and treatise author Hugh Henry Brackenridge, for example, asserted that because they settled the colony as Englishmen, the common law was each Pennsylvanian's birthright. William Penn's charter stipulated that the laws governing his colony would be "by the general course of law in England," until the laws were altered by the proprietors or the freemen of the province. Brackenridge maintained that the wholesale transfer of law from England to Pennsylvania would have been impractical, because law "founded in the nature of colonization" could not carry with it all the regulations of the mother country, "but such only as have *subjects to attach upon*" and that were "not excluded by the change of situation."[42] Americans could choose which laws suited their societies, but they could also reject those laws that did not.

Zephaniah Swift used strong language turning on the concepts of choice and consent when he asserted that Connecticut's first inhabitants "settled this country without the aide of the British crown" and were, therefore, independent from the beginning. They "were under no obligation to obey the government, or observe the laws of the country, from whence they emigrated." They could have instituted a completely different government and legal system, but instead they voluntarily received English laws "by the general consent of the people." After the Revolution the people of Connecticut again faced the choice of abolishing the English legal system or retaining it, and again they chose to keep the system, as far as it was "warranted by reason, and conformable to [their] circumstances." Swift pointed out that since the Revolution, Connecticut courts still studied English judicial decisions when they deliberated on similar questions. While this practice allowed state courts to incorporate English legal improvements in their own law, Swift was quick to add that these English precedents had "no intrinsic authority" in the American republics.[43]

Tapping Reeve elaborated on the importance of choice with regard to which parts of the common law were valid in Connecticut. If the colony's courts or "customs of the people by long establishment" adopted a particular common-law practice, or if the assembly voted to make it part of statute law, only then did it become part of the law in Connecticut. Where applicable, Connecticut officials adopted the common law of England, but they also freely rejected those parts of the law that they did not consider applicable to colonial circumstances. Connecticut courts generally considered common and statute law previous to Henry VIII binding, and all decisions in English courts of common law after that time nonbinding, although American jurists still followed English decisions "when consistent with reason & applicable."[44] Strictly speaking, the common law of England had no authority in Connecticut, but judges and lawmakers over the years chose to adopt certain portions as part of their own law. When deliberating over "novel questions," Connecticut courts often resorted to common-law answers, as "*prima facie* evidence" of what was right. But at the same time, Connecticut courts were "at liberty to examine and reject" those parts of common law that were not appropriate to their locality's governance.[45]

James Wilson used Blackstone's theories about the transfer of the common law to Anglo-America to show that custom and choice worked together to make a more fluid system that accommodated changes in society over time. In fact, Wilson saw custom and choice as parts of the same process, for just as rules of common law were introduced by experience and custom, they could also be withdrawn by discontinuance and disuse. The beauty of the English common-law system, according to Wilson, was that the common law's "accommodating spirit" offered flexibility, and because the common law contained "the common dictates of nature, refined by wisdom and experience," it weathered centuries of invasion and revolution. Yet the common law always kept "the great ends of liberty . . . constantly in view."[46] Thus, according to Wilson, common law easily adapted itself to America's distinctive social needs.

Wilson used Blackstone's words to illustrate the common law's character, but he tailored the English professor's views to fit his own purposes. Wilson's rejection of the theory of America as a colony of conquest in favor of a theory of rights by settlement allowed him to argue for Americans' rights to choose which English laws were applicable to their new polities.[47] As the colonists modified their daily lives to fit their new surroundings, Wilson explained, they also changed their customs. Though they preserved the core of the common law while making revisions to their legal systems, colonists chose to streamline their legal practices to match their simple societies' needs. The common law's flexibility made it easily adaptable to the unique socioeconomic situations each colony faced.

Peter DuPonceau echoed Wilson's admiration for the common law's mutability. Because the common law was more "*malleable* . . . than written codes or statutes," it was well disposed toward constant, gradual improvement.[48] He quoted one of Wilson's charges to the grand jury on the common law's openness to refinement, assuring the reader that any new situations gradually helped the common law to attain "higher and higher degrees of perfection."[49] Maryland law professor David Hoffman effectively captured the common law's flexibility when he wrote that the system had "survived many ages, and many revolutions of manners, and [had] yet been accommodated to them all." This "peculiar" feature allowed the common law to retain "its *form,* while it . . . altered its *spirit*" in order to mold itself to the society in which it functioned.[50]

The common law's mutability gave American legists license to effect improvements they considered necessary to ensure its suitability to republican societies. James Wilson claimed that in so doing, Americans had resurrected a purer form of common law than that of England, bearing "a stronger and a fairer resemblance to the common law as it was improved under the Saxon, than to that law, as it was disfigured under the Norman government."[51] According to Wilson, Americans' elimination of feudal vestiges such as primogeniture and entail allowed a legal system born in an ancient monarchy to fit their new republican governments.

IV Economic, social, and cultural diversity among the American states meant that the nation's republican governments were not cast from the same mold. Yet, the common law could be adapted to a variety of local social and economic circumstances. Legal scholars considered this flexibility an essential quality for their polities and part of their Anglo-

American heritage. Colonial British America was a loosely bound empire with local power centers. The central authority was represented through an imperial constitutional structure, but Americans' colonial experience could be characterized as the evolution of a set of collective local identities. The power for lawmaking began on the local level, and most legists preferred it that way. As each locality absorbed other cultures, its leaders modified laws to suit the circumstances. Collective local experiences helped to shape the character of federal authority. After the Revolution, Anglo-American law was still the common foundation among the states, but deference to local variations and loyalties continued.[52]

The tension between local and federal control over law, however, was a central political issue in the early republic, and St. George Tucker acknowledged that tension in his version of Blackstone's *Commentaries.* The question of power dynamics among local, state, and federal governments had been a central point of debate during ratification of the United States Constitution, and the debates continued into the early nineteenth century. The Anti-Federalists, most of whom later found homes in the Jeffersonian Republican political faction, feared that the Federalist opposition was bent on consolidating power in the U.S. government. Tucker, a staunch Jeffersonian Republican, became particularly defensive of state sovereignty after the Judiciary Act of 1789 established the federal court system and gave the Supreme Court jurisdiction over state court decisions on federal questions. In a series of court cases in the 1790s, federal judges began to assert their authority over state laws when they believed states had overstepped their constitutional bounds. The Judiciary Act of 1801 provided even more reason for Tucker and his political allies to fear federal encroachment, despite the ratification of the eleventh amendment, which gave some protections to state sovereignty. To air his concerns over federal courts' assertion of common-law jurisdiction, Tucker published a dissertation on the history of common law in America in his 1803 edition of Blackstone's *Commentaries.* Tucker borrowed the Revolutionary-era defense of common law's authority in the United States and his Federalist colleagues' ideas about American choice and consent to erect his defense against the encroachment of a federal common law. He used history lessons that emphasized the unique nature of each colony's settlement and growth to reinforce arguments defending the local nature of the common law.

Tucker's writings reflected a concern, shared by his fellow Republicans, that ideas of federal uniformity could be taken too far. He used the history of each colony's distinct social, economic, and cultural development to show how these variations affected the evolution and diversity of American legal cultures. One of the central messages in his lectures on the common law's introduction into America was that one could identify no general theory or process by which the colonies adapted English common law. These variations made application of the common law in each colony "as various as their respective soils, climates, and productions." He used Virginia and New England as examples of the diversity of purpose, circumstances, and development among the colonies. In Tucker's version of colonial history, Virginia, "the most ancient of the British colonies," had been founded as a cooperative commercial venture between Crown and proprietor and enjoyed a harmonious relationship with Crown officials throughout the colonial period. Virginia remained staunchly loyal to England "even to the period when the revolution commenced." This loyalty, Tucker claimed, resulted in Virginia's adoption of a greater portion of the common law and statutes of England than perhaps any of the other colonies. On the other hand, the New England colonies "owed their establishment to that spirit of independency" that originated in their leaders' discontent with the established church and the Crown. Because the circumstances of New England's settlement revolved around a desire for religious independence, Tucker suggested that their propensity toward dissent could extend beyond religion and into government and law as well, making them more likely to improvise rather than adopt English law as extensively as had Virginia. Tucker could not envision how two colonies founded on such "discordant principles" could ever "be assimilated to each other," and he argued that a federal common law could never succeed in bringing such diverse social polities under one uniform umbrella of legal principles.[53]

Tucker next addressed the question of which parts of English law the states abolished or retained upon Independence. He stated that because the colonies rejected the sovereignty of the Crown, all laws securing the dependence of the colonies or respecting obedience to the king and his prerogatives were the first to go. The early state legislatures then turned to modifying, abridging, or annulling any laws that addressed issues of kingly office or government. For Tucker, an important consequence of the Revolution was the instant sovereignty of each state upon declaring independence from England. "From that moment," Tucker asserted, "there was no common law amongst them but the general law of nations, to which all civilized nations conform." Once each state established its own constitution and laws, separate and independent from all other states and all other nations, there were no laws in one state that were obligatory in another. Thus it followed that "although it might produce a general conformity in their municipal codes," the adoption of laws "was the separate act of each state." Each state retained the right to make changes or impose limits or restrictions within their own laws without the interference of any other state.[54] After briefly reviewing the contents of each state constitution with regard to adoption of English common law, Tucker concluded that although the common law had the force of law throughout the union, each state had independently "modified, limited, restrained, repealed, or annulled" the system to fit its own needs. Moreover, any future amendment, repeal, or annulment of common law would be up to the sole discretion of each polity. Because state legal modifications differed, in Tucker's opinion, it would be "altogether a hopeless attempt, to endeavour to extract from such discordant materials, an uniform system of national jurisprudence."[55] In fact, for Tucker, diversity of legal practices represented a natural, even desirable, result in a common-law culture.

St. George Tucker, James Wilson, and their colleagues wanted their students to understand that the English common law was unique expressly because societies could adapt it to their own needs and make it into American common law. They appreciated the honored place of immemorial custom within the common-law tradition, but they used the cautionary tales of ancient feudal corruptions to teach their students that custom could—and sometimes should—be undone. In the American legal tradition concepts of popular consent and popular choice had overtaken the veneration of custom. This shift of emphasis from custom to choice gave Americans the ability to create their own separate traditions and customs, not out of the fog of time immemorial but rather out of the distinctly memorable events of the establishment and development of colonies and the eventual, even more memorable, break with the mother country.

In their discussions about the common law's authority in their polities, legal scholars were not just talking about the law. History lessons about the common law's authority in America proved useful to legists as modes of instruction for a number of political and cultural purposes. Their praise for the common law's ability to adapt to local circumstances was not new. Indeed, that particular characteristic starred in the history lessons of many legal scholars on both sides of the Atlantic, before and after the Revolution.

The difference, for republican legal scholars, was that the common law now operated in their republics as distinctively American sets of legal principles. In James Wilson's law school lectures, delivered twenty years after his attack on the conquest theory, he praised the common law for weathering centuries of invasion and revolution while maintaining the flexibility and "accommodating spirit" that made it the ideal system for America's distinctive local needs.[56] The common law was now making history within the American republics, and the combination of American common law and republican government had created a society that, according to Wilson and his colleagues, was "materially *better*" than that of England.[57] American additions of consent and choice to their common-law traditions gave them a foundation on which to build their own political and legal cultures.

The post-Revolutionary generation of American jurists derived security from the ability to trace the origins of their system of laws back to a solidly visible foundation based on consent, choice, and new customs tailored to the needs of America's vigorous republican societies. Peter DuPonceau, for example, boasted that American legal and political institutions no longer depended on "uncertain traditions, but on the more solid foundation of written compacts."[58] The common law was an important point of reference for legal questions, but early national jurists began to look to it as a means of exercising justice, a system of jurisprudence that rested on the foundation of a written constitution. This tangible source of fundamental law was a novelty to the first generation of U.S. legal scholars, but it would become as much a part of American custom as were their own individual forms of common law.

2 American Constitutions and American Character

Americans made their emphasis on choice and consent tangible when they created their constitutions, which represented some radical departures from their English common-law roots. Revolutionary-era Americans had little desire to form their governments in the English image. After all, they had rebelled against England's ruling institutions. Yet, it was hard for them, even in a state of rebellion, to let go of English political forms. For Anglo-Americans, a constitution was not only a frame of government, but also a firmly entrenched part of their identity and a marker of their polities' character. According to Sir William Blackstone, the English Constitution protected the "absolute rights" of "even the meanest subject" from the arbitrary and despotic power that characterized the continental European monarchies. This "spirit of liberty" was "so deeply implanted" in the English Constitution that it had, over the centuries, protected Englishmen from the inevitable periods of oppression by "overbearing and tyrannical princes."[1] Of course, the legal scholars of post-Revolutionary America did not share Blackstone's confidence that the English Constitution afforded those protections.

Many of the new nation's legal scholars had been involved on some level with the framing of their independent governments. They were obsessed with the question of how the King-in-Parliament could have assumed so much power and therefore set out to teach the new generations of lawyers about the causes and evils of England's oppression. They also emphasized the innovative safeguards built into American constitutions to prevent such a consolidation of power in one branch of government.[2] Though early national legists did not provide many new insights in terms of republican political theory in their treatises and lectures, they continued to help define America's identity by echoing the republican sentiments and principles on which framers had based their new governments.

While they recognized the law and the Constitution's common roots, Americans took a different view of constitutions than the view prevailing before the Revolution. Although England's "unwritten" Constitution actually consisted of a series of documents, such as the Magna Charta (1215), the English Bill of Rights (1689), treatises, essays, judicial reports, oral tradition, and certain assumptions about the rights and liberties of Englishmen, the decentralized nature of England's Constitution created conflicting notions of the Constitution's meanings. This lack of clear understanding was, in part, responsible for the Revolution. In order to avoid a repeat of this confusion, Americans of the early republic conceived of their written constitutions as expressions of the central premises on which their societies rested. Besides putting the American frame of government in writing, the constitutions also placed the American people's collective character in tangible form. That character had existed before, but now men like James Kent, Zephaniah Swift, and St. George Tucker could not only tell their students and readers about the framers' ideas, but they could also show their audience these notions of a free and equal society created by and for the people.

The English may have been perfectly comfortable with unwritten protections enforced by the power of time immemorial, but American legists like St. George Tucker believed that a constitution should have more than mere custom behind it. The Virginia jurist, drawing upon the American colonists' pre-Revolutionary experience with the metropolitan government, warned that the absence of a set of written regulations endangered social rights. The unwritten English Constitution had "nothing of [the] visible form about it," and therefore its limitations of governmental powers were "uncertain." In America, however, the Revolution had given birth "to this new political phenomenon: in every State a *written* constitution was framed . . . and adopted by the people, both in their individual and sovereign capacity." For the first time in its history, Tucker boasted, the world "saw an original written compact formed by the free and deliberate voices of individuals disposed to unite in the same social bonds." Within these written compacts was the concept of sovereignty of the people and the responsibility of their public servants to follow the people's will. The government's power had limits, outside of which public servants could not venture without offending the greater power, that of the people.[3] The value of a written constitution, according to Tucker, lay in its use as a "beacon to apprise the people when their rights and liberties, [were] invaded, or in danger." The American constitutions' tangibility meant that rights could not "be impugned . . . or shaken."[4] With the advent of written constitutions, every man could know his rights and be able to refer to them, while maintaining a watch over his governments.

Placing their frames of government in writing was only one of many innovations. According to St. George Tucker, the framers had "carefully lopt off" of the English Constitution "every germ of monarchy . . . and feudal aristocracy" and kept those parts that they considered "republican" enough to retain for American uses.[5] The scholars then explained how, on this cleansed template, the former colonists built new polities that were based on innovative modes of rights protections. As American legists helped to tear down what they considered to be outmoded English social distinctions, they were helping to perpetuate the founders' confidence in the American citizen as self-governor. Legal scholars taught their protégés that the character of a nation was only as good as its citizenry, and that good citizens made for good leaders, which in turn created a good nation. The best way to achieve a nation of good character was to elevate average citizens to their rightful place of political power and authority. They communicated to their audience the Revolutionary vision that a well-informed citizenry that participated in their governments on local and federal levels would ensure the stability of the American republic. Moreover, the broader opportunity for public service and participation in government was a key distinction between the American republic and the oppressive monarchy in England.

As they described their nation's constitutional advantages over England, American legal scholars also expressed awareness that their polities were still works in progress, and not all of the pieces worked smoothly. They examined and critiqued their own systems, conducted comparisons of other local polities with their own, and shared ideas for improvements on local and federal levels. As they engaged in these conversations for improvement, legal scholars also recognized the importance of local variation in practice, in order to support economic and social differences that cultivated regional identities.

I

Because the people were at the center of America's governments, legal scholars devoted considerable time and space to discussing who had the right to exercise suffrage. Here they held to some English traditions, while also distinguishing themselves from their parent country. One custom worth preserving was the English government's parliamentary election process, which Nathaniel Chipman called one of the "democratic principles still alive in Britain."[6] James Wilson called the exercise of suffrage "the strongest bulwark of the British liberties."[7] Yet, American legists believed that they had created an even stronger republic by adopting more liberal voting qualifications. Blackstone explained that England's voting laws excluded "such persons as are in so mean a situation that they are esteemed to have no will of their own." Those persons who did not possess property had no individual will.[8] Because property ownership was restricted to a small percentage of the English population, that nation's electorate was far narrower than that of her former colonies.

American legists also recognized voting qualifications as important ways in which Americans could maintain local and regional differences. Chipman credited colonial settlers with importing these democratic values, establishing assemblies in the image of the Commons, and eventually improving on the English system by making all public offices elective.[9] Wilson saw America's commitment to a broader popular power reflected in the "generous and wise judgment" of the American Constitution's framers for allowing each state to maintain its individual qualifications for voting. He praised the United States government's confidence in the abilities of state legislatures to set fair guidelines for suffrage, and he noted that the action also showed the central government's appreciation of the social, economic, and legal differences that came with each state's unique development.[10]

Although they had established a broader electorate because so many more people owned property, American states still followed their English counterparts in emphasizing property ownership as the primary measurement of independence of will. To vote for members of a legislature was, to Wilson, "to perform an act of original sovereignty," and the weighty nature of the act required that "no person unqualified should . . . be permitted to assume the exercise of such preeminent power."[11] In America, however, the equality of opportunity afforded by ample land enlarged the pool of men capable of casting an independent vote, giving ordinary citizens a far greater voice in government. While land was more plentiful in America and the amount of real property a man had to own to merit political participation was comparatively low, no state was willing to allow those who did not own property to help select their representatives. When compared to his home state of Virginia, Tucker observed that English land ownership qualifications for voting were far more restrictive. Unlike Virginia's voting regulations, English copyholders "whose interest, in almost every other respect in their lands, seem[ed] to be equal to that of a free-holder," did not have the right of suffrage. This tradition, Tucker noted, significantly reduced the number of people who had the right to vote in England.[12] But Tucker did not object to the idea that one ought to own some property in order to vote.

Some American legists, however, criticized the belief that the best people to choose representatives were those who had an interest—meaning property ownership. Pennsylvanian Hugh Henry Brackenridge, for example, objected to any property qualification for the right of suffrage. Brackenridge declared that property ownership requirements contradicted the ideas of the ancient republicans, who lived in a time when "it was honourable to have enriched the republic, and to remain poor themselves." One did not have to own an estate to be honest, Brackenridge opined. Moreover, if he concentrated too much on pursuing personal wealth, a man had "in some measure" to neglect "the improvement of his mind." Those who owned extensive estates were even more ill-suited to hold elected offices, insisted Brackenridge, because "the man that has set his heart on riches, is lost to benevolence, and public spirit."[13] Brackenridge advocated universal suffrage, but he felt that this luxury had to be hedged with "proportionably powerful" restraints on public volition, "for the mind of man like the water of the ocean is subject to sudden and great agitation." He suggested several restraints, including assurance that the voters select "men of understanding" to fill public offices, a clearer division of power among the branches of government, and even more frequent elections than Pennsylvania's constitution already required.[14] These measures, Brackenridge believed, would ensure that citizens would be protected from corrupt office holders.

Nathaniel Chipman also believed that America's republics should shape their identities around a broader definition of "interest" in community welfare, which, for him, extended beyond property ownership. He asserted that in a republic "in which every thing ought to tend to a certain kind of equality," property seemed "not to be a just criterion." Chipman insisted that "the individual and social rights of man" were everyone's concern, whether or not they owned property. Too much reliance on property ownership as a qualification to vote opened the door to "a dangerous inequality of influence" and to the possibility that those exercising their influence would infringe on the rights of others.[15] Broadening definitions of the citizenry to include the unpropertied would cultivate even more interest among Americans.

Another safeguard against inequalities of influence came in the conviction that the new nation must cultivate an informed citizenry, although there was never any consensus about what, precisely, citizens ought to know. Revolutionary leaders firmly believed that republics could survive only if their citizens were knowledgeable. For these men, an informed public meant schools, a free press, a post office, and communication within social and political institutions, especially churches. Although the electorate was still almost exclusively male and white, the colonial political practices and the egalitarian impulse of the Revolution had widened the circle of those who could be politically active. If these political newcomers were to act responsibly, they had to cultivate the proper fundamental skills, such as reading and writing. Therefore, several states inserted constitutional provisions for the encouragement of education. Although many founders encouraged broader knowledge of public affairs, they still generally agreed that leading citizens needed to be better educated than the wider public. All white men had to be informed in order to be politically vigilant and to vote responsibly. Those who held office had to demonstrate a deeper preparation.[16]

Echoing fellow Virginian Thomas Jefferson's emphasis on the importance of an informed citizenry, Tucker praised American improvements in the manner in which laws were disseminated to the public. He scoffed at the English opinion that there was no need for formal promulgation to give an act the force of law. Although all English laws were available in print, Blackstone asserted that wide dissemination of new laws was unnecessary because every man in England was, "in judgment of law, party to the making of an act of parliament, being present thereat by his representatives" in Parliament.[17] Therefore, every man could be confident, without having to scrutinize legislation, that parliament worked in their interest. In a footnote to Blackstone's explanation of the English process, Tucker noted that Virginia laws were promulgated by printing and circulating copies of each law. Federal law spelled out a very specific process for disseminating all acts of Congress, which involved furnishing all states with compilations of U.S. laws and publication of every order, resolution, or law passed by Congress in at least one, and not more than three, newspapers in each state. In this manner, according to Tucker, all constituents could monitor the actions of their representatives and provide appropriate correction or approbation.[18] Laws widely publicized to a literate public helped to engage citizens in their polities' governance.

Although the early republics witnessed their share of discontent over unequal representation among white men on the frontiers—not to mention women and men of color—in their lectures and treatises, legists praised the safeguards that the framers erected to ensure an equal voice among all citizens and all states. Tucker asserted that the American Constitution guarded against lopsided apportionment in ways that England's did not. Every man "in his individual capacity," according to Tucker, had the right to vote in matters that concerned the community, and these safeguards made it impossible for "ten men in one part of the community" to "have greater weight in its Council than an hundred in a different place." Tucker contrasted this situation with that of England, "where a Borough composed of half a dozen freeholders" sent perhaps as many representatives to Parliament "as a County which contain[ed] as many thousands."[19] Wilson noted that Blackstone recognized the lack of a truly representative system in England when he admitted that the most beneficial potential alteration in the frame of English government would be "in favour of a more complete representation of the people." Wilson claimed that more equitable representation was another very important American innovation "in the science of jurisprudence and government." Great Britain's limited representative government was "by no means sufficiently extensive" because the electorate had no role in selecting the chief magistrate. The Crown, in turn, appointed judges so that the courts were not representative, and even in parliament representation was not "a predominating principle." On the other hand, the American states enjoyed "the glory and the happiness of diffusing this vital principle throughout all the different divisions and departments of the government." Representation was for Wilson "the chain of communication between the people and those . . . to whom they have committed the important charge of exercising the delegated powers necessary for the administration of publick affairs."[20]

On the receiving end of America's political "chain of communication" was the elected official, and legal scholars differed over who was qualified to hold public office. According to James Wilson, in a commonwealth, "the dignities of office [were] open to all."[21] St. George Tucker, on the other hand, preferred some property requirements for office holders, as long as they were not excessive. He found qualifications for office in the American states in general, and Virginia in particular, far more equitable and consistent than in England. The Virginia law professor thought that England's strict requirements with regard to property ownership deprived the nation of many fine public servants. In a republic, if the voters determined that a candidate's talents and integrity made up for his lack of estate, so be it. If a government required a sizeable estate to qualify for office, it could often happen that "men the best qualified in other respects might be incapacitated from serving their country." Adequate compensation for representatives' service would, in Tucker's opinion, secure them from undue influence.[22] While Hugh Henry Brackenridge agreed that American property requirements for office holding were more liberal than those of England, he believed that they ought to be even more liberal. A man who was interested in nothing but acquiring property constantly would be "thinking of what [could] be made" through possession of an office rather than thinking about the good he could do for his constituency.[23] For Brackenridge, good character was a far more important qualification for effective political leadership in America's republics than possession of property.

In addition to property qualifications, a few states employed age as another benchmark of personal character and effective leadership. England did not practice this restriction, and not all Americans approved of it. Wilson objected to some state constitutions' maximum-age restrictions, which kept men over sixty years of age from holding public office. He sarcastically remarked that the professional lives of some American public servants were disappointingly short. Wilson cited New York's constitution as a prime example of this sort of discrimination, in that the New York Supreme Court judges and the first judge of each county court could only hold office until the age of sixty. The Pennsylvania judge found it ironic that New York's constitution considered "a man . . . unfit for the first offices of the state *after* he is sixty; in Sparta, a man was deemed unfit for the first offices of the state *till* he was sixty."[24] The policy eventually affected his colleague James Kent. In 1823, as he approached his sixtieth birthday, Kent was forced to relinquish his post as chancellor of New York. After he retired from public life, Kent resumed his long-vacant post as professor of law at Columbia College and began composing his seminal *Commentaries on the American Law* from those law lectures.

American legists' debates over the nature of effective leadership extended to the question of how tightly representatives were bound to their constituents' advice and wishes. Blackstone wrote that members of Commons were not required to consult with or take the advice of their constituents upon any particular point, unless they believed it was prudent to do so. Brackenridge responded by quoting from Tucker's edition of the *Commentaries* that if a republic's power was derived from the people and if magistrates were the people's servants, one could not deny "that in a popular government the representative is bound to speak the sense of his constituents upon every subject, where he is informed of it." Brackenridge added his own emphasis when he repeated Tucker's assertion that "*the difficulty of collecting the sense of the people upon any question, forms no argument against the right to express that sense when they shall think proper so to do.*"[25] With this statement, Brackenridge not only set forth the expectation that representatives listen to their constituents, but he also implied that citizens could not be passive members of their polities. It was up to them to voice their opinions to their elected officials.

After emphasizing the constituents' right to instruct their elected officials, however, Brackenridge retreated from his stance and allowed that representatives held some freedom to decide questions of a general manner by their own conscience, calling it the representatives' duty to consider the good of the whole, the triumph of virtue, "if not of *wisdom.*"[26] Brackenridge knew firsthand about the political dangers involved in not following the wishes of his constituency. In the 1780s, while serving in the Pennsylvania Assembly, Brackenridge's own constituents accused him of going against their expressed wishes on the matter of debtor legislation. Against his constituents' wishes, then, Brackenridge had followed his conscience, which told him that the "whole body politic" did not possess "the means of information upon a great scale," and that the duty of "a faithful representative" was "*to respect the rights, but to distrust the impulses of the people.*"[27]

Zephaniah Swift agreed with Brackenridge's more conservative impulses regarding instruction of public servants. He insisted that a government by representation implied that representatives stood "in the place of the people" and were "vested with all their power" under the Constitution. Therefore, legislators were not bound by the instructions or will of the people, but rather they should pursue the measures that were "best calculated to promote the happiness and welfare of the community." The good of the community was, after all, any representative's goal once he took office. Therefore, he had to leave the parochial interests of his district behind to pursue the general welfare.[28] According to Swift and Brackenridge, elected officials had the right to exercise their own judgment, and if all worked as intended, the electorate chose the candidates who were capable of doing just that.

II

While legal scholars vigorously debated how far legislators could exercise their own discretion before overstepping their bounds, the matter seemed to be long-settled in England. According to Blackstone, every government needed a "supreme, irresistible, absolute, uncontrolled authority" in which sovereignty resided, and in England, Parliament was that body. The English legislative branch possessed the "wisdom, goodness, and power" to maintain order. He stated that acts of Parliament contrary to reason or impossible to perform were not valid, but if Parliament chose to enact such laws there was "no power that [could] control it."[29] The concept of parliamentary supremacy as Blackstone outlined it was a relatively new idea and not yet hardened into an orthodoxy among English jurists. When his *Commentaries* first appeared, many of Blackstone's contemporaries still believed that the English Constitution did in fact limit Parliament's power. In the first few decades of the nineteenth century, however, Blackstone's view of Parliament as the ultimate sovereign prevailed in England.[30]

St. George Tucker agreed with Blackstone that the power to make laws constituted the supreme authority, but he disagreed with Blackstone about who should possess that power. In England, this authority rested in Parliament, but in America, Tucker noted, the lawmaking power belonged to the people. Americans in turn delegated this right to the state and federal legislatures via their constitutions. These legislatures, however, had "no rights, nor authority, nor even an existence, but from the People."[31] Both federal and state constitutions derived "their authority and existence from the immediate act, and consent of the people" as expressed in the Bill of Rights. Tucker then directed his students to Emmerich de Vattel's discussion on popular sovereignty, stating that because the legislative body derived its "authority, and even its existence from that origin," an assembly never could claim superiority over its creators.[32] The highest power in America was the people, and only the people had the power to alter the form of government and put the execution of their authority into whatever hands they pleased.

In Wilson's estimation, the British Constitution was not the protector of citizens' rights but rather the "creature and the dependent of the legislative power." He condemned the English position that "the natural, the inherent, and the predominating rights of the citizens" were "so dangerous and so desperate a resource, as to be inconsistent with the arrangements of any government . . . which does or can exist."[33] He pointed out that Blackstone cited no precedent or court opinion for his assertion of parliamentary sovereignty because no such decision existed. Instead, Wilson used the notion of consent to reject Blackstone's assertion of parliamentary sovereignty. He began with Matthew Hale's statement that an act of Parliament was made when King, Lords, and Commons consented to that act. If this was the case,

Wilson suggested, any act required the assent of the King, who spoke for himself and represented the executive authority of the nation; of Lords, who spoke only for themselves and their heirs; and of Commons, who "assented for the people whom they *represented*."[34] Therefore, according to Wilson, the sovereign power did not reside in any one branch of the legislature, nor did it reside in the legislature as a whole, except in a delegated sense. Rather, the sovereign power was in the people whom, by their own consent, the legislature represented. Thus it was the consent, not the submission of the people, from which the supreme irresistible power of making laws originated. Once they had delegated their sovereignty to representatives, the people submitted to that delegated authority for the good of the whole nation.

Tucker, like most of his contemporaries, believed that the most important restraints against abuse of power were those that American framers had placed on the legislature. American suspicion of legislative power stemmed from colonial experiences with Parliament. When comparing the British King-in-Parliament with the U.S. Congress, Tucker used venomous language indicative of one embittered by parliamentary oppressions inflicted before the Revolution. He scoffed at the English people's "idolatrous veneration" of their parliament "as a palladium of political freedom which some partial deity had bestowed upon that favourite nation."[35] To Blackstone's assertion that the privileges of Parliament and its members were "indefinite, and depend[ed] upon their own construction" of their powers whenever the case arose, Tucker retorted that in America, congressional privileges were defined and limited by the Constitution in order to avoid just such inequitable and arbitrary rule.[36] He cited the game laws as examples of a "slight domestic regulation" that in the hands of an unchecked Parliament became a tool for depriving the people of their right to own and use firearms. Parliament also had unchecked power to determine the mode by which citizens petitioned the government, and it could prohibit public meetings to deliberate on national concerns. Neither the state nor the federal legislatures in America possessed power to regulate such popular action.[37]

Wilson noted that in the United States, the legislatures' authority was "very different from the supreme power" that Parliament wielded. State and federal constitutions placed the legislatures under strict control by providing checks "sometimes by the executive, sometimes by the judicial authority of the governments; sometimes even by a private citizen, and, at all times, by the superintending power of the people at large."[38] The U.S. constitutions hedged such legislative responsibilities as currency regulation, taxation powers, and commerce regulation with regard to ports and transportation. These precautions helped to eliminate dangers to state authority and diffused concern that a strong federal government might repeat some of the Crown's former oppressions.[39] America's citizen-centered republics, Wilson declared, could do without Parliament's mysterious political dealings, and he proudly stated that the Pennsylvania and U.S. constitutions clearly delineated the powers and limitations of their legislatures. He hoped that the federal government would eventually adopt the Pennsylvania Assembly's practice of opening all sessions of each house and all committee sessions to the people, an innovation that Wilson considered "highly beneficial both in its nature and in its consequences—both to the representatives and to their constituents" and provided effective safeguards to a system of curbs on legislative power that Wilson considered far superior to that of England.[40] More transparency in deliberations and debates represented an important check on abuse of power.

Tucker and Wilson also drew critical distinctions between the upper houses of England and America. Whereas Blackstone took pride in the hereditary nature of the Lords and looked upon the august body as the traditional counselors and defenders of the King, Tucker ridiculed the Lords as an absurd collection of hereditary and unqualified advisers. He illustrated his objections with Thomas Paine's remark that "the idea of hereditary legislators [or counsellors]" (Tucker's addition) was "as inconsistent as that of hereditary judges, or hereditary juries; and as absurd as an hereditary mathematician, or an hereditary wise man; and as ridiculous as an hereditary poet laureat."[41] Tucker preferred Virginia's practice of providing the governor with an advisory body, called the Council of State, which consisted of eight members chosen by ballot in the assembly. He likened this body to the King's Privy Council, with one important exception: while the Privy Council enjoyed many privileges and immunities that the average English citizen did not, Virginia's Council members possessed no special considerations other than immunity from arrest during their attendance at session.[42] Advisers were not members of an untouchable class. Rather, they were ordinary citizens who placed their valuable expertise at the disposal of the governor and assembly. Not even such expertise, however, was sufficient reason to bestow privilege in a republic.

Though most American legal scholars believed that America's republics should have no distinction of rank or privileges for public service, some also agreed that certain Americans were more qualified than others to hold an office in the upper house. Zephaniah Swift, for example, acknowledged that the "natural inequality of mankind, arising from superiority of ability and virtue," would inevitably give birth to a "natural aristocracy." While he assumed the existence of political and social elites, he also advocated for their separation from public servants of lesser ranks. Taking his cue from John Adams's reasons for advocating a bicameral legislature, he warned that when housed in the same representative body as the popular assembly, possessors of "genius, merit, and learning" could form dangerous alliances. Swift approved of the remedy of quarantining the natural aristocracy in their own branch of the legislature, so that they could not influence the popular assembly "to adopt rash and ruinous measures."[43] This segregation, Swift and many of his colleagues believed, could provide further safeguards to the rights of all American citizens.

Some legists did not agree with Swift's theory of segregation. For example, in a discussion about the federal legislature's structure, James Wilson expressed his dissatisfaction with the indirect election process by which Americans chose their senators. The Constitution required that senators be chosen by each state legislature, instead of through direct elections like those for the House of Representatives. The reason for this requirement, according to Wilson, was that the framers wanted to maintain "the material distinction, and, consequently, all the benefits which would result from the material distinction, between the two branches of the legislature." Wilson, however, believed that Pennsylvania's method of directly electing both houses of the legislature was more in keeping with America's identity as a set of free and equal republics. He cited the advantages of developing an esprit de corps among the members of each house, as the two bodies would become "rivals in duty, rivals in fame, rivals for the good graces of their common constituents." Additionally, members of each house would take care in their proceedings, knowing that they would fall under their colleagues' scrutiny.[44] This additional measure of transparency would keep both groups honorable and provide more security to the people.

III

Descriptions of the character of the electorate and its legislative representatives led to discussions about integrity of the executive as well. Sir William Blackstone described the English monarch as "the supreme executive power of these kingdoms" who, immediately upon ascending the throne, was invested with "all the ensigns, rights, and prerogatives of sovereign power." According to Blackstone, one of the attributes of the Crown was that the king, in his political capacity, was absolutely perfect. Not only was the monarch "incapable of *doing* wrong," but he was also incapable of "*thinking* wrong. . . . In him there [was] no folly or weakness."[45] But America's legal scholars attacked the conviction that England's executive was infallible, and they created an image of America's executive as imperfect and equal to all other citizens under the law.

That any man could be considered perfect, Tucker declared, was a unique form of folly. He asserted that England's King, Lords, and Commons "had often (as was to be expected from the weakness of human nature) done very wrong things."[46] English law, however, would not suppose the king capable of doing wrong, and therefore effectively placed him above the law. Before his subjects could hold him responsible for even "the most flagrant act of tyranny, or abuse of authority," they had to resort to a complete subversion of their Constitution. In the United States, however, "all notions of personal pre-eminence [were] consigned to oblivion," and Tucker hoped that such notions would "forever remain buried under the immovable mass of equal rights." In America, the chief magistrate was merely "a man, and fallible."[47] Because the framers considered a president capable of corruption, even treason, they provided for impeachment as means of removal from office and punishment for potential wrongdoing.

If, as Blackstone claimed, the king was perfect, then any of the executive's transgressions were the fault of the monarch's counselors, who worked as one with the king. Although the ultimate decisions were always the king's alone, Blackstone explained that any cases of public oppression stemming from the king's actions resulted from "the advice of evil counsellors, and the assistance of wicked ministers." Blackstone styled this advisory role of the king's ministers as part of the Crown's continuity, calling it part of the "unity of the executive."[48] Tucker challenged Blackstone's assertion as just another way of saying that the king was not responsible for his acts, and he remained above constitutional reproach. This concept of "unity," according to Tucker, destroyed the idea of executive accountability and deflected executive power to ministers and members of Parliament, which resulted in a corrupt and inefficient executive. The president of the United States, on the other hand, was "not clogg'd with any such Council" in cases that required immediate dispatch. Although the Senate could serve as counsel to the president should he require it, the executive only used senatorial advice under special circumstances. Regardless of who advised the president on any matter, Tucker asserted, the Constitution held the chief magistrate accountable for the consequences of his decisions.[49]

Part of the "unity" of the monarchy, according to Blackstone, was its hereditary nature, a quality that the English legist considered necessary to maintain order in the kingdom. A hereditary monarchy did not, however, mean that the king possessed a divine right to the throne but rather that the monarch inherited her or his position as supreme executive by general consent of the people from time immemorial. Blackstone admitted that an elective monarchy seemed to be the most rational choice for a society that valued the liberty of its people. If the citizens of a polity "could always continue true to first principles, uninfluenced by passion or prejudice, unassailed by corruption, and unawed by violence," elective succession would be desirable. Unfortunately, Blackstone lamented, men were not always so wise. Therefore, the English had created a hereditary executive so that they could avoid the confusion and upheaval that battles over the monarchy could cause. For Blackstone, the stability of the monarchy rested in its perpetuity, and under English law the king was said "never to die, in his political capacity." Although subject to the same mortality as any other human, the king "survive[d] in his successor."[50] This continuity in the monarchy, then, represented for Blackstone the key to England's stability as a nation.

Tucker dismissed as a "barefaced falsity" Blackstone's notion that hereditary succession spared a nation from civil war. He used England's own history to assert that hereditary succession caused more war than peace and often seemed to destroy "the very foundation" on which peace stood.[51] From the time of the conquest, Tucker stated, there had been "(including the revolution) no less than eight civil wars, and nineteen rebellions." He also ridiculed Blackstone's assertion that "'the king never dies.' . . . But Henry, Edward, or George may die, may be an infant in swaddling clothes, a superannuated dotard, or a raving maniac. Of what benefit is the immortality of the kingly office . . . in any of these instances?" Tucker deemed the elective perpetuation of the presidential office in America more reasonable. The Constitution provided for a vice president to assume the office in emergency and regular elections to choose a mature, qualified man to fill the position. Moreover, if the citizens misjudged a man's ability to be a good leader, they could vote the chief magistrate out of office at the end of four years.[52] The American frame of government, Tucker asserted, preserved its unity with an arrangement that was far superior to reliance on hereditary monarchy and the counsel of a confused and dependent body of men.

In describing the framers' replacement of the infallible and hereditary monarch with an elected executive, American legists helped to define an American political identity that relied not on the unity of hereditary lineage for their leadership but on the citizens' collective wisdom to choose the best man to lead. Whereas in England men owed their allegiance to the king in return for protection and justice, America's legal scholars pointed out that there was no such thing as personal allegiance to the magistrate in America. Allegiance was due only to the U.S. Constitution and government, and even the persons who administered the government fell under this same obligation. Men enjoyed certain rights that bore no attachment to any correlative duty toward any other man.[53] Wilson asserted that American liberties were not the gifts of princes but instead were powers that magistrates held at the behest of the people. Although they assigned a portion of their authority to elected and appointed officials, American citizens chose how much and what they delegated.[54] Therefore, the ultimate duty was to one another, the citizens themselves.

With regard to limitation of executive power, the legists discussed measures that America's constitutional framers took to guard against usurpation of power on the part of the executive and to shore up the magistracy against threats to its own power. The American presidency, devoid of the magical trappings of royalty and without hereditary continuity or sacred power, was far different from the English monarchy. Americans had to justify to the world, and to themselves, that their form of executive leadership could be strong and survive without anything holding it together except regularly scheduled popular elections. Wilson and Tucker did so by pointing to the checks on the president that kept him from assuming more power than his office allowed. They then showed their audiences how a magistrate elected from among the citizenry could function far more effectively, and with much more justice, than the infallible, never-dead king.

Tucker began his lecture on royal prerogative with the assumption that prerogative had been annihilated in America along with the monarchy. Many of these monarchical privileges were "rejected as nuisances by our government," while those still deemed necessary to the smooth operation of the nation were generally taken from the executive and handed over to the legislature. Tucker emphatically noted that according to Virginia law, the governor of that state could not "under any pretence exercise any power or *prerogative* by virtue of any law, statute, or custom of England."[55] Evidently, Virginia's framers were determined not to allow such abuse of power to happen simply because there was English precedent for just that kind of power.

One important protection, according to Tucker, was Americans' ability to procure justice against the executive. If an English subject believed that the monarch had committed a wrong against him, the subject's only recourse was to petition the king directly through the Court of Chancery. The king could grant the subject redress for injuries sustained, but as Blackstone stated, using Samuel von Pufendorf's words, a subject had "no way to oblige his prince to give him his due, when [the prince] refuse[d] it."[56] In Virginia, if a citizen had a complaint against the governor, he petitioned the Court of Chancery or the district court for redress. Unlike the English process, Tucker explained, correction of an act wrongly committed was not a "matter of grace," but rather a matter of justice. The constitution compelled the Commonwealth to do justice, whereas the English Constitution did not protect its subjects from the Crown's transgressions.[57]

Congress also shouldered responsibility for making all rules respecting U.S. territory and for the disposal of public property. For example, property of shipwrecks in England, if unclaimed, belonged to the king, but Tucker noted that Virginia law vested rights in the owner, regardless of how long the property went unclaimed. Tucker pointed to these reforms as evidence that personal property was even more sacred in America than in England.[58] He had little sympathy for Blackstone's complaint that it was impossible "to support that dignity . . . which a king of Great Britain should maintain, with an income in any degree less" than that which Parliament decreed at the time.[59] Tucker compared these royal riches to the American president's more equitable financial arrangement, which consisted of no compensation other than a salary that could not decrease or increase during his tenure of office.[60] From Tucker's perspective, the president's situation was a perfect example of civic republican behavior and in stark contrast to the greedy English royals.

The framers of the Constitution also transferred the chief magistrate's power to declare war to the legislative branch and placed his peace-making duties under the partial control of the Senate. Although the president, like the king, remained commander-in-chief of the army and navy and of the states' militia, only Congress could raise and regulate the fleets and armies or the fortifications within the union. According to Wilson, this arrangement was actually a renewal of principles of government "known in England before the conquest." This arrangement was indeed, Wilson claimed, one of the chief differences between the Anglo-Saxon and the Anglo-Norman governments. In the former, the *wittenagemote*, or chief, possessed the power to make war and peace "and was regarded as inseparable from the allodial condition of its members." Norman conquerors transferred the power to declare war to the sovereign, and that "branch of the feudal system" that was perhaps appropriate for "the depredations and internal commotions prevalent in that rude period" retained this power long after the elimination of the circumstances that had required it.[61] Thus, as Wilson explained, Americans had cleansed yet another feudal corruption from their governments and had created another distinction between their modern republics and the still-feudal English monarchy.

American legists also held up the presidential veto power as a distinction between American and English executive powers. Tucker called the presidential veto "a precaution . . . provided by the constitution against the hasty passage of impolitic or unconstitutional acts" and deemed it necessary to the balance of government, though unnecessary "to the completion of a law." Yet, the Constitution curbed the president's preventative role as well, by providing that the power of veto should apply only in those cases where the president presumed the Congress to have "acted unadvisedly through haste or oversight."[62] While the king's veto power was absolute in that without his assent no bill could pass into law, the president had what Tucker called a "qualified negative." If two-thirds of both houses voted to do so, Congress could overturn the president's veto.[63] James Kent considered the veto a way to protect executive power. He pointed out that although the president's "qualified negative" served as additional security against the passage of "improper laws, through prejudice or want of due reflection," it was principally intended as a "constitutional weapon to defend the executive department . . . against the usurpations of the legislative power." Kent explained that the lawmaking power was "transcendant" and that if the body possessing that power "be a full and equal representation of the people," there was great danger "of its pressing with destructive weight" on the other branches of government. Therefore, he thought it necessary to erect "strong barriers" like the veto to check the lawmaking power.[64] The barriers to legislative power did not, however, end with the veto power of the executive. Among the most important constitutional innovations was an independent court system, which was meant to provide an additional safeguard to American citizens' rights. It also provided another avenue through which citizens could exercise their sovereignty.

IV When they set out to construct their republican tribunals of justice, America's leaders wanted their courts to reflect the principles of popular sovereignty that defined their republics, and they wanted to make certain that their judges were effective protectors of personal security and private property. Framers knew that to accomplish these goals they had to prevent the courts from falling under the control of either the legislature or the executive. Though it took a while to produce the right balance of power, the eventual result of their efforts was yet another constitutional innovation, the independent judiciary.

In their lectures and treatises, scholars discussed which qualities framers chose to retain from their English judicial heritage and which features they created from local colonial-era experience or from their own visions of the ideal republican courts. These innovations and adaptations, legists believed, helped to shape American polities' identities as places where every citizen could participate in the meting out of equal justice. In the course of their lectures on the judiciary, every law professor in the early republic referred to those who administered justice in the courts as the preeminent protectors of personal security and private property. Legal scholars taught that for the judiciary to remain "the last bulwark against oppression," the institution had to remain independent and uncorrupted.[65] While St. George Tucker uttered this statement as if separation of powers had been a long-held notion, in reality an independent judiciary appeared for the first time in the republican experiments of the American constitutions. An independent judiciary, American legists pointed out, certainly did not exist in England, where the courts derived their power from the monarch.

In England, Blackstone explained, the king was the "fountain of justice" and as the ultimate arbiter of all disputes, he had "immemorially" exercised his authority to dispense justice. Blackstone hastened to add that by the fountain of justice he did not mean that the king was the "*author* or *original*, but only the *distributor*." Justice was not derived from the king, but rather he was the "steward of the public, to dispense it to whom it [was] *due*." The king alone possessed the right to establish courts of judicature and to appoint the judges who would assist him in executing his role as preeminent judge. Thus, all court jurisdictions were either "mediately or immediately derived from the crown," and all courts conducted their proceedings in the king's name.[66] The omnipresent nature of the king in his courts of justice meant that the judiciary could never escape from the orbit of the English executive. Blackstone declared that though the king could not personally distribute all justice, he was "always present in all his courts," and England's judges were "the mirror by which the king's image [was] reflected."[67] Judges of the nation's highest court worked closely with the king in an advisory capacity, which strengthened the ties between the king and his tribunals but also deflected accountability for any executive decisions toward those magistrates who already bore responsibility for judicial decisions.

Blackstone insisted that just because all courts derived their existence from the Crown and all judges owed their positions to the king, the judges were not obliged to do the king's bidding. Before the Act of Settlement that accompanied William III's ascent to the English throne, judges had held their offices at the pleasure of the king.[68] Upon that compact, however, the nobles and the new king agreed that to "maintain both the dignity and independence of the judges," their commissions would last for as long as they were on good behavior.[69] English judges kept their seats on the bench even upon the death of a monarch, and their salaries were "absolutely secured to them during the continuance of their commissions."[70] Blackstone boasted of the "distinct and separate existence" of the English judicial power as "one main preservative of the public liberty."[71] All of the rhetoric about an independent judiciary, however, did not change the fact that English courts of law were subordinate to the king.

Experience had taught Americans that the English court system was not the grand defender of English rights that Blackstone described or, at least, that the king did not grant equal defense to the rights of those Englishmen who lived outside of England. Those who lived in colonial British America did not have that same protection of impartial justice that Englishmen residing in England supposedly enjoyed. Judges appointed to colonial supreme courts of judicature served at the pleasure of the Crown and governor rather than on good behavior. Even justices of the peace, the local representatives of England's system of justice, by law served at the behest of the provincial governor. This arrangement left inhabitants of the colonies with little assurance that judges dispensed impartial justice, and it caused considerable political strife as colonies fought for judiciary privileges identical to those in England.[72] Those Americans who endured the injustices of pre-Revolutionary court systems were determined to protect U.S. citizens from similar bias on the part of their newly appointed judges.

The framers of the first state constitutions harbored recent and painful memories of the king's hold over provincial courts before the Revolution. To avoid similar executive control over their court system, most states first tried placing the judiciary under the control of their legislatures. This experiment, however, was not entirely successful. During the Revolutionary War, most of the state legislatures succeeded in amassing the bulk of governmental power. They then proceeded to absorb judicial power by such actions as reversing court judgments and interfering in the execution of laws. Most states eventually remedied this concentration of power by adding independent superior courts of appeals that assumed most of the appellate responsibilities originally granted to legislatures. The states' experience with unchecked legislative power led the framers of the federal Constitution to create an independent judiciary.

The American constitutions were the first documents to carry into full effect the absolute independence of the judiciary.[73] A separate and independent judiciary would, in James Kent's words, "keep the legislature within the limits of its duty."[74] And, of course, keeping the legislature in check was a central concern of the founders. While the English judiciary was always subject to being overwhelmed by Parliament and the king, in America tenure of office on good behavior, salaries that the legislature and executive could not reduce or increase, and written constitutions that limited the powers of the government's branches gave judges complete independence. Legal scholars taught that the judiciary had historically possessed what Tucker called a "natural feebleness" that left it in jeopardy of being "overpowered, awed, or influenced by its coordinate branches," which had "custody of the purse and sword of the confederacy."[75] In the United States, however, the judicial power was "a distinct, separate, independent, and *co-ordinate* branch of the government" expressed as such in the organic law of the states and the federal union.[76] Because of their novelty, the newly formed states became laboratories for experimenting with various permutations of an independent judiciary.[77]

The fundamental difference between the nature of the English and American justice systems was in the locus of power. While the "fountain of all justice" in England was the king, the foundation of the American judicial system was the people, as enforced by the state and federal constitutions. American law students and practitioners could see very clearly the differences in hierarchy simply by looking at the top of the appeals ladder in each polity. While the British Constitution placed the ultimate appellate power in the House of Lords, the American judicial system provided a higher court independent of the legislative branch to hear appeals. Under no circumstances, except for impeachment cases, was the American Congress involved in judicial concerns.

Not only would an independent judiciary check the other branches, but, most importantly, it would mete out the kind of impartial justice for which a model republic should be known. Legists such as Tucker and John F. Grimké of South Carolina emphasized the importance of job security and adequate and guaranteed salaries to a judge's independence from the legislature. Grimké considered the legislature to be "the arbitrary and tyrannical part" of government and asserted that a judiciary that was dependent on the legislature "for their continuance in office" would surely not provide impartial leadership.[78] For Tucker, the salary issue was also a matter of integrity. A judge had to be placed "above the reach of temptation" by fixing his salary at a level that made him self-sufficient and able to devote all of his time to the bench. Moreover, in order to attract men of experience to public service, Tucker emphasized the necessity for a salary that would provide appropriate compensation for a position that should be held in high esteem. This was a particularly sore point with Tucker, who resigned his position on the Virginia Superior Court under protest against inadequate compensation and the Virginia Assembly's lack of respect for judges.[79] Tucker observed at least one other flaw in American judicial practices. He wished that Americans would adopt the English prohibition against judges holding other offices during their time on the bench. By the end of the eighteenth century, two chief justices of the U.S. Supreme Court had already accepted appointments as "envoys to distant nations" while still "holding their offices in the supreme court of the federal government."[80] Although this practice had been common in the colonies before the Revolution, Tucker believed it corrupted an office that should be free from outside influence.

Legists in the American republics agreed that an independent judiciary was the key to maintaining citizens' personal security, but how did a free people keep the judiciary from encroaching on their rights? Nathaniel Chipman asserted that the abilities, integrity, and independence of the judges were "a shield, both to the rulers, and to the people," but there had to be a remedy if a particular judge did not exemplify these virtues once in office. There were no popular elections by which the people could hold judges accountable, and while the executive appointed judges, there the dependence on the chief magistrate had to end. Holding office on good behavior meant that should judges become corrupted or commit maladministration of office, the people could call for their removal by impeachment. Chipman also noted that in the state of Connecticut and some of its sister states the legislature could also remove a judge from office for activities that might not be serious enough to warrant impeachment proceedings, yet that undermined "respect and public confidence" in the office. The legislature initiated this removal through an address to the executive, and to prevent abuse of this form of removal, two-thirds of both branches of the legislature had to concur.[81] With these safeguards, Chipman and his colleagues believed that American statesmen had created courts that were independent enough to protect citizens' property and security, but not so independent as to become a threat to the citizenry.

In fact, instead of intimidating citizens, American courts were streamlined to permit more accessibility. Legists contrasted America's simpler judicial hierarchy with Blackstone's description of England's complex system of inferior and superior courts. The English jurist's lengthy synopsis included descriptions of at least thirteen courts of public and general jurisdiction throughout the kingdom, seven kinds of ecclesiastical courts, military and maritime courts, and ten different kinds of private courts, including such seats of justice as the Court of the King's Forest and the Commissioners of Sewers.[82] Although Blackstone's chapter on England's courts of special jurisdiction had little to do with Virginia law, St. George Tucker insisted that his students carefully study that section of the *Commentaries*. He believed that any student of the law aspiring to a seat in the legislature should pay special attention to Blackstone's descriptions of the functions and histories of this tangled web of courts, which for any aspiring statesman served as valuable cautionary tales about uncontrolled bureaucracy. While he refrained from direct criticism of England's complicated maze of courts, Tucker expressed admiration for recent attempts at reform in Middlesex, where they had streamlined the litigation process and thus significantly reduced the cost of bringing action in their local small claims courts. Tucker praised this attempt to prevent "a multitude of vexatious actions in the superior courts" and to give honest creditors opportunities to recover their small sums at minimal expense to them.[83] Even in a polity as ancient and complex as England, simplicity could be a virtue.

Although American judicial hierarchies were less confusing than those of England, they were not uniform among the states. Law students spent considerable time learning the idiosyncrasies of their home state's legal system, and law professors and legal treatise writers devoted ample space to describing the local and federal judiciaries in detail. Many states shared common elements within their court systems. In most states the county courts dispensed local justice, and justices of the peace or sheriffs served as local magistrates. Most of these overseers of local justice still had little or no training in the law, as had been the case in colonial times. If they did not do so immediately, most states eventually established some sort of district court system for which judges rode circuits to dispense justice in matters of more financial worth or gravity than the county courts could handle. Generally the states also had appeals systems, complete with independent courts of last resort to hear appeals from the inferior state courts.[84] There were, however, many local variations on these themes.

Hugh Henry Brackenridge's *Law Miscellanies* provided a snapshot of Pennsylvania's judicial hierarchy in the first decades of the nineteenth century. Brackenridge practiced law in Pennsylvania's backcountry and was therefore accustomed to the exigencies of law on the frontier, where few trained lawyers settled. Many of the judicial roles he described, such as the justice of the peace, county courts of common pleas and quarter sessions, and the state's supreme court, were typical of most states. However, Brackenridge's description of the quarter sessions' personnel revealed the importance that this frontier judge placed on a simplified system of justice. While the president of quarter sessions was a judge properly trained in the law, associates were, according to Brackenridge, not necessarily "*legal characters.*" In other words, they did not always possess schooling in the law. However, they represented the value that Pennsylvanians placed in the wisdom of the ordinary citizen. Brackenridge stated that associates were "of great use . . . contributing to the advice of good sense and moral reason and giving weight to authority" in the county courts. Associates were primarily responsible for taking recognizances, setting the amount of bail, assessing fines, and performing other basic tasks.[85] For Brackenridge and many other men mired in the practical considerations of everyday lawyering, "good sense and moral reason" carried far more authority than status or education.

South Carolina's court structure differed from that of other states in that it had no layer of appellate courts, and John F. Grimké applauded that omission within his polity. Grimké praised South Carolina framers for avoiding the "enormous expence" and the "impoverishment of individuals" that a court of appeals would have inflicted on the state. He accused English courts of appeals of being "constituted in favor of the rich" because it was so costly to bring an appeal before England's higher courts that only the wealthy could do so. Moreover, the lack of a jury in the Anglo-American appellate process disturbed Grimké. Whenever he saw "this palladium," the jury, removed from a court of justice, Grimké wrote, he was "immediately led to the conclusion, that the liberty and property of the citizen [were] rendered more precarious." In South Carolina, instead of what Grimké considered an inefficient appeal system, an appellant could procure a new trial with jury and judge within the existing court structure, provided he showed just cause.[86] This innovation, Grimké concluded, made South Carolina's appeal process a model for other states.

Despite Grimké's praise for a court structure that he considered superior to most of the other states and certainly to that of England, he saw other South Carolina judicial practices that he believed to be inadequate to the republican model. The practice of allowing all witnesses to be present for all other witnesses' testimony, Grimké claimed, made it easy to form conspiracies against the accused. Additionally, the accused had to pay the fees of the ministers of the court, a practice that Grimké said compelled "the innocent to pay for the proof of that innocence." Perhaps most important in South Carolina's case, Grimké noted that the state's district courts did not ride an adequately accessible circuit for citizens living in the rural upcountry. The South Carolina judge insisted that courts should sit in locations convenient to all they served. No complainant, Grimké declared, should have to incur an unreasonable expense or inconvenience of travel and time to seek redress. This lack of local justice deprived the citizen "of one of his most valuable privileges," and he was thus "proportionably oppressed."[87] This oppression, Grimké insisted, should never exist in America's republics.

Like Grimké, St. George Tucker still saw many imperfections in his home state's court system. He voiced his concern about problems in circuit court procedures as laid out in the Virginia constitution. The judges of the General Court acted as district magistrates, riding circuit throughout the state in groups of two. Because of the appeals system in which three of the judges constituted a court, and the circuit system in which two judges rode circuit together, the court's magistrates had little opportunity to "establish that uniformity which is much to be desired in judicial decisions." This lack of cohesion resulted in frequent "want of concert in the opinions of the judges," which undermined the court's credibility and clogged the superior tribunal with numerous appeals. Another procedural problem that Tucker feared could cause even greater damage was the structure of criminal trials. Two judges were necessary to constitute a criminal court unless the prisoner petitioned to be tried with only one judge present. Frequent illnesses or other incapacities sometimes made it impossible for two judges to sit at a criminal trial. Very few accused criminals petitioned the court for trial, unless of course they thought circumstances to be in their favor by doing so. If two judges were not available for trial at the next court, the prisoner, regardless of the severity of his offense, had a right to be freed on bail. If there was no court to try him a third time, the prisoner was automatically discharged. Because of this two-judge rule, Tucker claimed that "some of the most atrocious offenders that were ever brought to the bar of a court . . . have escaped punishment."[88] This flawed process did not meet Anglo-American standards of justice and by Tucker's estimation was an innovation that Virginia could do without.

Even after Independence, some states styled certain of their courts after English models. For a long while after the Revolution, Connecticut's superior courts continued to bear more of a resemblance to those of England than to those of its sister states. In England, the House of Lords was the court of last resort, and colonial Connecticut's judicial system followed that model.[89] Connecticut leaders did not immediately draw up a new constitution upon declaration of independence from England. Rather, they chose to retain their colonial charter as their frame of government. At the time of the break with England, the Connecticut legislature still exercised most judicial power. Through the next decades Connecticut's General Assembly gradually created inferior courts, but the legislature remained the state's highest court of appeal until 1818, when the state ratified a new constitution.[90] Connecticut's small geographical size perhaps lessened the necessity for immediate change, and that state's court system continued to evolve slowly.

Even after the Connecticut legislature had created a separate system of courts, these tribunals could not boast independence in the same manner as their fellow states. The General Assembly still retained certain powers that Zephaniah Swift did not consider conducive to impartial justice. The state legislature established the Supreme Court of Errors in 1784 to help relieve some of its judicial burden, and the General Assembly initially appointed the superior court judges annually, a practice that Swift called "most exceptionable." He insisted that judges could not be treated like legislators, because the nature of their jobs differed considerably. "The responsibility of the legislature to the people," Swift explained, was "the security that good laws [should] be made." The judiciary, however, had a different responsibility, that "they should expound the laws justly," and to do so they had to be assured of their independence. In Connecticut, if a case came before the superior court for trial "between an influential character" who was "usually a member of the legislature, and a poor man without influence," the legislatures' annual appointment of judges to the superior court could favor the influential man. If, on the other hand, judges' independence was secured with service on good behavior, all citizens could better be assured of judges' impartiality.[91] The Connecticut Constitution of 1818 finally gave that assurance by providing for the superior court judges' tenure of office during good behavior. To ensure that judges remained accountable for their actions, the legislature made them subject to impeachment and removal, for misconduct, by a two-thirds vote of each house of the assembly.[92] Slowly, Connecticut's leaders erased what they considered to be imperfections in their judicial system. Some of these corrections involved shedding English legal tradition in favor of American innovations.

V

In some states, however, the framers thought that preserving a particular kind of English court might benefit its citizens. The court of equity, a body presided over by a chancellor, appeared in some states. England's chancellor was, according to Blackstone, "the keeper of the king's conscience" and the "general guardian of all infants, idiots, and lunatics." He exercised jurisdiction over the Court of Chancery, in which there was a court of common law and a court of equity. The court of common law's jurisdiction included those cases concerning wards of the king, personal actions to which any officer of the court was a party, and other various instances. By the mid-eighteenth century, however, the chancellor's common-law tasks were a very small portion of his overall duties. Blackstone admitted that "so little [was] usually done on the common law side of the court" that he could find few examples of cases brought before the chancellor at common law.[93]

The equity side of the Chancery, however, had grown in importance through the generations. Although the court of equity's history was unclear, Blackstone surmised that in ancient times when a court of law gave a "harsh or imperfect judgment," the person who thought himself wronged by the verdict appealed directly to the king and his Privy Council. Eventually, they began to refer the matter to the chancellor, "who mitigated the severity or supplied the defects of the judgments pronounced in the courts of law, upon weighing the circumstances of the case."[94] This custom of bringing appeals in equity to a separate court slowly became common law, and the chancellor assumed these duties as the major portion of his judicial responsibilities.

Some American states also established a court of equity modeled after the English chancery court, and they often gave it jurisdiction over the kinds of cases that England's ecclesiastical courts would have handled. This particular court had become increasingly important in England as a mitigating force in the rule of law and the rigid observance of precedent. But Maryland's David Hoffman cautioned that the distinction between common law and equity was often difficult to discern. He pointed to what he characterized as the confusion that even the great Blackstone experienced when trying to differentiate between equity and common law. Hoffman probably characterized Blackstone's definition as "confused" because the court's origins lay in the king's power to bend the law. Equity was, according to Blackstone, one of the mysteries of the Crown. When common-law precedent provided what in the Crown's view was too harsh a judgment, the court of equity could, upon weighing the circumstances, mitigate the severity of the sentence to rectify the defects of the case.[95] Instead of bringing monarchical grace and mystical power into his definition of equity in America, Hoffman preferred to use Zephaniah Swift's definition of a court of equity. Swift's treatise on the laws of Connecticut described a court of equity as acting "according to the dictates of conscience" and aiming at "the attainment of abstract right and perfect justice." Hoffman explained that a court of equity had the power "to abate the rigour, correct the injustice, and supply the deficiency of positive law" in cases where it was apparent that "such effect was not the design and intent of the law." However, if the complaint flowed "as a direct and necessary consequence from the principle of law, adopted upon a calculation to promote the general good," a court of equity could not interfere.[96] For Hoffman, reason and individual rights trumped the mystical power of the king's mercy.

Virginia also adopted the English tradition of a court of chancery, with jurisdiction over all persons and cases in equity with a value of at least thirty-three and one-third dollars. St. George Tucker explained that in colonial Virginia the general court had all the powers and jurisdiction of a court of chancery but that upon Independence Virginians chose to separate the court of equity from the court of law. It was not long, however, before these separate equity and common law jurisdictions began to blend together again. In 1777, when the court was first organized, the legislature allotted three judgeships for the tribunal, but in 1794 they reduced this number to one. By 1830, James Kent listed Virginia as a state in which there was no independent court of equity.[97]

Other states, however, never created a separate chancery court, because they did not believe that their republics needed that English institution in order to mete out impartial, yet compassionate, justice. Hugh Henry Brackenridge explained that Pennsylvania did not have a court of equity, nor did they need one, "for *equity is a part of our law;* and all our courts exercise *equitable jurisdiction.*"[98] Fellow Pennsylvanian James Wilson concurred. In his lecture on the judicial department he required that his students pay close attention to the subject of equity despite the absence of a court of chancery in his state. He used Aristotle's definition of equity, "the correction of that, in which the law is defective, by being too general."[99] Wilson explained that in making laws it was impossible to foresee every detail and every case in which that law might be used. There would, then, always be exceptions in which judges should "become the arbiters, instead of being the ministers of the laws." The Pennsylvania judge cautioned that judges should only use this power when and where "the strongest and most convincing reasons appear for using it," for example, when a decision that followed the law would go against the "spirit of the law" or against the "motive which prevailed on the legislature to make it." When equity was defined in this sense, every court of law was also a court of equity, and when applied to the interpretation of the law, it was an expression "synonymous to true and sound construction."[100] For Wilson, equity and common law could not be separated.

Wilson cautioned his students not to place the two kinds of justice in contradistinction to one another, because to conclude that a court of law decided without equity and a court of equity decided without law would be "greatly erroneous." He pointed out that all courts, not just those of equity, should be bound to explain the law according to the intention of those who made the law. Conversely, a court of equity was just as bound as courts of common law to abide by precedent and rules of law. In both chancery and common-law courts, "rules of property, the rules of interpretation, and the rules of evidence" were the same. There were, however, some material differences in the two courts. For example, at common law courts individuals could not be witnesses in their own favor and could not be obliged to furnish evidence against themselves. The court of equity, however, could examine the accused under oath. In courts of common law, trial was by jury, and common law required that all witnesses be present in court and give testimony viva voce. In chancery, however, witnesses could give written depositions and need not be present in court.[101] These differences in modes of confrontation between accuser and accused created two distinctive forms of justice. The potential for inequity was all the more reason to combine law and equity, according to many American legists.

One would expect that as the retired chancellor of New York, James Kent would have provided a clear sense of the place of equity in American law. This was not, however, the case. In his *Commentaries on American Law,* Kent rarely mentioned courts of chancery in the states. He allotted one extensive footnote to the subject in which he listed the various modes of dealing with equity jurisdiction among the states as of the mid-1820s.[102] Kent's lack of concern with the chancery court reflected an increasingly common attitude that, as Hugh Henry Brackenridge and James Wilson had pointed out, law and equity should not be separated, particularly in the atmosphere of equitable justice that America's republics cultivated. Therefore, practically speaking, by the 1830s law students and practitioners did not need to know the special functions of a court of equity unless they still lived in one of the few states that preserved the distinction between common law and equity. The notion of equity in the law remained a key point of study for legal practitioners, however, and James Wilson would have been pleased to see Judge Joseph Story's treatment of equity in his *Commentaries on Equity Jurisprudence* (1836). This important work provided law students with an American alternative to Blackstone's English interpretation of a law of equity that existed outside the common law. Story's treatise recognized American courts' blending of common law and equity into one American mode of justice in the fashion that Wilson, Brackenridge, and Kent had described and placed the mitigating force of equity squarely in the center of American law, as all jurists' "conscience."[103] American jurists envisioned that in their republics, with proper checks on power, a judge's conscience should contribute to the protection of individual rights.

VI Despite the gradual incorporation of equity into America's common-law courts, precedent maintained a privileged status in the new nation's legal institutions. Americans inherited a legal culture steeped in the veneration of custom, but America's European settlers encountered legal situations that were without precedent. Land and inheritance issues, slavery, and the presence of Native Americans with territorial claims necessitated legal modifications that had nothing to do with English customs. Moreover, when Americans broke their ties to England, they also severed all obligations to follow British precedents. American legal educators taught that although precedent still held a prominent place in their courts' decision making, practitioners also had a right to question its validity under certain circumstances.[104] By questioning the place of precedent in their law, Americans also explored citizens' places in governance. Did the power of choice extend to the overturning or modification of important institutions like legal precedent?

Blackstone's answer to that question would have been a qualified no. He argued that the foundations of the common law rested on the authority of maxims and rules that enjoyed general usage from time immemorial. Precedent, the legitimation of legal custom, took place in the courts and thus determined the law in England. One of these established rules, Blackstone wrote, was that judges were to abide by legal precedent when deciding any litigation. This strict adherence to precedent kept the "scale of justice even and steady . . . and not liable to waver with every new judge's opinion." In essence, every judge was sworn to determine, "not according to his own private judgment, but according to the known laws and customs of the land." Judges were not delegated to pronounce new laws but rather were sworn to maintain and expound the old ones.[105] Therefore, judges had limited power to ignore or change precedent.

While he believed that Englishmen owed a rigorous "deference to former times," Blackstone admitted that there were exceptions to this rule. If a past determination was "most evidently contrary to reason," or even more so if it was contrary to divine law, judges could rule against precedent. Blackstone did not consider this reversal a creation of new law, but rather a vindication "of the old one from misrepresentation." In other words, when judges ruled against "bad law," they were merely correcting a mistake that one of their predecessors committed. Bad law, in Blackstone's opinion, could not be called law, because it was contrary to reason, and that which did not follow reason was not law.[106]

American legists treated precedent with only slightly less veneration than did Blackstone, and they too emphasized the value of prior decisions in determining the validity of causes in their own courts. James Wilson asserted that a judge "should bear a great regard to the sentiments and decisions of those" who had deliberated and offered judicial decisions before him. This sort of deference to a point of law, simply "because one man or a succession of men have said it in law," was, Wilson explained, perfectly logical. In certain sciences, "a peculiar degree of regard should be paid to authority," and according to Wilson, the common law was one of those sciences. He echoed Blackstone's sentiment that judicial decisions were "the principal and most authentick evidence . . . of the existence of such a custom" as was entitled to form a part of the common law. The Pennsylvania jurist cautioned each judge to remember that it was "his duty and his business . . . not to make the law, but to interpret and apply it."[107] Despite Wilson's insistence on Americans' rights to choose, he recognized that custom still occupied an important place in the nation's legal culture.

Deference to precedent, however, only went so far. Tapping Reeve observed that there were "certain *maxims* universally acknowledged & received as principles of the common law" and that those maxims or precedents were the first resort of any judge. But he warned that precedent represented "the evidence of what the common law" was, as "handed down by wise men," rather than the law itself. Reeve cautioned his students to distinguish jurists' pronouncements from legal principles.[108] Moreover, if precedent failed to yield an answer, the court had "nothing to resort to, but the dictates of reason & justice which [were] written in no volume but that of nature & which [were] indelibly impressed . . . on the mind & heart of man." When a judge's decision hinged on this natural law, his opinion immediately became "a *precedent* for future Courts to resort to." Therefore, while it was true that judges did not make the law of reason, Reeve believed that at such times as there was no precedent for their case, judges could make decisions agreeable to the law of reason and thus "establish a rule as part of the Common Law which was no part of it before." This procedure, Reeve insisted, was the only way by which "novel" cases could be settled.[109] Whereas Reeve limited judges' discretion only to the novel, others stretched American judicial license a bit further.

Zephaniah Swift used his state's colonial history to argue that Connecticut judges were not bound by the authority of precedents at all times and that they were specifically not bound by English precedents. The only certain rule that directed the student of the law, Swift wrote, was the practice and decisions of their own courts, and Swift even went so far as to claim that colonial jurists in his home state considered the common law of England "as auxiliary" to their statutes, rather than conceiving of it as "the basis of their jurisprudence." From the first settlement, Swift explained, Connecticut's founders enacted many colonial laws that were significantly different from English law. Therefore, the common law's validity in Connecticut depended on the assembly's approval and the authority of the courts to admit it as law, and not on any statute or other declaration specifying the validity of the common law in Connecticut. According to Swift, the state's legislature and judiciary also had power to choose which English precedents they honored and which they did not. Whereas Connecticut courts had given "new force and evidence to a principle part of the common law of England," Swift claimed that they also rightfully chose not to honor certain aspects of precedent that did not fit within their republic.[110]

The one obstacle Swift saw to the Connecticut judiciary creating its own discrete body of precedent was the fact that although courts were not at liberty to depart from prior decisions in similar cases unless those decisions were repugnant to reason, few reports of Connecticut cases had been published. In the 1780s the legislature passed an act requiring judges of Connecticut's Supreme Court of Errors and the superior court to place the grounds and reasoning behind their arguments in writing and to register these written records with the clerk of court. This act, Swift believed, was a start, but he also feared that until these Connecticut case reports appeared, the state's courts would remain judicially dependent on England. Without these written reports, Connecticut lawyers and judges were obliged to "trust the memory of man" or to rely on written English precedent.[111] In some cases, jurists were forced to resort to their English roots, whether or not they were comfortable with the prospect.

Reliance on English precedent was a distasteful idea for many legists in the early republic, and Peter DuPonceau seconded Swift's assertion that even in the colonial era America's magistrates had deviated from English legal opinions. In an address to the Philadelphia College of Law, DuPonceau noted that before the Revolution, judges in colonial tribunals "shewed a disposition to accommodate the law to the local circumstances of the country" and that after Independence they had continued this practice, in some states even completely rejecting English precedent. For example, Pennsylvania and New Jersey passed laws prohibiting their courts from citing British authorities in decisions passed down after the Revolution. DuPonceau did not approve of such a summary prohibition. He complained that it applied "the axe to the root of the tree" and was an "ill judged and inefficient remedy, but at the same time a solemn warning to Judges" about "the manner in which the people wished the law to be administered."[112] Whether these ideas originated with "the people" or among judges, Massachusetts attorney general James Sullivan agreed with DuPonceau that these exclusions were "sudden, rash, and improper." However, he was certain that such anti-English sentiments originated in "a strong love to our national independence."[113] Both Sullivan and DuPonceau found it hard to fault Americans for demonstrating their nationalistic sentiments, even if they did so at the expense of reason.

DuPonceau recognized the necessity of following English precedent in certain circumstances, but Supreme Court decisions indicated a swing back toward a much more rigid adherence to English judicial decisions, which also concerned him. The high court itself was an innovation unlike anything in England. Justices who sat on American courts of last resort felt their way through uncharted territories, bounded by narrow jurisdictions. To establish a good reputation among the European powers, the new republic had to appear confident that its judiciary was equal to, or better than, the parent country's system. To that end, DuPonceau cautioned his audience that American jurists would not gain the respect of British judges "by servilely echoing their decisions and opinion." Rather, they would earn respect by "shewing them that the science of jurisprudence [was] not exclusively theirs, by decently contradicting them when a proper occasion offer[ed], and by correcting their errors when discovered," while at the same time accepting their corrections of American judicial errors.[114] Equal status required that U.S. courts establish their authority while also recognizing that English precedent could still be useful.

Many legists looked on precedent as a double-edged sword that judges also could use to block, rather than encourage, evolution of the law. Although they believed that precedent was the key to the perpetuity of the common law, they feared that if jurists relied solely upon narrow interpretations of precedent to make law, they could make no improvements in their law. Nathaniel Chipman warned that judges had for generations adhered to a number of ancient legal decisions, "however obscure or uncertain the principles upon which they were founded," even "when the state of society, and of property," had been "very different" from the contemporary situation. Times had changed, and Chipman lamented the judges' hesitation to upset the order of immemorial law. Instead, they left many obsolete precedents to await legislative remedy, rather than addressing those changes from the bench.[115] James Wilson also harbored reservations about strict adherence to precedent. Despite his caution to judges to refrain from "making" the law, Wilson warned that although observation of precedent might "prevent the trouble of investigation," it could also "prevent . . . the pleasure and advantages of improvement." Wilson counseled his students to walk a fine line between respect for established legal opinions and "blind assent" to the dictates of the past.[116]

Hugh Henry Brackenridge cautioned his audience against the tendency to become too attached to precedent, because it was necessary for law to be mutable for improvement's sake. The frontier jurist blamed the "timidity of judges," with perhaps too great "a respect for the profession," for this desire to stick closely to the decisions of their predecessors.[117] Brackenridge recognized that the nature of the English legal system required acknowledgment of precedent when deciding cases, but he cautioned the reader to use his own faculties of reason as the final deciding factor. He advised his audience that "the first lesson to a student of the law ought to be, to distrust authority. A mere automaton of decision" was, to Brackenridge, "little better than the machine that plays chess by springs."[118] A more independent attitude was necessary to allow the American judicial system to grow into its own institution.

When Brackenridge, Chipman, and their colleagues pointed out these limitations on the usefulness of precedent, they were reacting at least in part to Blackstone's own concerns about English courts' tendencies to overturn judgments or throw cases out, citing technical errors or breaches of precedent. This "literal strictness of the courts," according to Blackstone, caused a "great obstruction of justice, and ruin of the suitors," and American jurists vowed to avoid such mistakes in their newly formed systems of justice.[119] They took Blackstone's warning to heart, that if they allowed precedents to govern absolutely, "the law would be the same 500 years hence," as it was then, and instead of changing "with the manners & customs of the people, . . . it would remain a stale & antiquated rule without spirit or meaning" and in its obsolescence would be "erroneous & unjust, . . . unfit & inapplicable" to America's changing societies.[120] They could not form exemplary republics on stale laws.

For Blackstone's American disciples, the way to avoid the dangers of "antiquated," "erroneous," or "unjust" law was to educate oneself on the principles on which each particular precedent was founded. Armed with this knowledge, if a jurist found that a law did not conform to such a principle despite repeated recognition in the court opinions of "men of learning," he could safely declare it to be "not law."[121] Without this knowledge, he was bound to perpetuate the narrow mistakes of the past. As one of the Litchfield students put it, if a scholar of the law neglected to educate himself on the principles behind a court decision, knowledge of precedents alone, though useful, did "not make a genuine or liberal Lawyer, but only a technical one."[122] America needed better than merely "technical" lawyers to maintain and improve its distinctive republican legal systems. It was most important that these young lawyers be well informed. They were, in effect, representatives of the people, and they had to be prepared to decide whether any precedent should retain its authority. Therefore, the principles behind the precedent were crucial components to their law educations.

When they addressed the creation and development of the American court system, the republic's first legal educators and writers communicated a dual lesson to their audience. The first part of this lesson was that America's leaders had invented the very finest constitution and court system the world had ever seen. St. George Tucker boasted that while English courts generally provided the models with which American framers began to fashion their tribunals, local circumstances introduced a variety of new forms that, "by imperceptible and gradual changes, [had] lost all resemblance to the British original." He considered these changes for the best, and at the time that he wrote his treatise he confidently asserted that in no other country were there so many efficient courts of judicature whose jurisdiction was "competent to afford relief in all cases." Americans had taken the modes of proceeding at common law and had created from them a system that was faster and more equitable than their English predecessors. This new and better system was still capable of improvement, but Tucker pointed out that these improvements had to grow gradually, from experience.[123]

Now that they believed that they had created the finest court system in the world, American law professors and treatise writers admonished the next generation of lawyers to keep it. Their tribunals were still works in progress, and just as Revolutionary-era leaders made adjustments to achieve independent judiciaries, contemporary tribunals needed adjustments as well. American legists were also aware that the changes would not cease with the next generation. It was up to the citizens to make sure that their judicial institutions kept pace with their societies.

VII

Even if they did not make the law their profession, American citizens still contributed to the administration of justice in their polities. For many law professors and treatise writers, the very finest part of their English judicial heritage, and one that was most felicitous to their republics, was the jury. Blackstone called trial before one's peers "the grand bulwark" of every Englishman's liberties.[124] Juries were, according to Blackstone, used in the earliest Saxon colonies in Briton, and some historians claimed that the Britons themselves, "first inhabitants" of the island, also used juries. The feudal system made use of the jury trial, and this ancient practice was a central privilege outlined in the Magna Charta. Blackstone insisted that the history and varieties of trial by jury should be part of every gentleman's education, because he would be "frequently called upon to determine in this capacity the rights of others, his fellow-subjects." This ancient practice, Blackstone believed, was the key to maintaining every man's "own property, his liberty, and his life."[125] Legal scholars in the early republic echoed Blackstone's sentiments about the necessity of the jury to the maintenance of a free and equal system of justice. Just as in other political and social circumstances, however, the words "free" and "equal" carried different meanings in America than in England, particularly when it came to the question of who should sit in judgment of his peers. In America, just as suffrage was broader than in England, so was the pool of potential jurors. Because of this broader American concept of representation, juries served justice from a different perspective. America's legal scholars described juries as alternative representative bodies, as additional symbols of popular sovereignty, and as powerful checks on the actions of judges.

The jury's importance to free and independent justice was a theme that professors and law treatise writers described as a part of their British heritage made better by American equality of opportunity and by the securing of these rights through written constitutions. In seventeenth- and eighteenth-century England and America, courts were the most accessible arm of government because townspeople witnessed the actions of government officials firsthand, and because, particularly in America, a broad cross-section of ordinary citizens took part in this brand of local decision making. Local governance functioned in great measure through the courts, as judges and juries spent most of their time on day-to-day cases of petty crimes and neighborhood squabbles. Juries interpreted both the facts and the law in these local cases. Many local magistrates had no more legal training than their fellow townsmen and members of the jury; therefore determination of fact and law based on common sense rather than technical knowledge of the common law was the norm in early Anglo-America.[126] The jury's role in "finding" the law meant that jurors contributed to the determination of specific cases as well as the alteration of common law to fit local customs. This power of local decision making, which often crossed the boundary into lawmaking, gave the jury a forceful representative voice in local government that endured beyond the Revolution and became part of the new polities' frames of government.[127] By the Virginia Bill of Rights and the U.S. Constitution, Tucker asserted, every man accused of wrongdoing had the right to demand the cause and nature of the accusation, he was able to face his accusers and witnesses to the offense, he had the right to call for evidence in his favor, and he was entitled to receive a speedy trial by a jury of his peers.[128]

James Wilson praised Blackstone's depiction of juries as another mode of popular representation. "To be tried only by men of one's own condition," Wilson stated, was "one of the greatest blessings" as well as "one of the greatest securities" that a man could enjoy. Unlike present-day trials that demand the impartiality of judge and jury through lack of familiarity with the circumstances and central figures in a case, in the early republic magistrates wanted jurors who were familiar with the people and places involved in a trial. Wilson stressed the facility of appointing jurors who were familiar with the characters of the witnesses, the plaintiff, and the accused. He warned that a jury comprised of a selected body of men from outside the community, who were removed from the context of the dispute, left much to chance. It was much better if the jury consisted of "a competent number of sensible and unprejudiced jurymen" summoned from among the local citizenry for each particular cause. These representatives of the citizenry would not only be able to determine the facts of the case, but they could also judge the credibility of the witnesses. If juries consisted of local citizens familiar with the circumstances surrounding the incident in question, "truth," Wilson concluded, would "be estimated by the character, and not by the number" of those who gave testimony.[129]

In his lecture on juries, Wilson acknowledged that it might seem extraordinary to employ "twelve men, untutored in the study of jurisprudence," as "the ultimate interpreters of the law, with a power to overrule the directions of the judges." When one looked closely into the specifics of such a responsibility, however, Wilson pointed out that the decision of guilt or innocence often hinged on such factors as the character and conduct of the witnesses and, sometimes, on the character and conduct of the prisoner. The jury, Wilson concluded, was "the fittest to make the proper comparison and estimate" of these factors, and to leave the determination of guilt or innocence to them was, therefore, most reasonable. Juries certainly could, and did, make mistakes, but Wilson assured his students that because they were constantly rotated in and out of their offices as jurors, these mistakes could "never grow into a dangerous system." Wilson was certain that the "native uprightness" of a jury's sentiments would not bend "under the weight of precedent and authority." Besides, these rare mistakes were not without redress. If a grand jury incorrectly indicted an accused criminal, a verdict of innocent would surely result. If a petit jury wrongly convicted, the court had the power to grant a new trial.[130] These safeguards provided additional assurance that, if one man or group of men erred, the institutional structure provided opportunity for proper correction.

Nathaniel Chipman also noted the peculiar place that "plain sense, conversant only in the common business of life, and the common characters of men," held in the American courts. While the average freeholder might not possess the "professional and systematic knowledge" of those men more learned in the law, Chipman asserted that it was perfectly logical for men to acquiesce more readily to the verdict of a jury than the opinions of judges. Judges were viewed as "a distinct class, placed above the common interest and common feelings of the citizens." Because judges could hold the prejudices of their class about certain questions, juries had to be "taken from the substantial class of citizens" to counterbalance the interests of more learned men.[131] South Carolina judge John F. Grimké also recognized the importance of a jury composed of men whose background and experience might mirror that of the accused. "However illegal their conduct," Grimké insisted, "however enormous their offences," all men were entitled to a fair trial by their peers.[132]

Americans also looked upon juries as protectors of citizens' rights and a check on the power of the judges. For Nathaniel Chipman, this was just as true of grand juries, which considered whether there was sufficient evidence for a trial, as for petit juries, which passed judgment on the guilt or innocence of the accused. Under criminal law, the grand jury protected the rights of the accused by guarding "the innocent from the infamy and oppression of a public accusation" and impartially brought "forward the guilty to trial for their crimes." All juries were disinterested parties, "taken from the body of the people," who acted "as a shield between the accused, and the interested passions, or malicious attempts of private prosecutors."[133] This sort of "intervention between the people and the officers of the law" was not just an important symbol of the protection of rights within a free republic.[134] It also symbolized the exercise of popular sovereignty in the support of or protection against the powers of government.

James Wilson pointed out that although propertied Englishmen enjoyed the privilege of jury service, they could not share in this exercise of popular sovereignty nor could they enjoy the equal distribution of the burden of this sovereignty as Americans did. He reminded his readers of his previous discussion on the manner in which the people had delegated the legislative, executive, and judicial powers in their constitutions. The people, Wilson pointed out, retained for personal exercise authority to decide guilt or innocence in criminal cases and to determine the validity and degree of injury in civil cases. Wilson called this authority both a burden and a power. As a burden, it was too heavy to be imposed on any one man whom the people might appoint for that purpose. It was also too great a power for the people to confer permanently on any one man or body of men. Because responsibility for determining guilt or innocence was distributed among all of the citizens, no one man felt its burden or its power too strongly.[135] Diffusing the power of judgment protected individual rights, and rights protection was a lynchpin of the American character.

While legists celebrated the existence of trial by jury in America, they also sensed that internal and external forces were working to diminish the jury's authority in certain kinds of cases. They perceived this development as a threat to the reputation of that mode of trial and thus also to personal liberty. For example, Grimké noticed among some South Carolinians a lack of willingness to serve on juries. Courts were still barely accessible to those who lived in South Carolina's sparsely settled upcountry, obliging jurors to travel farther afield to serve. The resulting loss of time and wages made citizens reluctant representatives on the court. Grimké looked to practices in states "to the Northward" for a solution to this problem. He suggested that South Carolina courts pay jurors a small sum of money for attendance to their duty so that potential jurors did not have to make financial sacrifices while performing their responsibilities to the state.[136]

Payment for services, however, did not always resolve problems surrounding the selection of qualified jurors. St. George Tucker perceived a marked decline in the character of men who served on some juries in Virginia, and he attributed the problem to a "disregard to the characters and qualifications of jurors" on the part of the magistrates charged with selecting those officers of the court. He complained that in some parts of Virginia, juries were not "composed of the most respectable freeholders in the county" but rather consisted of "idle loiterers about the court, who contrived to get themselves summoned as jurors," so that they could collect pay for their service in the courts. These unfit representatives of the people frequently misunderstood or mishandled evidence, resulting in increased numbers of retrials. While qualifications for jury service existed in Virginia law, Tucker proposed a bill for amending the law concerning juries. He included remedies such as observance of property qualifications for all county and district jurors and also listed a number of less-tangible qualifications in the bill, such as honesty, discretion, and intelligence, all qualities that he hoped would bring "ability, integrity, and impartiality" to the courts. He also proposed excluding from jury duty persons who practiced certain necessary occupations, such as clergy, doctors, or overseers or managers of plantations, and he provided that officers of the government or the court also be excluded from service. Additionally, Tucker suggested that those reputed to be "conspirators, barretors, . . . swindlers, gamblers" or "idle haunters or frequenters of taverns" also be excluded from the jury rolls.[137] Tucker believed that these strict regulations, if the courts' magistrates followed them, would save the mode of trial by jury from disrepute in his home state.

While he may not have believed that all men were appropriate candidates for jury membership, Tucker jealously guarded the right to trial by jury and nervously observed a trend in Virginia's courts toward summary proceedings. Blackstone defined a summary proceeding as one that provided for the dispatch of a criminal or civil complaint by a judge working without the intervention of a jury. The English jurist gave several examples of the kinds of trials that could take place without a jury in England, such as violations of excise laws and specific petty offenses brought before the justice of the peace, such as common swearing, drunkenness, or vagrancy, or civil cases involving matters of ecclesiastical jurisdiction such as marriage, excommunication, or "general bastardy."[138] Tucker disapproved of the entire notion of summary proceedings, and he assured his students and readers that many of the English species of summary trial were obsolete or never had been practiced in America. The Virginia legist warned, however, that summary judgments on proceedings "without the solemnity of a trial by jury" had increased rapidly in the recent past. Though Virginia's legislature created the Court of Chancery with the intention of trying all cases before a jury, in 1783 they repealed that portion of the article requiring a jury trial. In its place, the assembly established the option of a summary trial in the Court of Chancery. The chancellor could still order a trial by jury in his or any other court but also could try matters of fact by himself, solely on his discretion. Other instances in which jury trials could be bypassed were cases at common law in which the sum in question was very small or those in which a public officer had to answer for an alleged delinquency. Additionally, cases requiring "the most speedy aid to prevent [the plaintiff] from suffering by the defendant's default" and cases in which the defendant had already received "the utmost indulgence of the law" were also eligible for summary proceedings.[139] This movement toward more frequent summary trials did not sit well with Tucker.

Through their own examples of constantly seeking improvements in their governments, legal scholars taught their audience that they continually had to question the effectiveness of their institutional processes and to make changes when necessary. Despite their willingness to experiment, Tucker and his colleagues believed that the custom of jury trials was one English feature worth preserving. Moreover, through American republics' practice of broad participation in their juries, they believed that American framers had improved the institution and had infused more common sense and equity into their legal system with their improvements. Therefore, they tried to impress on their audience the importance of preserving the institution of the jury, which, Tucker declared, the framers of the Bill of Rights "held *sacred.*"[140] The seemingly incompatible qualities of veneration of custom, willingness to experiment, and openness to change had become important components of the American republics' identities.

In performing their tasks as educators, legal scholars helped to demystify old forms of the government while building up the political body of the sovereign people in their place. As James Wilson put it, in England, the "people" was a group scarcely noticed, or if noticed at all, they merely were "considered as the body, of which the king [was] the head," and were "viewed as the subjects of his crown and government." In Pennsylvania, on the other hand, the people were the polity, and in the United States they were "in the foreground of the constitution: 'We the people.'" According to Wilson, America's citizens formed an artificial person, a body politic that he described "as a complete body of free natural persons, united together for their common benefit." This body of individuals, Wilson wrote, possessed an understanding and a will that it used to deliberate, resolve, and act politically. It possessed interests and expected to perform certain obligations in return for enjoying certain rights. "To this moral person" Wilson assigned, "by way of eminence, the dignified appellation of *state.*"[141]

In effect, American legists' lectures described how Americans had replaced a mystical monarchy and sovereign parliament with a sovereign body called "the people." American citizens created and protected their constitutions, and in turn their written constitutions protected them from the dangers of a corrupt legislature and overbearing monarch of the kind they believed existed in England. Legal scholars' depictions of a corruptible and uncontrollable sovereign parliament provided a mirror for the virtues that a sovereign citizenry could bring to their republics. This reflection helped to perpetuate the Revolutionary identity of America as the ideal political order built around a reasonable and collectively wise citizenry. These descriptions of the ultimate sovereign helped to define for the next generation of Americans their identities as members of societies created by and for the people.

America's legal scholars communicated the idea that innovative constitutional protections were products of the American character and that, in turn, the nation's character boasted deep roots. They were able to create an image of a citizenry that possessed equal political influence because of the economic opportunity available to an unprecedented number of people within the nation. Its open societies stemmed from the seemingly unending supply of land and the wealth that this land, and other forms of property, brought to the nation's denizens. And yet, chances to gain wealth and influence did not extend to all inhabitants of the new nation. As legists advertised the nation's constitutions and laws as tangible evidence of Americans' superior character, they had to contend with darker images of restrictions and oppression alongside the images of openness and opportunity.

3 Property Acquisition and Inheritance

In America, James Wilson declared, property was "of more consequence than life or personal liberty."[1] With this statement, Wilson combined English traditions of exclusive property rights with the American experience of upward mobility through ease of property acquisition to produce a snapshot of American attitudes toward property and status in the early national period. From the first British colonial settlements, the abundance of land and the absence of a hereditary aristocracy to monopolize that land were central to forming American identities. This key point of difference between American and English societies meant that American property law worked under a distinctive set of cultural definitions. American legists agreed with their English counterparts that one of the most important functions of government was to protect property. But unlike the English, Americans owed no superior for their property or its protection. Instead, the state and federal governments protected the right of property ownership for all citizens. These fundamental differences in the nature of property ownership led to numerous American departures from English property law, particularly with regard to ownership and conveyance of real property. As they described the origins and evolution of their property law, American legists drew upon the unique circumstances that made freer modes of property ownership and conveyance possible. The abundance and low cost of land created new dynamics of acquisition. Many fathers hoped that their children would maintain the family estate, but a fluid economic and social structure meant that real property easily changed hands, even moved outside of the family, and fathers and sons had choices as to who would work on and inherit family land. America's more fluid property exchange made England's restrictive conveyance and inheritance laws unnecessary in the New World, and colonial courts and assemblies often disregarded confining English customs of primogeniture and entail in favor of more practical and egalitarian practices.[2] Upon Independence, each state legislature reaffirmed colonial regulations on property transactions, and in some cases the new states made property acquisition and inheritance laws more liberal.

While they acknowledged that their property laws shared a history and many technical definitions with English law, American legists wanted their audience to comprehend that Americans had not just modified common-law tenets to fit their societies. Instead, America's legal scholars posited that their legislatures had invented a completely different kind of property law, particularly with regard to the laws of descent. These egalitarian innovations, they asserted, better reflected the American character. Legal scholars designed their discussions of property law to highlight the ways in which the states had cleared away all feudal property laws and had replaced them with rational and egalitarian laws tailored specifically to each state's needs. Moreover, each state crafted its own set of regulations for ownership and conveyance of property. Distinctive American property laws not only helped to illustrate the development of American identities, but also portrayed one way in which the law preserved local and regional identities.

I

Along with the conviction that the government should protect citizens' property, the fundamentals of property ownership in America were still recognizably English, down to the historical narrative of the evolution, definitions, and categories of property ownership. Legal scholars were happy to borrow definitions and histories from their English counterparts, but they readily contrasted English notions of property held at the behest of the king with America's more equitable absolute property ownership. While they borrowed common-law terminology, American legists when necessary modified the definitions to give them more republican meanings.

Legal scholars cribbed freely from Blackstone's lengthy dissertation on the history of private property ownership. The English jurist began his lectures on the history of private property by exploring its natural law origins. At first, men owned all things in common. Man's possession of an object lasted only as long as his immediate need for that object. As the world's population increased, men began to "entertain conceptions of more permanent dominion . . . and to appropriate to individuals not the immediate *use* only, but the very *substance* of the thing to be used." This measure prevented conflict in the world's increasingly populous societies. Still, the land itself remained common until the "art of agriculture" encouraged men to produce goods out of the soil. The resulting desire to maintain ownership of those parcels he had improved introduced the idea of "a more permanent property in the soil." A man ultimately claimed title to a parcel of land through occupancy. Until that original owner abandoned the property, it was his in sole proprietorship.[3]

Tapping Reeve borrowed and condensed Blackstone's descriptions of English property law's feudal origins into a series of lectures on the historical roots of American property law. Originally, Reeve explained, donors granted estates to feudal chieftains in exchange for the fidelity of the grantee, and these chieftains owned England's estates only for the duration of the donor's will. Eventually, in order to secure the loyalty of their subjects and their subjects' heirs, the chieftains began to grant estates to heirs. In England, an heir could only be the eldest living son of the owner, and no collateral relation could inherit from the grantee.[4] There was no "alienation" or buying and selling of land at a price until the crusades necessitated the sale of small portions of real property to raise money. As England's local chieftainships gave way to a consolidated monarchy, the king became the lord and ultimate donor of all lands. Gradually, purchase of property became more common, although landholders could not dispose of their property by will until the reign of Henry VIII. Inheritance was still confined to those men who directly descended from the first purchaser, or what they styled "the blood of the first purchaser."[5] These customs regulating descent may have been necessary in England, but from the first settlements in America, they proved far too restrictive.

The first English colonists understood that the New World was the ideal field of experimentation with different modes of property ownership. As James Wilson and James Kent noted in their lectures, the first American settlements tried to return to simpler societal arrangements that included holding all property in common, but these experiments with common property bore "uncomfortable" results.[6] Virginia's first leaders originally planned to trade and produce goods jointly and to deposit and withdraw all supplies from common stores for the first five years of the colony's existence. Instead of promoting cooperative production, however, this plan led to "idleness and immorality." A similar experiment at the Plymouth Colony "was found to be injurious even with that small, simple and pious band of immigrants."[7]

The drive for individual property ownership proved to be too firmly engrained among New World settlers for them to subordinate their desires for personal gain to colonial leaders' version of the common good.

From these stories of the early settlers' experiments with common property, Wilson and Kent concluded that although equality of opportunity was a key to America's commercial and social superiority, equal access to property did not provide the same results. They asserted that the right to private ownership of property was most conducive to the industry and progress that helped their republics to thrive and to shape their nation's character. Wilson contended that man was "intended for action" and that the natural and appropriate reward for "useful and active industry" was property. Exclusive ownership of property promoted "economy and care," prevented disorder, and facilitated the development of "distinct professions and the division of labour."[8] When a community chose not to hold property in common but instead allowed "a free circulation" of property and abolished such restrictions as perpetuities, entailments, claims of primogeniture, and "inequalities of descent," Kent claimed, the laws of nature would "themselves preserve a proper equilibrium . . . and dissipate the mounds of property as fast as they accumulate[d]." For Kent, the moral of these tales was that "the state of equality" that accompanied common property did not "suit the present condition of man" and was actually "against the laws of our nature."[9] The natural state of man was one of individual ownership and individual gain.

Kent's description of private property as a catalyst for commercial expansion was far more enthusiastic than any of the earlier treatise writers. By the time he had published his *Commentaries* in the 1820s, Kent had the advantage of seeing his nation's land mass double and the population increase significantly. Despite war and economic hardships, America's commercial success was evident by the first few decades of the nineteenth century, and Kent and others of his generation attributed much of the growth to the incentives provided by the nation's equitable property laws. Individual gain contributed to the general welfare of the nation through the growth of American commerce. Kent pronounced that the incentive to own private property had cultivated an individual industriousness that in turn had benefited America's economy and commercial society in general. The right to property ownership, Kent explained, was "graciously implanted in the human breast, for the purpose of rousing us from sloth . . . and stimulating us to action." As long as a man acquired property according to the law, his right to that property "ought to be sacredly protected," and the exclusive right of transferring property to individuals of the owner's choice, Kent wrote, followed "as a natural consequence" from the right to possess property. According to Kent, the "natural and active sense of property" was the cornerstone of social improvement, which led to "the cultivation of the earth, the institution of government, the establishment of justice, the acquisition of the comforts of life, the growth of the useful arts, the spirit of commerce, the productions of taste, the erections of charity, and the display of the benevolent affections."[10]

Just as they had borrowed and adapted Blackstone's explanations of the history and nature of private property ownership, America's legal scholars also adopted common-law definitions and categories of property ownership and then made Americanizing modifications when necessary. Blackstone defined property as "that sole and despotick dominion which one man claims and exercises over the external things of the world, in total exclusion of the right of any other individual in the universe."[11] Property was divided into things real and things personal. Things real were immoveables such as lands and tenements. Things personal were moveable possessions like money, furnishings, clothing, and other goods. Under English law, real property did not consist merely of the tangible, or corporeal, soil of the land but also of many intangible, or incorporeal, rights and privileges that the owner automatically possessed. Together, these corporeal and incorporeal components comprised the *hereditament,* or the body of goods and privileges that one inherited or could devise to others.[12] Although some English definitions of real property still applied to American legal culture, their meanings were often modified.

In his lectures, St. George Tucker indicated that not all English incorporeal *hereditaments* still existed in America and that if they did exist, they had taken on more "republican" forms. For example, titheables, which in England were one-tenth of any yearly increases in profits of lands, stock, or other property that the owner presented to the church, took on a different character in Virginia. The Virginia government still assessed titheables for the maintenance of clergy, but instead of paying the tax on land profits, Virginians paid assessments for potential labor sources. Titheables included all males, slave or free, over sixteen and female slaves over sixteen in the household, the number of whom was assessed for the provision of the clergy. In this form titheables were not considered incorporeal *hereditaments.*[13] Moreover, the right of office and the right of dignities were not considered *hereditaments* in Virginia. No man, Tucker asserted, could inherit a public office in Virginia, nor was any man entitled to exclusive or separate privileges from the community. Although in colonial times the Crown had granted franchises to certain Virginians, the General Assembly annulled these privileges during the Revolution because it considered them branches of the king's prerogative.[14] From Independence on, republican governments leveled the playing field by eliminating such advantages.

American legists also borrowed English methods of delineating degrees of ownership, from limited to absolute possession. Blackstone defined the term "conditional fees" or "fees tail" as denoting landownership with any sort of limitation attached. These estates were limited as to who could inherit them or the length of time that the heir could remain in possession. For example, estates held only for the life of the heir or estates that could pass only to a male heir were conditional fees. Property held in fee simple meant that the land could descend to anyone, without restriction. Blackstone explained that those who held fee simple property in England were still beholden to the monarch and therefore did not own the property outright. Fee simple was not the same as an *allodium*, or absolute possession in a man's own right. Only England's monarch possessed allodial land. All English subjects' lands were therefore "in the nature of *feodum*, or fee."[15] In England, these limitations of ownership made sense, because of the strict hierarchies embedded in the English social structure. But Americans found the idea of dependence on a superior objectionable.

American legal scholars who touched upon the subject of property ownership made much of the fact that no landowner in America was beholden to a superior for his property. Henry St. George Tucker designated this presence of a superior as the fundamental difference between property ownership under the English monarchy and owning property in the United States. In England, Tucker observed, a man was merely "trustee for land held at the behest of the king," whereas in America, a property holder was "beholden only" to himself.[16] The history of this American form of land ownership stretched back before the Revolution. Massachusetts attorney general James Sullivan explained that in pre-Revolutionary America, "the foundation and source of the estate was considered as being in the Colony itself."[17] American legists branded English property-holding customs as pure feudalism, and they declared to their audience that American legislatures had jettisoned all vestiges of feudal property practices from their republics. James Kent observed that England held the dubious distinction, "above every part of Europe," of holding fast to the most ancient and universal feudal tenures, and he repeated Blackstone's statement that because the king was the benefactor of all landholders, he alone held real property in allodium. Kent borrowed Blackstone's words to explain that all lands in England were held by some feudal tenure, with the formal establishment of feudal tenures "in their genuine character" coming during the reign of William the Conqueror.[18] This ancient tradition may have been satisfactory for Englishmen, but it was not compatible with America's republican polities.

Kent and Reeve both noted that their state laws no longer held to Blackstone's distinction between the terms "fee simple" and "allodial." Although by English common law the term "fee simple" originally implied an estate held under a superior, by the late eighteenth century Connecticut and New York law considered estates in fee simple the same as estates held in allodium. The American definition of a fee was an estate of inheritance in law, belonging to the owner and transmissible to his heirs without restriction. An estate in fee continued forever, with no limited duration. Those estates that had conditions attached regarding the duration of a lifetime were merely freeholds and not fees.[19] In Connecticut, Reeve explained, a fee simple was "*alienable,* devisable, descendible to the *heirs general,* liable to dower, & liable in the hands of the owner to be *extended* for his debts tho' not liable to be *sold* for that purpose."[20] Nathaniel Chipman echoed his colleagues' opinions that although English law still represented a feudal restraint on land ownership, in Vermont the only laws that applied to the rights of ownership or transfer of property were those that applied to allodial rights. All real property in Vermont, Chipman explained, was owned absolutely, and the owner did not hold "even in idea, of a superior."[21]

In many states the desire to protect rights to absolute property ownership resulted in legislative measures that transformed common law into statute. St. George Tucker cited a Virginia law declaring that lands formerly held by the king's prerogative or granted by colonial officials in the Old Dominion had since the Revolution been allodial, possessed in the owner's own right without owing any rent or service to a superior. In that same act, the General Assembly explicitly prescribed that all land as of that date was owned in fee simple and not beholden to any superior.[22] Even though Virginians had declared independence and established a new government under a written constitution, they still felt it necessary to put this additional measure of independence in writing.

Because Connecticut's government continued to operate under its British charter long after the Revolution, it was crucial that the legislature establish citizens' rights to absolute dominion over their property. Zephaniah Swift helped to establish Connecticut's independence from English property law with his version of the state's property law history. He claimed that even under the initial charter, Connecticut's landholders did not labor under the same restrictions as their English counterparts. Connecticut's founders had "experienced the inconvenience of feudal restraints upon landed property" and were "determined to hold their possessions by the freest tenure . . . and clearest title." He speculated that if the colony had been settled "under the direction and controul of the British crown" that their lands would have been burdened with "all the restraints of the feudal system." The colonial charter, however, imposed only minimal tenure restrictions on landholding. Thus, upon Independence the legislature could easily remove the light restraints by statute. In 1784 the Connecticut legislature confirmed that all lands previously held under the behest of the king were from that date forward considered allodial. Swift also noted that the legislature had recently passed an even stronger act declaring that even though Connecticut's charter from Charles II proclaimed that all lands were held at the behest of the King of England, this obligation no longer existed after the state's independence from Britain. Instead, at the break with the parent country, Connecticut's citizens "became veiled with an allodial title to their lands." The act further declared that every proprietor in fee simple possessed "an absolute and direct dominion and property in the same."[23] Thus, Connecticut completed its declaration of independence from England's property-holding restrictions even as its government still functioned under the former British charter.

II

English and American modes of alienating and acquiring property also held many similarities, though American legists tried to distinguish their own forms as far as possible from those practices of feudal descent. In England and America a man could acquire land through purchase or descent. The word "purchase," as Blackstone pointed out, had a much broader meaning than merely the "vulgar and confined" application to acquisition by "bargain and sale, for money, or some other valuable consideration."[24] The legal meaning of purchase encompassed five methods of acquiring title to estates. The first method was escheat, "one of the fruits and consequences of feodal tenure," in which property was forfeited to the lord of the soil because the line of heirs to the property had become extinct, or because there was no one legally capable of inheriting.[25] Next was title by occupancy, or taking possession of things that previously belonged to no one, a rare mode of acquisition in eighteenth-century England.[26] Third, title by prescription, or claim of immemorial use, was another rarely invoked English method of acquisition.[27] The fourth method was title by forfeiture, in which the owner forfeited the land as recompense for an illegal act of negligence. In England, the conviction for a crime or misdemeanor was grounds for forfeiture of property.[28] Finally, one could acquire land by alienation, the method that Blackstone called "the most usual and universal" mode of transferring real estate. Alienation meant the conveyance or purchase of property in its limited sense, by which estates were "voluntarily resigned by one man, and accepted by another."[29]

The practices of escheat and forfeiture of property constantly reminded American law practitioners of their escape from an oppressive system of property ownership. Even ownership in fee simple, the parent country's highest form of property possession, was, in James Gould's words as recalled by Timothy Follett, "nothing more than a feud."[30] According to English legal theory, all lands were given to their owners by the lord of the see, in return for military and other services. These lands were in turn handed down to the original donee's descendants. Should there ever be a time, however, when the blood of the donee's line became extinct, the lands reverted to the descendents of the lord of the see, which in England's case was ultimately the Crown. Estates could also be forfeited if the original donee's "blood be attainted." In other words, if he committed certain crimes such as treason, the Crown could revoke claims to the land. Additionally, in England, if there were no more descendants of the whole blood or if descendants were bastards, who were incapable under any circumstances of inheriting, the land escheated. Other reasons for taking an action of escheat were if the descendant was an alien or if the heir was "a monster, which hath not the shape of mankind, but in any part evidently [bore] the resemblance of the brute creation."[31] Blackstone also mentioned that by statute enacted during William III's reign, "every papist" who did not "abjure the errors of his religion by taking the oaths to the government" was incapable of inheriting or purchasing real estate in England. His Protestant next of kin could hold the estate for their own use "till such time as he complie[d] with the terms imposed by the act" and rejected the Roman Catholic religion in favor of Protestantism.[32]

America's legal scholars took pride in pointing out that when it came to instances of escheat and forfeiture, American law protected property better than did English law. In most states, not even for treason could lands be taken away from the owner. In Virginia, Tucker explained, no conviction or judgment for treason, murder, robbery, or other major offense was to "work corruption of blood, or any forfeiture of estate." Even convicted criminals did not forfeit their property. They continued to hold the property as long as they lived, and after their death it passed to their heirs as if they had died intestate.[33] In New York, anyone convicted of treason as late as 1830 forfeited all personal and real property during his lifetime, but, according to James Kent, "the tendency of public opinion" had been "to condemn forfeiture of property . . . as being an unnecessary and hard punishment of the felon's posterity." When the convict died, the wife's dower was still protected, and conviction for treason did not "corrupt the blood of the offender," as it did in England. James Gould noted the existence of a similar statute in Connecticut that declared all lands held as allodial, and this law made the practices of escheat and forfeiture extinct in that state.[34] In 1790, the federal government also passed a law abolishing forfeiture of estate and corruption of blood for federal crimes. According to Kent, even English lawmakers by the nineteenth century were softening these harsh laws. A bill introduced into Parliament in 1814 abolished corruption of blood in cases of felony, except murder.[35] In this particular case, it seemed that English lawmakers followed the U.S. lead.

Though American legists summarily rejected the existence of a superior in the fashion of an English monarch, they acknowledged their state governments as the ultimate heirs to any unclaimed property. This shift allowed property to become a moral tool by emphasizing the idea that private possessions should be used to the best advantage of the community. In those rare instances where escheat of property became a reality in America, according to Kent, the state stepped into "the place of the feudal lord, by virtue of its sovereignty, as the original and ultimate proprietor of all the lands within its jurisdiction." It was, Kent gathered, the general principle in American law that when the title to land failed because there were no heirs, possession reverted to "the people, as forming part of the common stock to which the whole community [was] entitled." Kent compared American laws of property forfeiture to Roman law, in which property of deceased persons with no recognized heirs vested "in the public" and was "at the disposal of the government" in what Kent called "the universal law of civilized society." This principle, Kent explained, lay "at the foundation of the right of property," that if ownership of property failed, "the right must necessarily subside into the whole community, in whom it was originally vested when society first assumed the elements of order and subordination."[36] Again, Kent emphasized the idea that the central purpose for individual property ownership was improvement of the community. When individual ownership failed, the community could reassign the property for the common good.

Tucker also used the concept of private property as part of the community's common stock, and he asserted that it was for the collective good of the citizens that when there ceased to be anyone with a hereditary claim to property it reverted "to the common stock." As community property, it could be retained by the community or granted to another member, depending on which decision would be better for that locality. Tucker distinguished this idea of property serving the needs of a community from the "idea of feudal superiority which formerly prevailed" by explaining that the Commonwealth was not "the superior lord of the soil, but [was] regarded, strictly, as *ultimas haeres* only."[37] This interpretation allowed the community to maintain its right to the property in the absence of an heir, without assuming the presence of any kind of superior claim in the feudal tradition.

The Commonwealth of Virginia also assumed the moral obligation of managing any property belonging to persons deemed incapable of maintaining an estate, such as "ideots and lunatics," but by statute the state restored the property to the rightful owner when they returned "to right mind." If such an owner died before recovering from his mental illness, state officials distributed the property as if the owner had died intestate. In England, Tucker pointed out, such property would become the conserve of the king, and after the owner's death, the estate would revert to the heirs. Though this process was similar to that adopted in Virginia, Tucker noted that in England the king or his designated administrator seemed to have full use of the profits of an "idiot's" estate after "finding him necessaries," without accountability to the unfortunate person's heirs. In Virginia, men who were placed in charge of the property were fully accountable to the heirs of the property owner, thus providing what Tucker considered a morally superior system of custodianship.[38]

Tucker also observed that although Virginia had not abolished escheat, any case of escheat to the Commonwealth was rare, because, unlike in England, any blood relation, including descendants and ascendants, linear and collateral, and those of the half blood could inherit. The ascendible quality of real estate, made part of Virginia law in 1785, contradicted one of the fundamental maxims of the common law, which was that an inheritance should escheat rather than "violate the laws of gravitation." In Virginia, if there were no descendants or ascendible heirs, the estate was distributed evenly between the paternal and maternal kin. English common law, Tucker pointed out, allowed no such benefits to the paternal and maternal kin. Instead, English law "would rather the land should escheat, than descend to any other . . . than the blood of the first purchaser, how remote soever he may be from the person last actually seised."[39] In a new nation, with ample land and a more egalitarian spirit, England's narrow definition of heirship was impractical.

The laws regarding escheat and forfeiture varied little among the states and followed the same moral guidelines of communal benefit as other American property laws. Tapping Reeve noted that if no heirs existed in Connecticut, the property escheated to the "public," which had the right to dispose of the property as it saw fit. Reeve pointed out that New York also abolished the law of escheat in cases of criminal conviction or other "taint of blood."[40] Hugh Henry Brackenridge noted that "extinction of inheritable blood by civil means" did not take place in Pennsylvania. No forfeiture of estate could happen simply because there were no direct descendants, nor were estates confiscated if the owner committed an offense against the state. As in Virginia, in the absence of heirs, land escheated to the Commonwealth, and by act of the Pennsylvania Assembly in 1787, escheat to the Commonwealth could happen only if there was no will and if the deceased had no heirs or known kin, ascending, descending, half or full blood.[41]

In reality, the only lands that experienced a systematic process of escheat in America were those lands that the Crown held at the time of the Revolution. Tucker noted that in 1799, Virginia law nullified the Crown's control over royal mines, quit-rents, which were rent payments that freed tenants from other obligations to their landlords, and other reservations and conditions of patents. From that point on, the General Assembly declared, all lands granted by patent from the Crown were held in absolute and unconditional property, by fee simple. The government set up a system by which lands could be surveyed and specified the manner in which one could file a petition for lands or a caveat to petitions to protest the patent holder's right to lands.[42] In this manner, Virginia and other states created an orderly process by which open lands could be claimed and private holdings could be protected.

During the Revolution, debates raged over whether those who remained loyal to England should be deemed aliens and whether they should be allowed to keep their property in the former colonies. In his edition of Blackstone's *Commentaries,* St. George Tucker discussed the issues surrounding land confiscated from British subjects during the Revolution. By legislative act, British subjects who chose to remain loyal to the parent country became aliens and enemies of the United States and were therefore incapable of holding property in Virginia. With the treaty of peace came gestures of compensation for confiscated property, but by statute anyone still professing loyalty to the British Crown could not possess land in Virginia after the Revolution.[43] Zephaniah Swift placed Connecticut's confiscation of loyalist property under the category of forfeiture of estates for the conviction of a crime. He explained that during the war with Great Britain, people who "were adjudged guilty of the crime . . . of having voluntarily joined and put themselves under the protection of the enemies of the United States" forfeited their lands to the state of Connecticut. But Swift did not endorse the confiscation of lands for just any instance of treason. He blamed the exigencies of war for the legislature's enactment of such an extreme measure, and he emphasized the temporary nature of the law.[44]

Other legists also discussed loss of property in such exceptional times as the Revolution. While judge on the Virginia Circuit Court, Tucker heard the case of *Hunter v. Fairfax* (1794), which involved a dispute over Thomas Lord Fairfax's land in Virginia's Northern Neck. The question was whether the Commonwealth had confiscated some of Fairfax's land because he was a British subject who chose to remain neutral during the Revolution. Fairfax died in 1781 during the war between England and its former colonies, and his closest heir was at the time an alien enemy. According to common law, the heir's enemy status made the devise void, but the treaty of 1783 ending the war guaranteed British property against confiscation. Therefore, the land should have gone to the next eligible heir rather than being escheated to the Commonwealth. In the original case of 1794, Tucker decided in favor of the defendant, Fairfax's heir, and he ruled that the property had been improperly confiscated. The Virginia Supreme Court overturned Tucker's ruling, and the increasingly complicated case continued on appeal until the U.S. Supreme Court upheld Tucker's ruling in 1813 and again in 1816.[45] These Supreme Court cases carried far greater implications than the determination regarding confiscation of wartime property, but the idea that private property rights should be privileged over almost any other right remained at the center of the Supreme Court's decisions.

In this and other examples muddied by war and shifting allegiances, American law governing property ownership by aliens was largely more generous than in England. Writing on this subject in the 1820s, St. George Tucker's son Henry observed a curious construction of English common law that allowed an alien to purchase land in England, but his possession of the land was always tenuous. The king could take the land at any time because the law did not permit foreigners to hold the soil of the country. Tucker noted that because the alien did not have a right to hold the estate, the king "became the owner of what was thus without any other proprietor." But why, then, was any alien ever allowed to purchase land? Henry Tucker turned his answer into a jab at England by guessing that this puzzling practice may have originated in "the rapacity of the crown; or it may have been as a punishment to the alien" for not being English.[46]

Americans, on the other hand, demonstrated how the abundance of lands influenced their polities' openness to new settlers through their liberal citizenship requirements and state laws regarding property acquisition by aliens. James Kent made note of the U.S. relaxation of "the force of this rigorous doctrine" against landownership by aliens. Foreigners, Kent explained, were admitted into American citizenship "on liberal terms." The law required "only five years residence . . . to entitle them *and their families* to become naturalized citizens," and Kent believed that this generous policy implied "a right, in the mean time, to the necessary use of real property."[47] Once again, individual pursuits of progress quickly benefited the community as a whole. St. George Tucker observed that in 1783 Virginia's General Assembly had passed an act for admission of immigrants and determination of citizenship that encouraged the immigration of foreigners into the state by allowing them to purchase property whenever they wished. Any alien friends of the new nation who migrated into the state and gave satisfactory proof that they wished to settle in the state were entitled to rights of citizenship, except for political privileges. After residing in the state for two years and purchasing lands worth at least one hundred pounds or marrying a citizen of Virginia, aliens were able to hold, purchase, and inherit property in the same manner as citizens.[48]

Not all states were so charitable toward aliens, however. Zephaniah Swift noted that in Connecticut "aliens or foreigners" could not purchase or inherit land. This limitation was probably a result of Connecticut's small geographic size in the face of a large demand for land. Swift explained that in the early years of the settlement, when the new colony needed to increase its population, Connecticut's founders thought it necessary to offer foreigners the advantages of purchasing land. When the land became "fully settled and under improvement," however, the legislature thought it "proper" to exclude aliens from purchasing or inheriting lands. Connecticut's statute made no distinction between those living in or outside of the state. No aliens could possess Connecticut land. Moreover, any relations, no matter how much more remote than foreign relatives, who held American citizenship inherited in preference to foreigners. If there were no relatives except noncitizens, the property escheated to the state.[49] These safeguards could help to keep Connecticut's limited land resources undiluted by foreign blood.

Acquisition by alienation was the most common mode of procuring property in England and America, although abundance of land in the United States meant that purchasing real property happened far more frequently there than in England. From the early settlements through the nineteenth century, the opportunity to acquire land was open to a far wider range of people than in England. Tucker wrote that in colonial Virginia, one could procure land relatively easily, through petition to the General Assembly. The colonial assembly granted land patents under the authority of the Crown in Virginia, with the condition that the applicant had to seat and plant the land granted to him within three years from the date of the patent. If the patentee did not meet that condition, or if he failed to pay quit-rents on the property for three years, he forfeited the land. In 1720 the assembly limited the amount of land cleared to keep it in proportion to the amount of land "saved" or conserved and not cleared.[50] Early on, Virginians could see that their land resources were diminishing too rapidly for comfort.

Though settlers frequently acquired unappropriated and "waste" lands in the British American colonies, such settlements on unclaimed land were rarely, if ever, encountered in England, because in that country all land had long been occupied. Under English and American common law, "waste" land could mean any number of things. Waste essentially meant any destruction or material deterioration of land by the holder of the land. In the English tradition it could also mean any alteration that "changed the character or nature of the land, notwithstanding the fact that it was an improvement thereto."[51] In 1779 the General Assembly founded the land office of the Commonwealth and established the terms and manner of "granting waste" and unappropriated lands to new owners.[52] The legislation stated that claims to unappropriated land could be founded on charter rights, importation rights (for indentured service), purchase from the receiver general, legislative acts for up to four hundred acres of waste lands, or warrants from the governor for military service or other reasons.[53] One could acquire the waste lands by paying forty pounds for every one hundred acres and then registering with the land office to authorize a survey.[54]

Zephaniah Swift noted that, in Connecticut, anyone who was capable of owning property was also capable of alienating it to whomever he wished and on whatever terms he thought fair. By a late eighteenth-century Connecticut statute, Swift pointed out that even a married woman could purchase an estate without her husband's expressed consent. The husband could, however, void the sale simply by "declaring his disapprobation of the bargain."[55] In keeping with the prevailing attitudes of the time, Connecticut's legislators did not consider it a common good to allow women complete freedom with regard to property management.

The push for individual property ownership as an avenue toward communal improvement seemed to pay off. In the 1820s, James Kent enthusiastically told his readers about the results of America's progressive property policies, which he claimed distinguished the nation from all others in the world. Kent wrote that every citizen of the United States was "capable of taking, and holding lands . . . and every person capable of holding lands" could "alien the same at his pleasure, under the regulations prescribed by law." In no other part of the world, Kent proudly noted, was land "made such an article of commerce, and of such incessant circulation." This commercial vitality, according to Kent, marked America as a powerful society. He observed the same phenomenon in a more limited fashion in England, where houses and land were becoming "common means of investment" and, by the 1820s, were circulating "from owner to owner with unusual and startling rapidity."[56] This commercial expansion was by no means an exclusively American phenomenon, but abundant land and America's remarkably fluid society and economy placed that nation at the forefront of the world's commercial progress, thus shaping the U.S. reputation as a rising economic power.

III Regardless of the economic changes wrought by England and America's commercial progress, the most common way in which an owner relinquished property was still by death. As Blackstone pointed out, "naturally speaking, the instant a man ceases to be, he ceases to have any dominion."[57] Under Anglo-American common law, property descended in one of two ways: a property owner could devise his property by will or, if the property holder died intestate, the property descended to heirs according to a detailed set of local regulations. Colonial-era and early-republic American legislatures jettisoned many of the English feudal practices with regard to descent, and in their places they erected a completely different set of regulations governing the transfer of property from one generation to another. These divergent positive laws originated in the early years of colonial settlement, where there was no need or time for complicated land transfer processes. They not only differed from English laws of descent, but they also varied from one place to another, because local governments had always been responsible for the creation of their own laws of descent. By the Revolution, legists could boast that though the laws may not have been uniform within all states, each polity's leaders had formed their laws based on the common principles of equality of opportunity and protection of broad property rights. Moreover, they boasted, one probably would not find these same sentiments expressed so liberally in England.

St. George Tucker provided the best illustration of the way in which Americans treated their property laws as innovations that were vastly superior to the English common law. In his *Commentaries*, Tucker asserted that a Virginia act of 1785 regulating inheritance abolished the common-law rules of descent and erected "an entire new system of jurisprudence" in their place. The new system, Tucker claimed, stood at odds with the old because the framers' intention was to "eradicate every germ, and obliterate any former trace" of English common law where inheritance was concerned.[58] English property law, Tucker stated, had been established by "immemorial usage," while Virginia law evolved through "the mature consideration of the most eminent sages of the law . . . confirmed by the deliberate voice of the legislature." He found these two legal systems of descent "in continual and diametrical opposition to each other." The English system was "the offspring of feudal barbarism and prejudice," while the American system represented "the dictates of enlightened reason."[59] With this explanation, Tucker cast American notions of rational choice as superior to English impulses to follow tradition unthinkingly.

America's republican innovations in inheritance law could have been even more extreme and in some ways were not as much of a departure as Tucker would have liked to think. Some Revolutionary-era radicals called for even more drastic reforms, up to and including equal property distribution and abolishment of inheritance. In the end, state legislatures opted for more conservative modifications in inheritance law, primarily because of American admiration for common-law principles. Additionally, American legislators harbored the notion that property law existed to promote order, and, of course, extreme innovations like the abolition of inheritance would have brought chaos.[60] While they maintained the fundamental principles of inheritance and descent that were part of their English heritage, the states did, however, eliminate many of the feudal characteristics of the law of descent.

While the common law upheld a man's natural right to possess property, Blackstone acknowledged that the custom of ownership conveyance by "a set of words on parchment" represented a pure fiction of municipal law. Neither was there any basis in natural law for the son to "have a right to exclude his fellow creatures from a determinate spot of ground, because his father had done so before him."[61] Under natural law all property ownership, therefore, should cease upon death, "considering men as absolute individuals, and unconnected with civil society." Upon the owner's death the next "immediate occupant" could acquire a right in all of the deceased's property. This law of nature, however, had the potential to cause "endless disturbances" within civil society. To avoid conflict over vacated property, civilized governments chose to give a dying person the power to continue his property through disposal by will. If the owner was unwilling or unable to designate his own heir, municipal law determined who should be the deceased's successor. If municipal officials could find no heir, most civil governments, "to prevent the robust title of occupancy from again taking place," adopted the doctrine of escheats, by which property reverted to the authority of the state.[62]

Children's and other family members' right of descent, Blackstone posited, probably predated the right of devising property by will. Although the practice easily could be construed as natural, Blackstone cautioned that one easily could mistake for nature what had been "established by long and inveterate custom." Descent to children or other blood relations was "a wise and effectual, but clearly a political, establishment." The permanent right of property was "merely a *civil* right" and as such was a logical way to "make a man a good citizen and a useful member of society." Blackstone rationalized that peaceful transfer of property to a person of the owner's choice prompted the owner to take better care of his property. Therefore, the municipal law of England directed the vestment of property ownership in the person whom the last proprietor chose to succeed him.[63]

While most legal scholars agreed with Blackstone's assessment of descent as a positive-law invention, James Kent argued that because the practice had been based on reason and was universally accepted, descent was indeed rooted in natural law. Kent followed the Dutchman Hugo Grotius's view that the right to transmit property by descent to one's offspring was "dictated by the voice of nature." Ignoring Blackstone's cautions to the contrary, Kent claimed that the "universality of the sense of a rule or obligation" was enough evidence for the practice to claim foundation in natural law. The idea that the children of the property owner should have title to the property after his death was "in accordance with the sympathies and reason of all mankind," and this "better title of the children," Kent claimed, was recognized by all nations and founded in "the order of Providence."[64] Kent may have neglected Blackstone's warning not to mistake immemorial custom for nature, but the practice, so deeply embedded in their culture, appealed to Anglo-Americans' sense of order.

Kent admitted that the specific rules of descent, however, came under the purview of a "positive institution," and while American legislatures modified common-law rules of descent from the time of the first settlements, they also copied some English common-law definitions regarding inheritance.[65] Kent agreed with Blackstone that the disposition of land by will came much later than other kinds of land transactions, because it was simply assumed that the children had first right to succession on the death of the parent.[66] Although Kent noted that the law of succession was often more logical and orderly than the "fluctuating, and oftentimes unreasonable and unnatural distributions of human will," it was generally understood that every man should enjoy the free disposition of his own property, because it furnished "one of the strongest motives to industry and economy." Although a sense of "absolute right of property" brought about the use of testaments, Kent assured his readers that the law of nature adequately safeguarded against any "great abuse" of the power of disposition of property by will "by connecting our hopes and wishes with the fortunes of our posterity."[67] The desire for orderly transfer of property and visions of individual and community prosperity helped to perpetuate this custom.

Although there were some restrictions about who could inherit by will and testament, most of the positive laws of inheritance governed descent of that property for which there was no will. In his lengthy chapter on acquiring title to property by descent Blackstone listed a series of rules, or as he called them, "canons of inheritance," by which any English property held by owners who died intestate was transferred to the proper heirs. Blackstone's canons fell into three broad points: first, property could pass only to lineal descendants, and it could never ascend to an intestate's lineal ancestors; second, English heirs had to be of the whole blood of the first purchaser, and heirs of the half blood were excluded from inheritance; and, finally, English law always preferred male to female heirs and preferred the eldest son over his younger brothers. The common-law customs of primogeniture and entail reinforced this preference of male heirs.[68] Within these canons, many American legists found significant differences between English and American practices regarding descent, and these differences also produced significant variations among the laws of each state.

The first rule in Blackstone's volume was that, by English law, inheritances could only lineally descend to the issue of the property owner but that they could never ascend to parents or other ancestors. This maxim, Blackstone posited, was founded on a principle of natural reason that the possessions of the parents should go first to their children, "as those to whom they [gave] being, and for whom they [were] therefore bound to provide." While he admitted that the exclusion of parents and all lineal ancestors from succeeding to the inheritance of their offspring did not exist in other countries, Blackstone defended the rule against critics who labeled it "absurd and derogating from the maxims of equity and natural justice." Because all principles of succession were constructs of a state's municipal law, Blackstone insisted that it was not unjust for a society to establish its own processes for transferring property from one man to another. Whatever rules a state thought proper to prescribe were within the bounds of reason, as long as they were not contrary to natural law.[69]

The American states did not follow England's lead on this peculiar feudal custom restricting conveyance of property to a man's descendants rather than to his lineal ancestors. The omission of this restriction from colonial inheritance laws probably had much to do with the circumstances colonists faced as members of tiny settlements in a vast New World. Kinship networks on this side of the Atlantic were limited, and particularly in the southern colonies, mortality was high. In many early settlements it was not unusual for disease to leave young families without one or both parents, for male heirs to die before parents, or for women to marry several times and have children by more than one husband. Therefore, colonial governments relaxed common-law inheritance practices to accommodate the exigencies of life and death in the New World.[70] Revolutionary-era state legislatures and courts officially assimilated these more flexible inheritance customs into American law, and legal scholars deemed the innovations of lineal ascent "very great improvements" on English common law.[71] Zephaniah Swift considered the inclusion of parents in the line of succession "warranted by the ideas of mankind." He asserted that it was just and proper to give the estate of a person who had no lineal descendants or siblings to the parents, "who . . . had the care, trouble[,] and expense of his support" during his childhood. He claimed that American lawmakers had risen above "the prejudices" that were "usually entertained in favour of long established institutions, however impolitic," to adopt just and reasonable rules.[72] Once again, American notions of justice and reason won out over what they believed were outmoded English customs that had little to do with America's own traditions and needs.

Local polities seemed to take all possible protections into consideration as they laid out their inheritance laws. There were many variations among state laws governing ascent, most of which placed restrictions on who could inherit and when. For example, Virginia inheritance law prohibited a parent from inheriting from a minor child who died without having children if the property descended to him upon the death of his other parent. This change, St. George Tucker concluded, came about to protect a minor's life from a dishonest guardian who also happened to be next in line to inherit the child's property.[73] Other state restrictions imposed limitations on women as heirs, such as the New York law that prohibited a mother from inheriting outright from a child who died intestate without wife or children. The mother was excluded, Kent explained, "lest, by remarrying, she would carry all the personal estate to another husband, in entire exclusion, for ever, of the brothers and sisters" of the deceased.[74] While she was barred from inheriting the real estate, the law privileged the mother's right to personal estate over the deceased child's more remote relations.[75] Kent also pointed out that in New York and Pennsylvania, if the inheritance came to the intestate from the mother's family, the mother could take the estate for life only, after which it would go to the intestate's siblings or their descendants. If there were no siblings, the mother inherited the estate outright. He listed other states' variations on the mother's right to inherit from her intestate children, noting that the most restrictive laws against the mother's inheritance were in New Jersey, where she was completely excluded from inheriting. The states giving the mother the most favorable terms of inheritance were Illinois and Louisiana, where she and the father took equal portions of the inheritance.[76] The more liberal terms of inheritance in these two states may have resulted from earlier French or Spanish legal influence. The civil law of these nations tended to favor more equal distributions of assets.

In his next set of canons, Blackstone claimed that the rules governing heirs of the whole or half blood were actually rules of evidence designed to trace the heirs back to the original purchaser as best they could, when evidence of exact descent had disappeared over time. The collateral heir of the person who last owned the property had to be his next collateral kinsman of the whole blood. This arrangement meant that the heir must descend not only from the same lineal ancestors as the owner of the property but also from the same couple of ancestors. At common law, if the only living relations were those of the half blood, then the estate escheated to the Crown. This "total exclusion of the half blood from the inheritance," Blackstone pointed out, was yet another quality that was "almost peculiar" to English law, and he noted that it was "looked upon as a strange hardship" by those "unacquainted with the reasons" on which it was grounded. He explained that this rule simply represented another way to assure that the property descended straight to an heir who shared the blood of the first purchaser, and he explained away this "harsh" rule by falling back on a familiar excuse. Because all laws of inheritance were constructs of the government and not a part of natural law, "only upon a like supposition and fiction" did the common law entitle landholders' siblings, whether relations of the whole or half blood, to inherit at all.[77]

The idea that only those descendents of the whole blood could inherit had no force in America, though both James Kent and Tapping Reeve noted the wide variations among the laws of the states with regard to the distinction between heirs of whole or half blood. Kent called Blackstone's "rule of evidence" argument for the exclusion of half-blooded heirs "artificial" and boasted that the American law of descent seemed founded on better principles of reason. To Kent, it seemed of little practical necessity to search out the first purchaser and to ascertain whether an heir to the estate, perhaps generations after the original purchase, was of full blood, when it was obvious that the heir was a blood relative of the intestate. Kent listed a number of states, including New York, that made no distinction between heirs of whole or half blood.[78] In his treatise on the law of descents in America, Reeve marveled at the variety of laws regarding this and other parts of the law of descent. He observed that in some states the law gave preference to whole-blooded relatives over those of half blood, although the manner of that preference varied greatly. Reeve devoted several pages of his treatise to these variations, listing New Hampshire, Massachusetts, Rhode Island, Vermont, North Carolina, and Georgia as states that by 1825 did not privilege whole-blood over half-blood relations. Other states gave varying degrees of preference to whole-blood relatives. For example, New Jersey gave preference to any relation of whole blood, no matter how remote, to closer half-blood relations. Other places, like Virginia, gave half-blood relations half as much estate as whole-blood relations.[79] Although some polities retained vestiges of English inheritance traditions, transitions in American inheritance practices reflected the fact that America's ample land and history of higher mortality mandated the establishment of new practices. These practical considerations seemed to take priority in most places over the idea that protection of property rights meant that the property had to stay among those with the purest blood. Instead, an orderly and expedient transfer of property sometimes required legal innovations.

IV The third set of Blackstone's general rules of descent dictated that male offspring should inherit before the female and that, when there were two or more male offspring, the eldest male only should inherit. If there were no male children, the females would inherit the estate together. The English legist speculated that the preference for male over female heirs arose from the policy of the feudal constitution, whereby no woman was capable of performing the military services for the purpose of which the feudal system had been established. Instead of abolishing the law "like many Norman innovations," however, Henry I enforced it. Blackstone assured his readers that although the law seemed harshly disposed toward female children, it still was better than Salic law, an ancient code of law derived from the Salic Franks, which forbade women from inheriting at all. Instead, the English law of inheritance allowed daughters to succeed in the absence of sons, thus "steering a middle course, between the absolute rejection of females and the putting them on a footing with males." The only times in which the right of sole succession prevailed when only female heirs existed was for inheritance of the Crown, "wherein the necessity of a sole and determinate succession [was] as great in the one sex as the other" and also with respect to female dignities and titles of honor, when the king saw fit to continue the father's title through the daughter.[80] Continuity of leadership and privilege, in rare instances, necessitated the bending of gender restrictions.

The preference of male over female heirs extended to collateral inheritances as well. The common law privileged kin derived from the blood of the male ancestors over those who were blood relatives of the female, unless the lands in question had descended from the woman's side of the family. Blackstone suspected that this rule owed its origin to the canons requiring that every heir must be of the blood of the first purchaser. Because English law generally favored male heirs of lineal descent, judges faced with questions about the heir of a particular estate assumed that the first purchaser, and the last tenant of the land, would have been male. Again, he attributed this attitude to the feudal principle that males, not females, could perform the personal service necessary to acquire an estate.[81] The European culture dictated that men occupy exclusive places of privilege in matters of war and honor.

Blackstone explained that originally the Greeks, Romans, Britons, Saxons, and even the feudalists divided the lands equally among all children or among all male children. When emperors began to create honorary titles of nobility, however, they found it necessary "in order to preserve their dignity" to make estates descendible to the eldest son alone. The inconveniences that accompanied splitting estates, such as dividing military services, the "consequential weakening of the strength of the kingdom," and enticement of younger sons to take up with the "business and idleness of a country life" instead of being serviceable to themselves and the public by engaging in mercantile, military, or ecclesiastical employments made it necessary to change inheritance practices to favor the eldest male offspring. Blackstone noted that the county of Kent proved one exception to the practice of primogeniture in England. There they preserved *gavelkind* tenure, which provided for the joint inheritance by all sons or some variation of this practice of partible inheritance as local custom dictated.[82]

Many British colonists rejected primogeniture and exclusively male inheritance in America, where regional variations in availability of land, kinship networks, mortality rates, and economic circumstances affected inheritance customs.[83] Kent allowed that, though parts of colonial America retained the English law of primogeniture, even before the Revolution some colonies had rid themselves of the law. A Pennsylvania law of 1683 and a Massachusetts law of 1692 abolished primogeniture, though the eldest son still received a double portion.[84] Post-Revolutionary legislators in Massachusetts had some trouble deciding whether America's brand of social equality translated to inheritance practices. A 1784 Massachusetts law confirmed the eldest son's double portion, but that measure was repealed in 1789. After that date, all offspring in Massachusetts inherited equal portions.[85] Rhode Island followed suit in 1770, and New York, New Jersey, Maryland, and Virginia lifted primogeniture after Independence. In pre-Revolutionary Connecticut and Delaware, the eldest son received only a double portion by law. In Connecticut's case, Zephaniah Swift explained that though the colony's founders disregarded the feudal practice of primogeniture, "their reverence for the bible," and perhaps some remaining desire to perpetuate the family through the eldest son, "induced them to copy from the law of Moses" the regulation conferring a double portion on the eldest son.[86] James Sullivan also posited that the law of Moses inspired the practice of double portions, but he introduced the theory that it was "a piece of respect to the English laws, and an apology for departing from" the law of primogeniture. Regardless of the reasons behind America's shift away from primogeniture, Sullivan asserted that "where there is no family dignity to be maintained by the opulence of one branch," there was no incentive to continue the practice.[87] The more egalitarian nature of American societies eventually brought down the aristocratic practice of favoring one son over other children.

After Independence, American inheritance laws rarely privileged males over females, nor did they favor the eldest child over the others. All children, regardless of gender or age, came into their inheritance at the same time and took equal portions. Swift observed that the idea of double portions for eldest sons seemed unnecessary in the republican climate, and therefore in 1792 the Connecticut General Assembly repealed that part of the state's inheritance law and placed "all the children . . . upon the same footing."[88] John F. Grimké of South Carolina also noted his state's republicanization of inheritance practices with the repudiation of "the old absurd principles of the English law of bastardizing all a man's children except the eldest son, or the issue of such son."[89] St. George Tucker pointed out that the Virginia Assembly had abolished the right of primogeniture in 1785 along with the preference for male heirs over females. Until 1790, however, the eldest daughter possessed the right to inherit the principal residence.[90] When Virginia rescinded that law, they put an end to a rare, local instance in which women held a legal advantage over men.

Not only was the law of primogeniture incompatible with republican notions of freedom, choice, and equality of opportunity, but Tucker also asserted that the general idea of the eldest son inheriting all his father's property contradicted reason. He showed his students just how illogical the custom of primogeniture was by an English example in which a man's property extended to such "incorporeal" hereditaments as office, including for the nobility a seat in the House of Lords. Tucker ridiculed the notion that the eldest son invariably inherited the "Virtue or Talents" that one needed to hold such an office, and he used biblical references to prove his point. "The *first born son* of the first Man," Tucker reminded his students, "was a Murderer. The first born of Abraham (by a Concubine it must be confest) was an outcast from Society, his hand was against every man, and every man[']s hand against him."[91] In the unpublished version of his lecture notes, Tucker extended his critique of primogeniture into contemporary society, taking a jab at one of Great Britain's most prominent families. He pointed out that in their own day Virginians had seen "the eldest Son of a *Chatham* a dignified Cypher, whilst the youngest . . . inherited the Talents, and succeeded to the Glory of his father."[92] Tucker was probably referring to the sons of William Pitt, first earl of Chatham. Although Pitt's eldest son John also had a political career, William Pitt the younger followed in his father's footsteps, becoming prime minister in the years following the Revolution.

Hugh Henry Brackenridge asserted that it was everyone's duty to improve the earth and everyone's right to be able to own land. Therefore, according to Brackenridge, primogeniture's unequal distribution of property thwarted what should be the intent of every man, to "people and improve the earth." He pointed out that Pennsylvania law did not privilege male heirs, but rather that "all the children, lawful issue, or their representatives" were "entitled to succeed to equal parts of the real estate." Brackenridge believed that a more equitable distribution of land like that practiced in the American republics would "increase . . . happiness to mankind" and bring prosperity to the community.[93] The practice of attaching communal prosperity, social and cultural progress, and happiness to broader property ownership grew in popularity as the nineteenth century, and the nation, matured.

In the 1820s, Kent applauded the valuable benefits that more equitable inheritance practices had brought to America and used these broader American practices to assert a sense of superiority over the English and their continued reliance on feudal laws of descent. At least, Kent noted, English statesmen had moved beyond Blackstone's argument that primogeniture and preference of male heirs remained necessary for the "stability of the hereditary orders." Instead, Englishmen placed increasing emphasis on the economic advantages of primogeniture as being "favourable to the agriculture, wealth, and prosperity of the nation, by preventing the evils of an interminable subdivision of landed estates." They contended that breaking farms into small parcels, and the subsequent division of those parcels into even smaller sections with each succeeding generation, would result in "a redundant and starving population, destitute alike of the means . . . and of the enterprise requisite to better their condition." After due consideration, Kent agreed that for England's needs these arguments might be valid. He stated that primogeniture might be a logical practice under monarchical governments and among the "crowded population of England, Ireland, and France." But Kent called the custom of primogeniture "incompatible with that equality of right, and that universal participation in civil privileges," which was the "constitutional policy of this country to preserve and inculcate." When a polity's leaders debated over appropriate inheritance laws for their citizens, Kent asserted that factors such as the "genius of the government, the character of the people, the amount of cultivated land, the extent of territory, and the means and inducements to emigrate from one part of the country to another" weighed into the ultimate decisions. In the American states, Kent boasted, "the extraordinary extent of . . . unsettled territories, the abundance of uncultivated land in the market, and the constant stream of emigration from the Atlantic to the interior states" operated sufficiently to maintain both the integrity of family estates as well as to preserve the broad opportunity for citizens to acquire additional property. Should the idea of partitioning ancestral lands prove too painful or injurious to the family, in some states, Kent noted, the eldest heir had the option of paying the other heirs for their shares and maintaining possession of all lands.[94] Otherwise, equality of opportunity and freedom of choice, central features of America's identity, dictated that the states possess more equitable laws of descent.

While Americans generally embraced more progressive inheritance practices, some vestiges of English customs remained in certain parts of the new nation. According to Tapping Reeve of Connecticut, for example, although the law required partible inheritance for those estates whose owners died intestate, when property owners divided their estates by will, the eldest son still "regularly inherit[ed]."[95] Connecticut's limited land resources could provoke such concerns over inequitable inheritance practices, and Reeve's impressions might have been accurate in some instances. One study of Connecticut inheritance practices shows that while Connecticut landholders may have favored certain sons in some wills, it was more common for them to reserve more land for their sons at the expense of their daughters.[96]

The worry that primogeniture still existed in America was not limited to

Connecticut legists, however. In the 1790s, James Kent privately expressed the concern that the "harsh" practice of male preference still potentially existed in his home state. He believed that the principles of male preference in inheritance had been "pretty much abolished" by acts of the state assembly but worried that loopholes in New York law could allow the practice, "in certain cases," to remain in effect "and [to] intrude their rigorous Dicta on our Courts of Justice."[97] The remains of feudal practices even surfaced in the letter of the law in some states. For example, if there were no lineal or collateral descendants and the property was directed to ascend, in Virginia the nearest lineal male ancestor was preferred over the female ancestors.[98] America's progressive inheritance laws only went so far.

Although America's laws of descent placed more power in the property owner's hands, if he went to the trouble of making out a will he was not entirely free to dispose of his property as he wished. American landholders did not have to contend with restrictions of entail, but in some instances they still had restrictions on what they could and could not devise away from their families. For example, while all other states followed the common-law practice of allowing a testator to "devise all his estate to strangers . . . and disinherit his children" if he wished, Louisiana exhibited its civil-law heritage by retaining the doctrine of forced heirship for all children. Kent found this sort of assured inheritance unnecessary because he believed that American children were sufficiently safeguarded through parental affection from an abuse of the power of free devise. A more general set of practices among the states called for the will to be void under several circumstances, such as the birth of a child after a will was drawn up, the birth of a posthumous child, or a marriage after a will was drawn up.[99] A single woman's will was revoked upon her marriage, although in some states, if she survived her husband, the will could be revived and be considered as valid as if she had remained single.[100]

V In England, the common-law custom of entail was an even stronger restriction on the making of wills than any regulation in force in the United States. Entailment of an estate involved the limitation of its descent by specific terms or to specific beneficiaries, instead of allowing the estate to descend to any heir without restrictions. Even the head of the household could not alter the entail. The common law limited this practice to real property, meaning any lands and those incorporeal hereditaments attached to the land, such as rents, commons, offices, and dignities, and according to Blackstone, the purpose of the restriction was to keep estates intact and in the families of the original donee.[101] Such a practice sometimes caused hardship for the heirs of entailed property. Taxes and other liabilities that accompanied the inheritance could drain a family's finances while leaving no recourse but petition to Parliament for release from the entail. These liabilities, however, did not seem to sway Blackstone, or many other English landholders, from the conviction that preservation of an estate was of prime importance to the maintenance of England's social orders. An English landholder felt pressing obligations to his family because he considered himself the family's trustee for an estate that he could pass on to his progeny. The holder of the estate was obligated under the common law to preserve the estate intact and unharmed for his heirs.[102] Some American legists interpreted entail not so much as a way to preserve inheritance for offspring, but rather as English society's way to keep land away from anyone but the aristocracy.

Tapping Reeve explained to his students that the sole purpose of entail was "to preserve all the landed property in the hands of the nobility." The practice arose, according to Reeve, from "the proud aristocratic spirit of the feudal chiefs . . . who could not endure the idea of seeing their estates aliened from their families." They began to grant estates to their children and "the heirs of their bodies," and eventually the custom evolved into common law, restricting descent to the family of the grantee "*ad infinitum.*" Eventually, Reeve explained, the practice of "docking" an entail became a popular way to facilitate the transaction of land to someone outside the line if a particular parcel of the estate proved to be too burdensome for the heirs.[103] Zephaniah Swift was less charitable toward the practice of docking entails as an English remedy for their outmoded practice. He explained that though entail became "extremely inconvenient . . . and detrimental to the public," the English could not bear to rid themselves of the venerated custom. Thus, they layered "the collective fictions of fines and common recoveries" to aid in docking entailments, rather than abolishing the outmoded practice altogether.[104]

While Swift's home state did not allow entail, it still sanctioned a form of entail only for the "first original grantee" that did not carry with it any of the English version's perpetual burdens. In other words, Connecticut lawmakers had transformed entail into a life estate, after which the state's law automatically terminated the estate tail. James Gould explained that

Connecticut's legislature decided to modify rather than abolish entail because although a man had the right to devise his property in any manner he wished, the legislature considered an estate tail to be inconsistent with the laws of Connecticut.[105] This form of abbreviated entail, therefore, bowed to the wishes of the devisor while still preserving Connecticut's preferred practice of partible inheritance. According to Swift, this modification carried all of the advantages, yet none of the "restrictions and incumbrances," of entail that "perplexed and embarrassed" Englishmen.[106] He refused to equate the Connecticut practice with the English form of entail. Instead, Swift preferred to believe that his state's lawmakers had merely borrowed the term and introduced it into their own jurisprudence with a modified meaning.

Late eighteenth- and early nineteenth-century American legal scholars' arguments against the custom of entail generally depicted the practice as contrary to the republican freedoms and rights for which Americans had fought. St. George Tucker taught his students that by common-law practice, colonial Virginians originally sanctioned and even preferred entail. Immediately after the Revolution, however, Virginia's legislature decided that "entails would be the means of accumulating and preserving great estates in certain families, which would not only introduce all the evils complained of in England," but the practice would also "be utterly incompatible with the genius and spirit of our constitution and government." Therefore, acts passed at the first session of the assembly after the Declaration of Independence declared all estates and any slaves previously held in fee tail after that date to be held in fee simple. Although anyone could devise differently in his will, if an estate-holder died intestate, his estate would be divided among his heirs and would not be held in tail.[107] Tucker concluded that this act changed the entire course of descents, making Virginia's law of property contrary to common law.[108]

Tucker's words influenced Hugh Henry Brackenridge's work on Pennsylvania law, in which he lauded the General Assembly's determination to abolish a practice that could do nothing but "usher in many of the evils manifest in England." He criticized Pennsylvania's assembly for not reacting in a manner similar to that of Virginia, and he noted that the statutes of entail were, though not explicit in Pennsylvania's laws, implicitly recognized as part of the law. By 1794, his state had enacted many changes to inheritance laws such as allowing partible and ascendible inheritance, but Pennsylvania still had not dealt "a final blow to the feudal system." Before Pennsylvania's laws of property and descent could be "in all particulars, accommodated to a republican government" and free from English feudal influence, Brackenridge insisted that the law of entail "must go."[109] Any vestige of feudalism, particularly within the law of real property and inheritance, could tarnish the Commonwealth's reputation.

James Kent's *Commentaries* provided a national perspective on the elimination of entail from American laws. Like Tucker, Kent credited Virginia with being the first state to abolish estates tail officially in 1776, and he listed the states that followed suit soon thereafter. By the 1820s, the doctrine of estates tail was "quite obsolete" in most of the country. Other states, such as Vermont, Indiana, Illinois, South Carolina, and Louisiana, seemed never to have had laws of entail, though Kent admitted that there were also some states, such as New Hampshire, Alabama, Mississippi, and Connecticut, in which the status of estates tail was vague or in which entail was still legal in some limited fashion.[110] Kent concluded, however, that these modified forms of entail still extant in some parts of the country held "increased power over the property . . . and greater facility of alienation" than the English form of entail. He described some states' unwillingness to part with such restrictive inheritance laws as part of a "desire to preserve and perpetuate family influence and property," which prevailed among all humans. He warned, however, that "the lustre of families, and the entailments of property" were, "like man himself, perishable and fleeting."[111] Therefore, the action most in keeping with America's character would be to abolish entails and allow for more flexible inheritance practices.

In a change that reflected greater emphasis on America's commercial expansion in the 1820s, Kent added the enjoyments of free commerce and social and economic improvement to the list of rights that entail curtailed in England. He again suggested that this promotion of commercial growth through more liberal inheritance law was a superior feature of America's society and law. Entailed estates did not "stimulate exertion and economy," he wrote, because they had "a tendency . . . to destroy the excitement to action" in the heir and to result in "an accumulated mass of property" in the hands of a long line of "idle and . . . vicious" lineal descendants. Kent deemed entails "unfavourable to agricultural improvement," and he posited that the practice removed "a very powerful incentive to preserving industry and honest ambition." He recommended entailments for monarchical governments "as a protection to the power and influence of the landed aristocracy," but he maintained that such practices had "no application to republican establishments." In the United States, Kent boasted, wealth did not "form a permanent distinction." Every individual possessed equal rights and was "equally invited, by the genius of the institutions, to depend upon his own merit and exertions" for social and economic advancement. For Kent, these republican calls to individual action and improvement were incompatible with a culture that depended entirely on inherited lands, names, and reputations.[112] They were, however, perfectly in keeping with American polities' superior senses of equality and civil liberty.

VI

American ideas of equality were not always quick to progress beyond English roots. Preservation of traditions in Anglo-American law was nowhere better illustrated than in laws pertaining to women, property, and inheritance. It is apparent throughout Blackstone's canons on inheritance that English law severely limited married women's property rights. Only under rare circumstances could a married woman possess or convey property. Although single women enjoyed somewhat broader rights to property in America than in England, they still possessed far fewer privileges than their male counterparts. States limited their power to convey or manage property that they held in their own names. Women were subject to the authority of their fathers until they married. Upon marriage, women came under the dominion of their husbands. In England and in America, a married woman was considered a dependent, one who required protection under the law and was generally incapable of holding or disposing of her own property.[113] According to Blackstone, marriage made the husband and wife one person under the law, meaning that "the very being or legal existence of the woman [was] suspended during the marriage, or at least . . . incorporated and consolidated into that of the husband." Upon marriage, the wife became, according to the legal terminology of the day, a *feme-covert*, "under the protection and influence of her husband, her *baron*, or lord."[114] Because of her status as dependent on and "inferior" to her husband, a married Englishwoman could not execute deeds or devise by will lands to anyone without her husband's approval.[115] Nathaniel Chipman's comments about a *feme covert*'s property rights are particularly illustrative of the prevailing attitudes in the late eighteenth century. With regard to conveyances, Chipman noted that "the acts of femes covert, and idiots are absolutely void."[116] In other words, women and the mentally incompetent possessed no legal voice. Lumping women in with the mentally or intellectually impaired was as common in the United States as it was in England.

A woman's status in America was not so different from her status in England, and, in fact, women were the losers in the bid to simplify American courts. Because few states maintained separate courts of equity, and no colony or state ever established ecclesiastical courts, women did not have a buffer between them and the more rigid common law.[117] Single women often enjoyed the freedom of managing their own property without the intervention of a male relative. As soon as she married, however, a woman's legal personhood and all her property became her husband's possessions.

Not all legists believed that women were incapable of managing property. Tapping Reeve opposed in principle these traditional Anglo-American restrictions on women's property rights, and he reputedly allowed his wife, Sally Burr Reeve, to manage as she saw fit the property that she brought into their marriage. Connecticut law, according to Reeve, provided that if a woman made a will while single and subsequently married, the will was automatically revoked by her marriage. Reeve thought this rule ridiculous. "Surely," he scoffed, "her understanding [was] not impaired by marriage." The law obviously did not consider a woman deprived of her volition upon marriage, because courts still held her accountable for her actions and the law required her consent to convey the lands that she brought into the marriage.[118] However, Reeve was in the minority. Even the more progressive legists of his time found it difficult to relinquish legal control over their wives' property.

Other scholars tried to defend laws that curtailed women's legal authority by pointing to some measures of progress. Reeve's colleague Zephaniah Swift explained that the law had been more restrictive in Connecticut's early years. During the first settlement of the colony, the husband could alienate his wife's lands without her permission. This custom, Swift explained, arose because land was of little value during that period. As the colony became more settled and land increased in value, the legislature took action to protect the wife's limited rights to her property. Therefore, although Connecticut law still gave husbands "absolute power" over their wives' personal property, wives gained at least a limited say in the disposal of real property.[119]

In rare cases, women were allowed to reserve some of their family's property through premarital agreements. Widows were most likely to draw up these agreements and could thus control property left to them by first husbands or fathers. Because fathers usually brokered prenuptial agreements, such contracts may have represented concern over their daughters' marriage choices. If they could not control whom their daughters married, fathers could at least protect some family property.[120] Connecticut law declared that if the woman's husband and father agreed before the marriage, they could make the wife's personal property inaccessible to the husband and payable for debts on her death. Any surplus after debt payment went to her next of kin.[121] This practice, however, was rare. Additionally, under certain circumstances a husband had no right to certain kinds of real property if he survived his wife. For example, chattels real that were devised to the wife for her sole use, property of which she was in possession as executrix, or property separately settled to her went not directly to her husband but to her administrator upon her death.[122] Reeve admitted that Connecticut showed "some reluctance" to adopt any law allowing a married woman to have some real or personal property that was separate from that of her husband and over which he had no control. He noted that in the early nineteenth century it was sometimes "customary to convey directly to the wife." To protect her inheritance, however, the conveyance needed to state explicitly "the intention that she have it for herself."[123] According to the notes of Litchfield law student George Flagg Mann, by the mid-1820s it was more common for real or personal property to be given to a woman for separate use, either by agreement between the father and husband or by the husband directly. In such cases, Mann noted, the property was in effect "a Trust in the husband."[124] With this measure, any control that a woman gained over her property remained in the shadow of the men on whom she depended.

At the time that Reeve wrote his *Law of Baron and Femme*, there was considerable debate as to whether a woman had the capacity under common law to devise her own property. Some believed that she could not do so, while others contended that under the common law of England, if a wife possessed property that was hers alone, she could "as freely devise it as any other person," as long as her husband's rights were not compromised. Reeve spent a good deal of time mulling over the question, not in terms of precedent and legal authority, but rather according to what he believed was "reasonable and right," yet still consistent with legal principles. He used many of the same criteria in this debate as he had in his discussion of a woman's right to own and manage her own property. Surely, he reasoned, there was nothing in the nature of marriage that prevented a woman from devising. As in the case of conveyances, her understanding of such a transaction was not impaired simply by her marriage, and if she had been "sufficiently discreet to devise . . . when unmarried," she did not lose that ability upon her marriage. Reeve dismissed the English practice of privately examining the wife regarding her consent to a conveyance as an "imaginary guard." A wife who was unwilling to convey, he reasoned, yet had "yielded to the importunities of her husband . . . as to proceed in the business" would never "stop short on such an examination." Therefore, if she could convey with his consent, why could she not devise with her husband's consent? In Reeve's opinion, if the law would simply admit the wife's liberty to devise her own property, then "all danger of coercion" would be at an end.[125] Reeve chose to believe that his state's lawmakers followed his line of reasoning and allowed the wife the power to devise her own property.

In the 1820s, James Gould noted a small change in Connecticut's law governing the wife's power to devise. Though the state still revoked the will of a married woman if she died before her husband, Gould indicated that a widow could revive a will she made before her marriage if she survived her husband.[126] James Kent approved of Connecticut's more progressive law but noted that in New York it was not the case that a wife's will was revived on the husband's death. He explained that according to the rulings of several judges, as well as a provision of the *New York Revised Statutes* of 1830, the marriage left the will no longer subject to the wife's control. Therefore, a New York widow could draft a new will after her husband's death, but she could not revive one made before her marriage.[127] These acts opened a small window on women's ability to control certain assets that they brought into a marriage.

While the wife legally gained "nothing by marriage during the coverture," if her husband died intestate she was generally entitled to one-third of her husband's personal property after payment of debts, as well as all the land of which her husband was seized during their marriage, but this inheritance was merely a life estate, or dower. Laws protecting the widow from destitution at the hands of an unscrupulous heir were similar to that of the common law and generally uniform throughout the states.[128] As James Sullivan explained Massachusetts law, the heir of an estate was obliged to protect the widow's dower. Other laws reinforced a widow's right to her dower and provided for issuance of a writ of dower if the heir refused to assign the widow her portion.[129] James Kent called dower a "humane provision" intended for the "sure and competent sustenance of the widow, and the better nurture and education of her children." The custom, Kent observed, "had continued unchanged in the English law to the present times"; with various local modifications, it had been adopted as part of the municipal jurisprudence of the United States.[130] The limitations on an heir's discretion were not simply part of an altruistic tradition. Rather, providing a widow with some income, even if it was significantly less than that which she enjoyed during her husband's life, kept many women from seeking alms from their communities.

In notes regarding a case determining a widow's right to dower, St. George Tucker traced the origins of common-law regulation from the "old" English version to American laws that he considered to be more protective of widows' rights. He referred to Blackstone's version of the laws, which stated that by ancient English common law a man "could no more deprive his wife of her thirds . . . of his personal estate . . . by his will, than he could of her Dower in the Lands whereof he died siezed of an estate of inheritance." That law, however, evolved to a point where the wife's safeguard was "totally abolished throughout England," and a man could "dispose of his personal Estate as he please[d] . . . by his will, and the claims of the Widow[,] children[,] and other relations to the contrary [were] totally barred."[131] Tucker observed that a 1672 Virginia law restrained the husband "from depriving his wife (by his will) of her share of his personal estate, without her own consent, express or implied."[132] Virginia law required that a woman be given a "privy examination" to ensure that her husband was not coercing her into selling the land. If there was no record of the examination, the deed did not bind her or her heirs.[133] Tucker also noted that while the English common law gave the testator the option of granting his personal effects to his next of kin or to his widow, Virginia law gave preference to the widow. Additionally, in Virginia slaves could not be sold away from the widow for payment of debts unless there was not enough personal estate in other forms to cover the debts.[134] Slaves were often significant portions of Virginians' property and therefore could provide considerable financial security to widows. Tucker meant his description of Virginia's protective laws to create an image of Virginians as more charitable toward the defenseless, but he neglected to mention that this protection of slave property was not part of English law, because England did not sanction the institution of slavery.

Hugh Henry Brackenridge noted similar changes in Pennsylvania law, which carried the same dower of one-third of lands and tenements during the wife's lifetime. If there were no children from the marriage, the wife received one-half of the real estate, including the main residence, for use during her life. Pennsylvania's law also required that a woman be examined privately, apart from her husband, to ensure that she freely consented to land being conveyed away from her inheritance. He noted what he deemed a "material change" that the Pennsylvania Assembly enacted in 1797. By common law, if it was the "clear and manifest intention of the testator" that a specific property be devised to the widow in lieu of a dower, the widow had a choice between accepting the dower or accepting the devise. Pennsylvania's act of 1797, however, mandated that if the testator wished it, the wife must take the devise in lieu of the dower. The same was true in Connecticut, according to Reeve.[135] Neither Brackenridge nor Reeve offered an opinion on this modification to the common law, although the restriction seemed to imply that where women were concerned, American law did not allow choice and consent.

Despite some local limitations, widows' rights to dower were generally protected from usurpation because the husband could not convey away the wife's dower unless she agreed to the move without coercion. Connecticut law also directed that the wife was entitled to a life estate of one-third of the real estate her husband owned at his death, but the husband could, "*by his own deed* bar her right of dower."[136] If, however, there was evidence that the husband conveyed away his property "in contemplation of death," the wife could still claim her dower. Connecticut's slightly more liberal divorce laws were also reflected in the state's inheritance laws, in that, unlike English law, if the couple were divorced through no fault of the woman, she was still entitled to a dower.[137] The only cases in which a Connecticut widow could not inherit her dower involved those in which she was the faulty party in a divorce or if she eloped with an adulterer. Additionally, if the wife was not an American citizen, she could not legally inherit, because in Connecticut, "altho' an alien may hold property if it is not taken from him, which it is always liable to be, yet it can never descend from him."[138] In this instance, Connecticut's laws bore equal restrictions on men and women.

In a peculiar twist to the theory that a widow's dower was a way to protect her from destitution at the hands of an unscrupulous husband, Reeve mentioned a Connecticut law that specified that a woman "by force carried away" and forced to marry against her will was not entitled to a dower, even if she later consented to remain married to the man who carried her away. Although Reeve doubted that this common-law restriction could escape a compassionate judge or jury in his own state, he admitted that such a marriage was technically void, because "a marriage ought never to be deemed valid where there [was] no consent."[139] It seemed that under certain circumstances, an emphasis on consent as part of the American legal character could injure a married woman.

While free white males benefited greatly from the Americanization of property ownership and inheritance law, women gained little ground. Elimination of the feudal practices of primogeniture and entail potentially gave women equal opportunity to inherit with their brothers, but America's polities had not yet abolished the feudal practice of men gaining control over their wives' property and legal personhood upon marriage. Moreover, American legal scholars generally did not object to these restrictions. As they discussed women and property rights in their treatises and classrooms, legists tended to concentrate on rights to dower and other measures that they believed protected dependent women from destitution. On the whole, then, legal scholars believed that with a few modifications, English property and inheritance laws were still adequate in order to deal with women's property rights.

In 1801 James Sullivan wrote that

> the principles of a fee simple estate, the power of making a disposition of it, by a devise, in a last will and testament, and the distribution of intestate real estates among all the children or relations of the last proprietor, are powerful objections to all tyranny. These principles, planted in the soil, are the seeds of genuine civil liberty . . . [they] awaken that ambition, which is of the family of virtues, stimulate industry, the only true source of wealth, and prohibit the increase of authority by any other hand than that of merit.[140]

Unquestionably, America's improvements on English property law gave the new nation a sense of superiority that legal scholars encouraged as they discussed the liberal property laws that facilitated America's growth before and after the Revolution. Though they remained within the English orbit of property custom more than they cared to admit, they could also claim many important innovations, particularly under inheritance law. Legists even went so far as to claim that American inheritance laws were "utterly opposed to . . . the common law of England" and that the republican innovations in laws of descent had resulted in an "entire new system of jurisprudence."[141] Perhaps these assertions were a bit too zealous, as such radical claims denied the pervasive influence of the English culture and common law on American societies. American lawmakers tended to preserve common-law language of inheritance even as they stripped away the feudal parts of property law. While American improvements on English property law may not have represented the birth of a new system of jurisprudence, they certainly represented some important modifications that reflected the radically different social and economic opportunities available to Americans. Many of these innovations stemmed from the common law's foundation in local custom, a characteristic that helped to preserve local identities within property law. Because local governments had possessed the responsibility to protect their citizens' property from first settlements, much of property law grew from local custom. This local governance of property transfers meant that no two states' property laws were alike. America's legists described this diversity in their lectures and treatises, but they also found many common features among the variations in property laws.

The common law's flexibility also lent itself to the peculiar circumstances under which Americans often had to navigate. The seemingly endless supply of land in America stood in contrast to England's cramped quarters. The abundance of territory was the single most important component to the making of American identities, and to the creation of American property laws. America was a land—or a group of lands—in which one could find equality of opportunity illustrated through their broader property laws. In practice, however, the more expansive U.S. property laws did not benefit everyone. The same commercial and territorial progress that legal scholars celebrated as a hallmark of the American character worked to the disadvantage of some of the nation's inhabitants.

4

The Question of Slavery in the New Republic

Zephaniah Swift once boasted that Americans lived in a country where the "constitution of government, the system of law, and the administration of justice" secured "to every member of the community the highest political felicity." They had created a union of ideal republican polities founded on the principles of liberty and equality for all. Unfortunately, according to Swift, America also owned the distinction of being "the origin and theatre of the most extensive slavery known in any country."[1] As Americans strove to set themselves apart from England by showing off their superior republican governments and laws, slavery was a stigma they could not overcome. In the backs of their minds, and increasingly on the tips of their tongues, the question became, if American government and law represented a tremendous improvement over English government and law, how could they explain their republic's preservation of such an oppressive institution as slavery?

The American Revolution was about freedom and the preservation of natural rights, but it was also about protection of property. Few Americans were willing to take notions of freedom to the extreme of relinquishing property, regardless of whether that property was in things or persons. Some Americans began the Revolution with noble intentions of somehow erasing slavery from their new republic, but they soon realized the cost of such a move. They then turned to rationalizations that enslavement in America was really a better existence for blacks than that which they would have had in Africa.[2] Even in the Northern states, typically considered "free" states, slavery existed into the nineteenth century, and even when emancipation came, in many places it was a gradual process that took decades to complete.[3] As they struggled to rid themselves of this most unrepublican institution, Americans faced growing criticism.

One of their critics was Sir William Blackstone, who in his *Commentaries* unequivocally denounced the institution of slavery as "repugnant to reason" and contrary to "the principles of natural law."[4] Blackstone's condemnation of slavery stung, particularly because Americans knew that it was not just one Englishman's sentiments but rather that the opinion spread throughout England and into much of the outside world. Critics singled out the United States as a crucial site of this unjust practice, but slavery represented a state of disgrace that many Americans did not feel they should have to bear alone. They believed that they were merely the heirs of an institution that had existed in many forms and in many places, including the ancient republics and, perhaps, even in England itself.

As they dealt with the legal workings of slavery in their lectures and writings, American legists felt compelled to condemn its existence. At the same time they tried to justify its presence in America. Legal scholars were among the first to wrestle with the moral and historical questions about the nature and evolution of American slavery. They used Blackstone's words to help them accomplish this complicated and often contradictory set of tasks. The *Commentaries* served as a resource for historical background on the institution of slavery and for the common-law origins and practices of slave law. Just as important, Blackstone's harsh words against slavery served to frame American legists' own condemnations of the institution. His criticisms also stood for the outside forces that, at least in the first few decades after the Revolution, unified Northern and Southern Americans in a defense of their most unrepublican institution.

I

Just as any good lawyer would, American legists began their defense of slavery by searching for valid precedent. As they established their new governments after Independence, Americans looked to the ancient Greek and Roman republics for much of their inspiration, so it now seemed logical to look to these role models again to locate the roots of their form of slavery. To establish their institution's origins and to assure their students and readers that their immediate ancestors, the European settlers in the Americas, had not invented such an objectionable institution, they drew parallels between American and ancient republican slavery practices. Swift accused Rome and Greece, "so long erroneaously celebrated as the most excellent models of a free government," of unjustly subjecting the majority of the people under their governance to "the severity of domestic slavery." He grounded ancient slavery's origins in "the pretended right of conquest." Swift used Blackstone's dissertation on the origins of slavery, which Blackstone styled after Justinian's *Institutes*, to explain how slavery first arose from the state of captivity in war. According to ancient Roman law, a conqueror could kill his prisoners or he could spare their lives and use them as he pleased.[5] Roman law granted the master absolute power over his slaves, and the law designated the slave "the property of the master, as much as the beast of the field." Slave marriages were prohibited unless it was to the benefit of the master, and the master "at pleasure of his own hand took away the life of a slave . . . without any form of trial . . . and without being responsible to any tribunal." When war failed to furnish adequate numbers of slaves, "a mart" was "opened for the sale of rational beings."[6] Thus, a practice begun under the premise of "just war" became institutionalized when demand outstripped supply. James Kent pointed out that, compared to the United States, Greek and Roman slavery operated on a much larger scale. He told of private persons who owned more than four thousand slaves in Rome. In Greece, a republic that Kent believed practiced a milder form of slavery than that of Rome, the proportion of freemen to slaves was a bit more equitable at about four hundred slaves to every ninety freemen.[7] Although slavery may have been less severe in Greece, Kent still believed that the existence of the institution in the ancient republic could not "but diminish very considerably our sympathy with their spirit . . . and our reverence for their institutions." Kent noted that the severity of Greek slavery varied from place to place, and he credited the great philosophers' presence in Athens for encouraging the very mildest form of slavery in the republic. Slaves in that Greek polity had the right to sue their masters for excessive ill-usage. Athenian slaves could also compel their masters to sell them, and under certain circumstances they had the right to purchase their freedom. Slaveholders in the peripheral Greek polities like Thessaly, Crete, Argos, and Sparta were, according to Kent, subjected to far greater measures of oppression.[8]

Swift exhibited significant religious bias in his history of slavery. He credited Christianity with trying to eliminate slavery, despite Muslim efforts to enslave any within their dominions who refused to follow Islamic practices. Swift claimed that in the face of Christian attempts to abolish domestic slavery, Muslims strove "to rivet its shackles on all the nations of the earth."[9] Then he blamed Catholic Spaniards for reviving the institution when they began to colonize the New World. Swift's description of the inherently cruel and evil nature of the Spaniards bore traces of the Black Legend when he described how the Spanish forced Native Americans to "labour for the benefit of their oppressors." He credited Spanish priest Bartolomeo Las Casas with helping to save the Indians from slavery by suggesting that Spain import Africans to replace Native American laborers, who could not seem to endure the heavy labor required to build and maintain the New World's Spanish settlements. When the French and English began to settle other parts of the New World, they also took up Spain's practice of using African slaves to provide the strong backs needed to build their new cities and cultivate their lands. Thus, Swift lamented, the discovery of America proved to be a "most calamitous event to Africa."[10]

Like most of his contemporaries, Swift's sympathy for the African slave's plight was grounded in the conviction that no human being should be kept in a state of involuntary servitude. Overlooking the West Indies and Latin American slave systems, Swift branded the United States as the only Christian country in which slavery was tolerated to any extensive degree and the only place in which "the African . . . [was] deemed an article of property, and adjudged to have forfeited his natural rights, on account of the blackness of his complexion, and the inferiority of his intellectual capacity." He insisted that dissimilarity of complexion and inferiority of mind were not reasons to perpetuate the system. Those who justified such a system, in Swift's opinion, showed "the extreme baseness" of which humanity was capable. Such logic was merely a way of taking unfair advantage of the weak and defenseless.[11] These assertions did not mean, however, that Swift considered persons of African descent as white men's equals. He and most of his fellow proponents of abolition believed that Africans were their social and intellectual inferiors. Abolitionists were not necessarily working toward equality for blacks, but rather they wanted to end slavery.[12]

Instead of laying the blame for U.S. slavery on the ancient republics or the opportunistic European heirs to the slave trade, St. George Tucker tried to implicate England as a participant in slavery's perpetuation. He hinted that U.S. slavery, or at least some of the legal and social conventions governing the institution, might have grown out of the English common-law status of villenage. Blackstone described villenage as not strictly feudal, Norman, or Saxon but rather "mixed and compounded of them all." Saxon societies contained people who were "used and employed in the most servile works" and who belonged, "both they, their children, and effects," to the lord of the soil, "like the rest of the cattle or stock upon it." The Normans raised these slaves "to a kind of estate superior to downright slavery" yet still "inferior to every other condition." They called the state "villenage" and the tenants "villeins." These villeins, according to Blackstone, were either annexed to the manor of the land or to the person of the lord. If they were attached to the land, then whoever owned the land also owned the villeins. If they were attached to the lord of the manor, they could be transferred to another owner by deed. Lords often allowed them to till small plots of land in order to sustain their families, but the lord could dispossess them whenever he pleased. Villeins could acquire no property in lands or goods. The law did, however, protect villeins from "atrocious injuries of the lord." If the villein's master murdered or maimed a villein, or if he raped a female villein, also called a *neise*, the king could punish the lord. The state of villenage no longer existed in England. Over time, "the goodnature and benevolence of many lords of manors" allowed villeins to possess property and enjoy a measure of freedom. "In a regular course of descent," these measures of freedom became part of the common law and the benefactors of this leniency became known as "tenants by copy of court roll." Their tenure itself was described as a "copyhold." At the very least, these former villeins had established nominal customary rights to their tiny estates, which were still technically held at the lord's will. A statute of Charles II finally abolished villenage altogether.[13]

St. George Tucker acknowledged that the gradual abolition of villenage in England had "utterly extinguished" all "traces of slavery . . . such as at present" existed "in several of the United States." At the time of the first migrations to Virginia, the English did not bring with them "any prototype of that slavery" that took root in the colony soon thereafter. Nevertheless, Tucker tried to bind English and American institutions by dredging up numerous similarities between the conditions of villeins and slaves. For example, the term of a villein's services was "uncertain and indeterminate . . . such as his Lord thought fit to require." A villein was subject to the complete authority of his master and was liable to beating, imprisonment, and "every other chastisement his Lord could devise, except killing and maiming." The villein could not hold his own property, and in fact he was "himself the subject of property" and "as such was saleable and transmissible." Like real property, certain kinds of villeins were conveyed with the land to which they were annexed, and certain kinds of villeins were inheritable. Finally, Tucker noted, "the Slavery extended to the issue" though, unlike slaves, the child derived his social and legal status from that of his father. Thus, if the father was a villein, so was the child. U.S. slave codes declared that the child's condition followed that of the mother.[14] By pointing out these similarities between villenage and slavery, Tucker could argue that England's past labor practices were not so different from U.S. slavery.

James Kent also likened a villein's condition to that of a slave, and he added his own protest against contentions that English soil had always been free of slavery. Though Kent acknowledged Blackstone's claim that villeinage had long been an extinct practice, he observed that in England, "predial servitude" existed as late as Queen Elizabeth's reign,[15] contradicting a then-famous observation that "the air of England was, at that time, too pure for a slave to breathe in." Kent admitted, however, that the "personal servitude" that grew out of feudal practices of villenage never rivaled the severity or degradation of domestic slavery in Greece, Rome, or the European colonies in the New World. Although the feudal villein was unprotected "in his property" and subjected "to the most ignoble services," he was not "a villein in the eye of the law, except in relation to his master." To all others, Kent maintained, he was a free man, and his master was answerable to the king for "excessive injuries committed upon the vassal." Moreover, the "life and chastity of the female vassal" were protected under the law, though perhaps with an eye toward the realities of slavery in his own country, he admitted that this protection may not always have been enforced in practice.[16] He then assured his readers and students that regardless of what used to be in England, there was no such thing as slavery "in the sense of the civil law, or of the laws and usages in the West Indies, either in England . . . or in any part of Europe."[17] Kent connected England's past to slavery, but he also acknowledged that the English had managed to divorce themselves from slavery by the early nineteenth century.

American legists also agreed with and quoted Blackstone's words on slavery's incompatibility with natural law. The English legist had borrowed Montesquieu's principles of reason and natural law to provide his readers with a point-by-point rejection of Justinian's assertions that slavery was sanctioned through the law of nations.[18] Blackstone asserted that Justinian's three origins of the right of slavery were "built upon false foundations." Justinian's first origin was from a state of captivity in war, in which the captor had a right to his captive's life. According to Blackstone, natural law dictated that a man had no right to kill his enemy for any reason except self-defense. The circumstance of self-defense did not exist if an enemy had been taken prisoner. Moreover, Blackstone insisted that even a just war could not sanction the killing, maiming, torturing, or enslaving of a captured enemy. Justinian next asserted that a man had a right to sell himself into slavery. Blackstone pointed out that though a contract to work for another man was just, a contractual agreement for perpetual slavery was impossible. No man could voluntarily trade his freedom for a price, because every sale involved a quid pro quo, an exchange of like goods between buyer and seller. Because there was no equivalent for "life, and liberty," Blackstone declared, no such transaction was contractually possible. Besides, in theory, a slave could not own property independently of his master; therefore, logic dictated that the moment a man became enslaved, the price he received for the sale devolved to his new master. If the seller received no money for selling himself, Blackstone asked, of what validity could such a sale be? Justinian's last point on the origins of slavery was that a person could inherit the status. Children of slaves, "by a negative kind of birthright," were also slaves. Blackstone deduced that this right was automatically invalid because he had already proven the previous two origins false. Therefore, Blackstone concluded, no one could be a slave under the law of nations.[19]

St. George Tucker and Connecticut's James Gould applauded Blackstone's natural law argument against slavery. Tucker deemed Blackstone's assessment of Justinian "the most clear, manly, and convincing reasoning," and he added that even if slavery was justified for captives in a just war, Europeans could not claim that what they were conducting in Africa was by any means part of a just war. He accused Europeans of fomenting "a kind of perpetual warfare among the ignorant and miserable people of Africa" in order to furnish adequate "supplies of these unhappy people for . . . the slave trade." Moreover, Tucker asserted, Europeans violated any remaining notion of just war when they made "slaves of the *sellers* as well as the *sold*.[20] James Gould added to Blackstone's argument that slavery was not compatible with the natural right to contract between one man and another. He agreed with Blackstone that no one could give another person absolute and unlimited right over his own life or liberty, because no man could, under natural law, take his own life for any cause, nor could he transfer that right to another. A sale or transfer of a person's liberty was the "same as selling one's moral agency or free will."[21] The power of consent did not extend to self-enslavement under natural law.

If slavery was not sanctioned under natural law or supported by the common law, then the only other mode of sanction, according to Tapping Reeve, was positive law. In the United States the institution depended on local laws and usages sanctioned by Congress.[22] When it came to the question of whether slavery existed under positive law in Connecticut, both Reeve and his colleague Zephaniah Swift indulged in some wishful thinking. They tried to place their state in the best possible light, both historically and legally. Swift argued that the first settlers of Connecticut were "animated by the principles of justice and benevolence." They obtained title to their lands by purchase, not conquest, and they never attempted to reduce the Native Americans to a state of slavery nor to spill the blood of the natives "but in self defence." Although the importation of slaves was tacitly permitted, "it was never authorized by law."[23] Thus, Swift tried to distance Connecticut from slavery.

Reeve also tried to remove his home state from the controversy of slavery by insisting that he could find no avenue by which slavery legally existed in Connecticut. He deemed the institution "founded in violence and contrary to the laws of natural justice," and he claimed that Connecticut common law did not legalize slavery "other than what [arose] from holding some black men in servitude in defiance of the law of nature and the principles of the common law." Neither, Reeve insisted, were there any statutes in that state that explicitly recognized such a doctrine of slavery, although he did admit that they had statutes that assumed the existence of the practice.[24] Reeve explained that the institution was "an existing evil in the state," as were "other crimes and vices." Slavery may not have been sanctioned, but it was regulated by statute. So also did the state regulate adultery and drunkenness, Reeve observed, but one could not infer from those regulations that the Connecticut legislature sanctioned those crimes.[25]

Around 1808, when Reeve's protégé James Gould began to teach about the law of master and servant, the Litchfield lectures on slave law took on a more realistic and less apologetic tone. Although Gould made his antislavery leanings known, he did not try to hide the fact that the institution was still legal in Connecticut. According to Ely Warner's notes from the Litchfield school year 1808–09, Gould contended that slavery had, in fact, been legalized in Connecticut by statute. Gould was aware that his mentor, Tapping Reeve, opposed the conception of slavery in Connecticut as legal, and while he did not wish to undermine Reeve's authority, Gould's students needed to understand the law, not what Reeve believed the law ought to be. Gould explained to his students that Reeve was so much "opposed to this practice on the ground of natural law" that he was "unwilling to acknowledge" that Connecticut law explicitly countenanced slavery.[26]

Ironically, to uphold the "opinion of the profession in general in this state" that Connecticut law legalized slavery, Gould used the very same laws Reeve designated as evidence that Connecticut's lawmakers did not support slavery. Gould referred to statutes prescribing the rights of the master over his slaves, limitations of a master's authority over his slaves, prohibitions against certain activities of slaves, and particularly a statute providing for the gradual emancipation of slaves as proof that the Connecticut General Assembly acknowledged the existence of slavery with positive law.[27] Not only did Litchfield's students get a lesson on state laws of slavery and servitude, but they also learned that evidence could be interpreted in a variety of ways, even to prove opposing views.

With the possible exception of Tapping Reeve, American legists did not recount these histories of slavery to absolve their own republics of all guilt in the perpetuation of the institution. Their goal was to show that slavery bore a lineage that included the noble ancient republics and perhaps even England itself. These polities, they believed, also had to share the burden of guilt for perpetuating this mode of oppression. Their deflection of guilt, however, did not make the U.S. reality any different. Positive law protections of slavery existed in all of the states during the early national period, and the nation's legal scholars had to unravel the complexities of these laws for their students and readers.

II

Slaves held a singular status under U.S. law, in that they were part property and part person. The degree to which the different states considered them property or persons varied, however. Southern states tended to treat slaves more explicitly as property than Northern states. But in certain instances, Southern slave law recognized what some scholars call a "legal personality."[28] Northern states, on the other hand, tended to lean more heavily on laws that recognized slaves' legal personhood, and the common law that governed the relationship between master and servant was the preferred arena for these regulations. In New England slaves could testify for or against white persons in court, and under Connecticut law they could sue their masters if they felt they had been excessively abused. In all states, the person/property dichotomy was present. Slaves were taxed as various kinds of property in all states, yet in some Northern states they were legally permitted to possess their own property. The Revolution awakened an awareness of individual rights that led some states in the North and the South to make murdering a slave a crime.[29] Generally, however, slaves only gained a completely human persona when they acted against social norms.

The writings and lectures of St. George Tucker and the two Litchfield Law School professors provide ideal case studies for examining this person/property dichotomy. These legists' lessons revealed the ways in which common law influenced the regulations governing slavery. While their descriptions of regional slave law created further ties between themselves and England, they also revealed the widening regional differences in slaves' treatment under the law.

Slaves were, of course, property under the Northern and Southern law, but Southern states seemed to emphasize their status as property to a greater degree. St. George Tucker provided the most forthright assessment of slaves as property. He did not mince words about the fact that Virginia law explicitly labeled slaves chattel to be conveyed in any manner the master saw fit. Virginia was unique, however, in that the colony, and later the state, found it difficult to decide exactly what kind of property slaves were. In the introduction to his appendix on the laws concerning slaves as property in Virginia, Tucker repeated the definitions of the two kinds of property that existed under the common law. Real property included land and those objects that were "permanently annexed to" that land, such as buildings and the rent and profits attached to the land. Personal property included all moveable objects that "may attend the person of the owner" wherever he went. The difference, Tucker explained, consisted in the "immoveable and permanent nature of land; and in the moveable and perishable properties and qualities . . . of such things as [were] neither annexed to, nor connected with" the land.[30] For a good portion of the eighteenth century, and even into the first decades after Independence, Virginia law considered slaves not only as property but as "immoveable" property, the same as land. He admitted that some might consider it unusual that a slave, "whose breath [was] in his nostrils" and who was mobile enough to run away, might be regarded as real estate. As he had done with the institution of slavery in general, Tucker tied this peculiar property law to the English custom of villenage, under which villeins were annexed to lands. The fundamental difference between slaves' and villeins' ties to the land was that slaves in Virginia were liable to be conveyed to compensate for their master's debt, while villeins were not used to compensate for the debts of their lords.[31]

In 1792 and 1794 Virginia's General Assembly passed acts that transformed slaves' status from real property to personal property. The assembly apparently made this change in order to make the distribution of slaves from intestate estates more convenient. Slaves were still, according to Tucker, "considered as a kind of special assets," in that the 1794 statute forbade the sale of slaves for payment of debt unless the executor or administrator of the estate had exhausted all other resources. Slaves could be emancipated by will or deed under these acts, but should the deceased not have enough property of other kinds to cover his debts, executors could sell those slaves to satisfy the debts instead of emancipating them. Additionally, though the law declared slaves personal estate in other respects, the widow of a person dying intestate received only a life estate of one-third of her husband's slaves. Just as with any other real or personal property, if a woman slave owner married, her husband automatically came into possession of the slaves. Therefore, if the husband died before his wife, the slaves his wife owned before their marriage could be sold to satisfy the deceased man's debts. If the husband died before his wife and it was unnecessary to sell these slaves to cover his debt, the "widow's thirds" rule meant that she could conceivably only have control of a portion of the slaves over whom she had complete ownership before her marriage.[32] These limitations were true not just in Virginia, but also in other states.

Despite legal evidence to the contrary, Tapping Reeve had a difficult time accepting that Connecticut law looked upon slaves as property. Reeve did not let the fact that state law allowed the sale or conveyance of slaves keep him from insisting that there was no statute in Connecticut "declaring any class of men to be property." If blacks were legally property, Reeve asserted, "their owners might put them to any use to which they could put their other property and might kill and barrel them up." That action, Reeve asserted, was certainly prohibited by law.[33] Although James Gould was more realistic about the status of slaves as property in his home state, he agreed with his mentor that Connecticut's relaxation of slave laws made their form of bondage milder than that of Justinian's Rome. He believed that this claim of a milder slavery even applied to Southern states because, though by Roman law masters had complete control over their slaves' lives, Gould asserted that Southern masters could not, by the letter of the law, legally kill their slaves.[34] At least, by Reeve's and Gould's estimation, American slave laws were improvements over ancient forms of slavery.

Although slaves were still property in Connecticut, state law did not presume that a black person was a slave. If there was any question as to whether a person of color was, in fact, a slave, the onus fell on the person claiming ownership to prove his case. Asa Bacon observed in his Litchfield Law School notes that Connecticut law had "destroyed . . . the presumption of a negroe[']s being a slave" by placing upon the master the burden of proof that he held title to a slave. The Connecticut law apparently made proof of ownership rather difficult, and Bacon observed in his lecture notes that if the state's authorities were to enforce that rule as it was written it would "liberate every slave in Connecticut."[35]

Reeve also argued that according to his state's laws, the only thing a master really owned was his slave's labor. To prove his point he used the example of Connecticut's adoption of the common-law action of trover with regard to slave labor. Blackstone defined an action of trover as an attempt to recover damages against a person who had "found" or otherwise appropriated another's property and then refused to deliver the goods to the rightful owner, converting them to his own use instead.[36] By English common law, this action was for the recovery of property, and Reeve admitted that it was still an action of property in Connecticut, even when it applied to the appropriation of a slave. However, Reeve claimed that in Connecticut, such an action would not be to recover a slave who had been taken from a master, but rather it would only apply to the loss of labor during the slave's absence. Therefore, Connecticut courts did not sanction the "total" slavery that existed when a master owned the body of a servant. Instead, that state's law only acknowledged possession of a slave's labor, as "only a right in the master to the *perpetual service* of the slave" and not to the possession of the slave's person. Thus, Reeve reasoned that a slave in Connecticut was really an "apprentice for life, entitled to all the rights of an apprentice." Connecticut courts, Reeve insisted, did not consider the master "as entitled to the slave, as *property*, but only to his services," and they considered the sale of a slave "as in the nature of an assignment of an apprentice by the custom of London." The only difference between a slave and another servant in Connecticut was that a slave's time of service lasted his entire life. Besides this small detail, Reeve insisted, the state's courts considered slaves entitled to "the same rights as other men" and the common law of master and servant, not property law, governed their presence in that state.[37]

Under Connecticut law, a slave possessed a variety of other legal rights unknown to those slaves who lived further south, and many of these laws descended from the common law of master and servant. For example, though he could not earn wages in return for his labor, a slave could sell certain produce or other goods of his own making and could inherit property.

Additionally, like free servants, a slave was protected from his master's abuse, and if he felt himself wronged he could take legal action against his master. He used the example of a slave's suit against his former owner for selling him to "a difficult master" and thus separating him from his family. Although there was no decision in the case, Reeve explained that the court privately advised his first master to repurchase the slave and the master followed the court's advice.[38] Connecticut's lawmakers seemed to have reached back into equity traditions as well as the law of master and servant to govern dealings between master and slave.

In addition to possessing certain rights under the common law governing servants, Connecticut's slaves also enjoyed some of the same legal protections as other household dependents. In the early nineteenth century, James Gould compared the status of a slave to that of a minor child in Connecticut on at least two counts. First, he pointed out that Connecticut's courts upheld slaves' rights to possess property even against their master, "precisely like a minor child." Second, the state's Superior Court determined that the marriage of a slave to a free person with the master's consent was the equivalent of the slave's emancipation. Marriage was a contractual relationship, Gould explained, and a contractual relationship was "inconsistent with a state of slavery." He pointed out that this doctrine was also used in England in the case of minor children.[39] Customs traditionally connected with equity and the rights of dependent kin combined to soften the letter of Connecticut's slave law.

Though application of the law varied from state to state and punishments were generally more severe for slaves, regulations governing liability for property or personal injuries to those outside the household generally followed the common law of master and servant for both slaves and servants. Under the common law, a servant was expected to obey his master, just as a wife was expected to obey her husband. If a servant caused harm to another person or his property while in his master's service, complaints often could be brought against the master rather than the servant. If a servant committed an unlawful act by command of his master, both were liable, because the servant was only compelled to obey his master when the commands were "honest and lawful." The servant could, however, plead ignorance of the act's unlawfulness, and then the master only was liable. When injury arose out of the negligence of the servant alone, he was sometimes solely liable, depending on whether the injury resulted from the implied consent or tacit agreement of the master, or if the servant performed the work negligently or did not follow his master's instructions. Additionally, if a master did not properly train a servant for tasks that the servant was directed to perform, the master could be held liable.[40] Though slaves were sometimes held to different degrees of punishment for causing injury, they were often assumed to have the same degree of judgment as servants when it came to committing wrongs.

Under the common law, masters also possessed the right to correct all of their dependents, both free and unfree, within moderation. The definitions of moderate correction, however, differed depending on whether the person receiving correction was a slave, a servant, a minor, or, for that matter, the master's wife or child. Litchfield student George Flagg Mann wrote in the 1820s that the master's authority to correct his servants was usually by virtue of compact with the servant or his guardian, but not always. Mann gave as an example of this rule's exception the case of slaves, "such as exist[ed] at the South," because slaves, of course, did not contract their labor.[41] Laws in the Northern and Southern regions seemed to regulate the head of household's authority over his servants in similar ways, though in both regions much was left to the discretion of a magistrate or a jury should a servant file a complaint against his master. In Connecticut, the master could correct a slave or apprentice of any age, but neither he nor his wife could beat any other servant of full age without risking the legal departure of that servant.[42] Although Blackstone and others noted the master's right to give moderate corporal correction to his servants, James Kent observed that this sort of punishment could only be safely meted out to apprentices and menial servants while under age, because at that point the master was considered to be operating *in loco parentis*.[43] Although parents could, of course, use the rod to correct children, using such tactics on adults contradicted the spirit of a contract between master and servant.

St. George Tucker also applied Blackstone's rules of correction to the regulation of slaves in his lectures on Virginia's master-servant law, but his explanation showed that Virginians recognized less legal personhood in slaves than was so in Connecticut. He too noted that if a master or his wife beat a servant "of full age," the servant had the right to depart. Tucker pointed out that Virginia law did not prevent moderate correction, but the law did protect servants and apprentices—not slaves—from excessive correction. If a county or corporation court found a master to be abusive, officials could remove an apprentice and bind him to another master. Servants legally could be corrected by whipping on order from the justice of the peace, and as in

Connecticut, the servants had access to the courts for complaints of injury by their master. Slaves in Virginia, on the other hand, had no recourse in courts of law in order to protect their personal security.[44]

In their interpretations of their state's slave law as outgrowths of master and servant law, Connecticut's legal scholars took some slightly premature steps toward a reshaping of their polity's identity as a place without slaves. While Reeve and Gould could demonstrate some measure of progress toward the republican ideal of freedom within their slave law, St. George Tucker could not say the same for slaves' legal condition in Virginia. Despite Tapping Reeve's assertion to the contrary, however, both Connecticut and Virginia still regulated their slaves as persons *and* property. Connecticut's legists could express some pride in their states' relaxed legislation on slavery, but in the end, they knew that a few more legal privileges still did not add up to freedom.

III

Blackstone's *Commentaries* was so central to American legal thought and education, and American feelings of cultural inferiority to England were so persistent, that American legists could not avoid discussing the English master's condemnation of slavery in their treatises and classrooms. In his chapter on the law of master and servant, Blackstone declared that the law of England abhorred and would "not endure the existence of . . . slavery within this nation," and that English law decreed that any slave, "the instant he land[ed] in England," became a free man.[45] Legists' reactions to this declaration began with emphatic agreement that the institution had no place in a civilized polity, but they almost invariably ended with the insistence that the parent country had done much to perpetuate the institution in the United States. They also felt compelled to defend their own place in history by arguing that as repugnant as slavery was, America's republics had made it a much milder and more humane institution than in any other place or time.

James Wilson followed Blackstone's lead on slavery almost to the letter. The only words Wilson uttered on the topic in his law lectures were a condensed version of Blackstone's: that slavery was "unauthorized by the common law" and "repugnant to the principles of natural law." Using Blackstone's objections against Justinian's origins of slavery, Wilson called the reasons behind the origin and perpetuation of slavery "built upon a false foundation," because the common law protected everyone "in the enjoyment of their persons and of their property." After making those brief and heated remarks in his lecture on natural rights, the Pennsylvania law professor then turned his attention to the legal relationship between master and servant and never returned to the subject of slavery in his lectures.[46] It was not as if Wilson could strike a superior pose with regard to slavery on behalf of his home state. The institution was still legal in Pennsylvania at the time Wilson gave his lectures. Though Pennsylvania had been the first to pass a gradual emancipation act in 1780, Pennsylvanians did not abolish slavery until 1847.[47] For whatever reason, the Philadelphia legist chose to omit the details of his state's slave law from his lectures.

Zephaniah Swift, on the other hand, addressed the subject of slavery in Connecticut and the rest of the United States at length, and in doing so, he leaned heavily on concepts of honor and reputation, hoping that he could salvage his nation's image by arguing that the U.S. form of slavery was milder than some. He asserted that as the United States was the seedbed of republican liberty in the Western world, Americans were obliged to set the example of absolute liberty. Again ignoring the widespread presence of slavery elsewhere in the hemisphere, Swift lamented that the United States was the only Christian country that sanctioned slavery so widely and openly, and he prayed that it would be "to the glory of the present age to wipe away this reproach" from the land.[48] Swift chose to take some comfort in the erroneous notion that masters in the United States did not treat their slaves as cruelly as some other countries. He invested considerable trust in the collective and individual honor of American institutions and men when he insisted that slaves were always under the protection of the government and that their treatment was "always distinguished by that mildness and clemency which accorded with the characters of their masters." Besides, he added, slaves' situation was "preferable to what it had been in their own country," an improvement that Swift believed compensated for their loss of liberty.[49]

As he absolved his nation of the title of most cruel slaveholding country in the world, Swift laid the prize for the worst treatment of slaves at the door of England's remaining colonies. Swift advanced the "mortifying truth that the English in their West-India islands" had "exceeded any other nation in the cruel treatment of its slaves." He expressed astonishment that such a people, who operated under a government "which remained unrivalled till the establishment of the constitution of the United States, should be guilty of cruelties so repugnant to the spirit and principles of their government." While describing the treatment of slaves, Swift dredged up other memories of mistreatment at the hands of the British. He recalled similar instances during the Revolution when Britain exercised many cruelties against American prisoners of war, and he denounced these actions against both slaves and free white Americans as "an eternal stigma on their national character."[50] With these descriptions, Swift employed the strategy of elevating his own nation's reputation by deflating England's character.

Swift was not alone in his efforts to blame England for the existence of the peculiar institution in an enlightened age. St. George Tucker defended "the present generation" of Americans for their part in the perpetuation of slavery, arguing that it was not their fault that the institution existed. In his edition of the *Commentaries* Tucker included an extract from a 1772 petition from the House of Burgesses that, in his opinion, showed "the sense of the people of Virginia . . . on the subject of slavery at that period." The petition called the king's attention to a "calamity of a most alarming nature," the slave trade into Virginia. Petitioners deemed the importation of Africans for the purpose of slavery "a trade of great inhumanity" and asked the king to assist them in halting the trafficking of slaves into their colony. Tucker noted that the petition "produced no effect," and he charged the Crown with privileging "the interest of the English merchants" who profited from the slave trade over the "wishes of the people of this colony." Framers of Virginia's constitution included this "inhuman use of the royal negative" among the king's "acts of misrule" when they drew up their new frame of government. The former colony's legislature was so determined to stop the importation of additional slaves that, according to Tucker, during the tumult and confusion of the Revolution in 1778 it took measures to "crush forever so pernicious and infamous a commerce" by passing an act to halt the importation of slaves from Africa.[51] Tucker neglected to mention that one of the central reasons why Virginia's legislators pushed for the importation ban was because Virginia was experiencing an oversupply of slaves by the 1770s. Virginia planters, already deeply in debt, feared that a reduction in the value of their human property would drive them closer to financial ruin. Moreover, Virginians were concerned about the growing black population in their colony. The larger the black population, the greater the chance of rebellion.[52] However, Parliament's refusal to allow Virginia to curtail slave importation provided American legists with a convenient way to protest their innocence.

IV

Despite the self-serving motivations behind his explanations of petitions to end the slave trade, Tucker possessed genuine antislavery leanings. His sentiments regarding the evils of slavery were not unusual, even for a slave-holding Virginian. Just after the Revolution, slaveholders like St. George Tucker expected that the republican movement toward equality and liberty had somehow to include the emancipation of all slaves. He seemed to be no less desirous for the demise of that burdensome institution than were his colleagues to the north. In fact, he declared that the abolition of slavery in Virginia and the United States was his "*first,* and . . . probably . . . last, expiring wish."[53] On the other hand, his family's economic security and the desire to protect his property were of paramount importance to Tucker and to his contemporaries. He was concerned about the calamitous property losses that he and his fellow slaveholders would incur should the slaves be emancipated all at once. Tucker reconciled these contradictory impulses by proclaiming on one page of his edition of the *Commentaries* that slavery was "perfectly irreconcilable . . . to the principles of a democracy, which . . . form[ed] the *basis* and *foundation* of our government" and then, just a few pages later, by laying out a scheme by which Virginia slave owners could effect the eventual release of all of their slaves without immediate loss of any human property.[54] The slaveholding legal scholar possessed an uncanny ability to communicate the reality of free and enslaved blacks' legal status in Virginia, but he was reluctant to act on his moral convictions when his family's economic interests got in the way.

After learning of the gradual emancipation plans of Connecticut and Pennsylvania and corresponding with Jeremy Belknap and Zephaniah Swift about the details of their state's legislation,[55] Tucker decided to fashion a similar plan for his home state. In 1796, he published a pamphlet entitled *A Dissertation on Slavery,* which discussed the state of slavery in Virginia and proposed a gradual emancipation of Virginia's slaves. He later republished this pamphlet as an appendix in his edition of the *Commentaries.* Tucker proposed that the Virginia legislature enact a gradual emancipation process that would take approximately one hundred years to complete. His proposal provided for the emancipation of all female slaves born after December 31, 1800, and their descendents. These newly freed blacks would then be required to perform service for their former masters until they were thirty years of age to compensate "for the trouble and expence of maintaining them during infancy." After those eligible for freedom had worked out their obligations to their masters, Tucker hoped that the former slaves would migrate to the frontier on their own and form their own separate communities rather than remaining among the white societies in the east.[56]

The plan seemed to alleviate everyone's concerns. It would rid the state of an institution that was, in Tucker's mind, contrary to the central principles in Virginia's Declaration of Rights, that "'all men are, by nature *equally* free, and independent, and have certain rights . . . namely . . . the enjoyment of life and *liberty*.'"[57] A gradual release of slaves would also protect slaveholders' property because, Tucker proudly declared, it could be achieved "without the *emancipation* of a single slave." Additionally, his plan for abolition did not confer rights of citizenship among the freedmen, nor did it place the freedmen within Virginia society. Instead, his plan provided former slaves with "liberty of loco-motion," under which they could choose to "submit to that civil inferiority, inseparably attached to [their] condition in this country" or could "seek some more favourable climate, where all distinctions between men are either totally abolished, or less regarded than this."[58] Thus, Tucker created a scenario in which the black population and the problem of slavery could be made to disappear.

Despite Tucker's valiant efforts to please the republican consciences and the pockets of his fellow Virginians, his proposal for gradual abolition of slavery in his home state was "illy received" by the House of Delegates, which tabled the proposal without debate.[59] This action infuriated Tucker, who then decided to print the plan as a pamphlet in 1796. Although by 1803 he had begun to consider his emancipation plan a "Utopian ideal," he still felt strongly enough about it to reprint the pamphlet in his edition of Blackstone's *Commentaries* in 1803. However, Tucker himself never freed his slaves.[60] As the years passed, the Virginian still tinkered with his plan for gradual abolition in order to restore his state's honor, even though his convictions placed him in a shrinking minority. He did not publicize subsequent modifications to his abolition plan after 1803.[61]

In his *Dissertation on Slavery* and elsewhere, Tucker alternately condemned slavery as a cruel practice that was contrary to natural law and praised Virginians for making the institution into a gentler form of involuntary servitude. Tucker defended the practice of keeping human property by rationalizing that a slave's situation in early national Virginia was much better than it had been in colonial times and was certainly better than if he had remained in Africa. He pointed to innovations in the mode of trial for slaves brought up on criminal charges that, in his opinion, were "infinitely more beneficial to them . . . than formerly." Though they still were not entitled to trial by jury, slaves could plead for benefit of clergy for many offenses, although punishment was still more severe for slaves than for whites convicted of identical offenses.[62] Tucker claimed that the state's enforcement against "this unhappy class of people" was not only "*less rigorous than formerly*," but "perhaps milder than in any other Country" where slaves comprised such a large portion of the population.[63] His own conflicting sentiments over slavery may have blinded him to the realities of bondage in the Old Dominion.

Tucker also pointed out that the Revolutionary impulse toward liberty seemed to have paid off for Africans in Virginia through a 1782 act authorizing the manumission of slaves. The act provided for emancipation by will or by deed under the signature of the owner and when signed by two witnesses from the county court. Tucker insisted that there was "reason to believe that great numbers" had been emancipated between the passage of the act and the publication of his *Commentaries*. He quoted census numbers of 12,866 free persons of color and American Indians in Virginia, and he proudly pointed out that in 1790 there were "*more* free negroes and mulattoes in Virginia alone" than in "the four New England States and Vermont" combined. He proudly stated that the "progress of Emancipation" in Virginia was "much greater" than their "*Eastern* brethren" supposed. Tucker claimed that in the 1790 census there were 20,848 inhabitants of Virginia's Eastern Shore, of whom 1,185 were free persons of color, and over the ensuing decade this number had been "much augmented." By contrast, New York, New Jersey, and Pennsylvania combined, according to Tucker, had only 1,087 free persons of color in 1790.[64] The Virginia jurist did not mention the fact that these numbers also revealed the much larger slave population in his state as compared to the Northeast. In 1790, Virginia had by far the largest slave population of any state in the union, and New York, New Jersey, and Pennsylvania had miniscule numbers of slaves in comparison.

All was not better in Virginia's republicanized version of slavery, however. Even in those enlightened days of the early republic, Tucker lamented that the protection of a black's right to personal security was "confined to very few cases."[65] He described three degrees of slavery: political slavery, in which a nation was deprived of the right to be governed by its own laws by some outside force; civil slavery, in which individual liberty was "further restrained than . . . necessary . . . for the general advantage" of the polity or when there was an inequality of rights or privileges among citizens; and domestic slavery, in which one man's actions were subject to the control of others. The colonies, Tucker explained, were under a state of political slavery before the nation broke with England and established their own governments and sets of laws. Civil slavery, he claimed, still existed in "every government in Europe before the French revolution" and also existed in America before Independence. Moreover, Tucker asserted, civil slavery still existed among the free blacks of America, "notwithstanding the maxims of equality which have been adopted" in the states' constitutions. This sector of the population, he claimed, labored under "civil incapacities . . . almost as numerous as the civil rights of our free citizens." In Virginia free blacks could not vote or hold office, could not carry a gun or other weapon, and could be whipped for resisting a white person, among other limitations on their liberties. Slaves, however, labored under the most extreme degree of servitude, that of domestic slavery. Tucker described this state as carrying all of the burdens of civil slavery with "the weight of other numerous calamities superadded thereto."[66] He concluded that even with improvements in the treatment of slaves and the greater ease of manumission in the period just after the Revolution, individual rights of slaves still were "at times either wholly annihilated, or reduced to a shadow." Slaves had no recourse against their masters and no legal mode of protecting their families or themselves from harm.[67]

Despite his progressive ideas, Tucker supported the existence of a few fundamental laws that limited the rights and privileges of persons of color, whether free or slave. He advocated laws that prevented any free black from holding office or possessing any landed estate except as a lease of twenty-one years' duration or less. Virginia law prohibited slaves or free persons of color from testifying against a white person in a court of law, and blacks or mulattoes could not legally marry a white person. If a white and a person of color were convicted of intermarriage, they were subject to one year's imprisonment.[68] Although Tucker felt twinges of guilt for the injustices of slavery, he, like many of his contemporaries, did not believe that African Americans possessed the intellectual ability to function as whites' equals in society. Therefore, they should not possess all of a republican society's privileges.

While his fellow Virginians chose to ignore his proposal for gradual emancipation altogether, Tucker's publication drew some measure of attention from Northern abolitionists. After Tucker's *Dissertation on Slavery* appeared in print, a Northern abolitionist named Robert Pleasants accused Tucker of harboring prejudice against blacks, because of his assertions that people of color could never hold full citizenship in U.S. societies. Tucker straightforwardly acknowledged that prejudice was "so prevalent in the present generation, that were I of a different opinion I would leave it to time to eradicate." He warned Pleasants that while this prejudice still prevailed, it was not wise to extend civil privileges to blacks, "for their numbers and those of the whites being nearly equal[,] if they could acquire any share in the administration of the state we should soon behold two parties formed and enlisted by nature under different banners whose contests would probably convulse the state."[69] Within his rhetoric about patience and moderation, it is hard to tell just what Tucker believed about blacks' intellectual potential. It is clear from Tucker's other writings, however, that the Virginia jurist did not consider blacks and whites capable of living together in peace or equality.

Tucker believed that if Virginia were ever to realize the republican dream of a free and equal society, the freedmen would have to leave that society to form their own separate communities. Sometime after 1803 he revised his treatise to include an elaborate resettlement plan for freed slaves. He explained that although he was once inclined to colonize the freedmen on the Florida peninsula, he was concerned that its proximity to Cuba and other West Indian islands made the plan risky. These islands were "already fill'd with negroe Slaves, who may in time follow the Example of those in St. Domingo . . . and form nations of Barbarians and pirates." Instead, he thought that the recently acquired Louisiana Territory might be ideal because of its sparse settlements and reputedly steamy climate, which Tucker believed to be much like that of Africa. He devised a complicated township plan that surrounded the freedmen's settlements with white settlements. Tucker envisioned government-provided incentives to white tradesmen, artisans, clergy, and teachers to settle close to the freedmen and to offer their services and examples. Once the free persons of color were capable, they could assume civil offices within their townships.[70]

In even later revisions of his plan for emancipation, apparently penned around 1821, Tucker suggested that the Florida treaty between the United States and Spain had given the government the perfect opportunity for resettlement of former slaves west of the Rockies "without danger to the future peace and happiness of the United States." He suggested allowing one-eighth of the western territory for freedmen and the balance of the territory for resettling American Indian nations. If each of the freedmen's settlements were surrounded with white townships as he had previously proposed, he expected that no injuries would come to white societies and that the "asylums" for freed blacks could furnish laborers for the white farmers in the surrounding western townships.[71]

Thus, even into the 1820s Tucker still pursued the republican ideal of a free and equal society in which those who once had not been free would be relocated to another society in which they could be equals. There they could pursue their own dreams of liberty and equality. But by the 1820s, Tucker's labors on his emancipation plan were secret.[72] Although he carefully recorded his plans, he apparently told no one of his newest ideas on the relocation of slaves and revised his plan only for his own peace of mind.

Tucker's preoccupation with the problem of removing freed slaves from his society revealed a deep flaw in his and others' dreams of free and equal republics. Tucker and many of his counterparts throughout the United States did not believe that persons of color could ever be their social or intellectual equals. Therefore, if the United States could free itself from the burden of slavery—and this prospect looked far dimmer in the 1820s than it had thirty years earlier—then the only way to achieve the ideal of an equal society was to remove those who they believed were inherently unequal. If persons of color remained, the society could perhaps achieve a measure of freedom, but it could never be the ideal republic that offered equality of opportunity for all citizens. It would still fall short of its Revolutionary ideals.

V

James Kent provided a unique window on one Northern lawyer's personal and professional sentiments toward slavery from the Revolutionary era to the late 1820s. His voluminous collection of papers spanning over fifty years of his life and career as lawyer and judge provides a few clues about the forces that shaped his writings on slavery in his *Commentaries on the American Law.* Although slavery existed in New York until the legislature abolished the institution in 1827,[73] Kent probably never owned slaves. He did, however, employ black servants, at least a few of whom held valued places in his household. In a 1792 letter, Kent's father, Moss Kent Sr., discussed the transfer of a black servant to James's household. The elder Kent indicated that the servant was willing to move to New York and to work for James. Moss Sr. instructed his son to contract with the man for "moderate wages" and to provide proper clothing for the domestic servant. Nine years later, James Kent wrote in his journal about his distress over the loss of his servant Jack, "an excellent negro of the age of 20." While riding circuit with his master, Jack was kicked in the stomach by a horse and died several hours later.[74]

As a young lawyer caught up in the post-Revolutionary antislavery movements, Kent was in favor of emancipation, but he apparently harbored mixed feelings about the African race and the place of Africans in his society. In the mid-1780s, Kent and his friend John Cotton Smith carried on animated correspondence about the newly formed society to emancipate slaves in New York, but Kent was skeptical that emancipation would come about simply as a result of the Revolution. Additionally, he resisted his friend's assertions that all enslaved Africans should be freed immediately. Smith objected to Kent's ideas that Africans were inferior products of tropical climates, a theory Kent had adopted from Montesquieu and one that Smith dismissed as "erroneous." He refuted Kent's assertion that mere geographical location had branded the African nations "with a total destitution of those illustrious virtues and qualities which characterize the polished inhabitants of northern climes." Smith asserted, over Kent's objections, that Africans had leaders among them who were capable of forming "as much juridical policy" and displaying "as many arts in government" as "those coroneted kings—enshrined in the pavilions of sensuality—and deaf to the cries of wretchedness and oppression assailing them from every quarter of their dominions." Kent, however, did not agree with his friend's estimation of Africans' abilities to govern themselves, and he registered his support for the gradual emancipation plans that neighboring states had begun to adopt.[75] Many of Kent's contemporaries believed, as he did, that gradual emancipation would allow whites to prepare blacks for independent lives while also protecting masters from the catastrophic financial consequences of immediate emancipation.

Forty years after his exchange with Smith, and over twenty years after Tucker's cautiously optimistic treatise on slavery in Virginia, Kent published his American *Commentaries*. In the ensuing years the New York jurist had witnessed a gradual but incomplete loosening of slave regulations in most Northern states and a tightening of slave law in the Southern states. While he was careful to maintain a diplomatic tone throughout his discussion of slavery, Kent's analysis made his readers aware of the increasingly sharp divergences between slavery's legal status in the North and the South.

Kent first addressed England's position on slavery. Though he lauded English courts' efforts on the behalf of slaves who brought complaints before that country's bar, Kent challenged Blackstone's assertion that English law freed any slave "the instant he land[ed] in England."[76] In England's favor, Kent cited the *Somerset* case of 1772, in which the courts freed a slave who had accompanied his master from America to England on the premise that there was no law protecting slavery in England.[77] He also discussed a similar case in which a slave by the name of Knight, who was brought from the West Indies to Scotland by his master in 1778, successfully petitioned the courts in Scotland for his freedom. The court ruled that the law of Scotland did not recognize slavery and thus did not recognize the master's claim "to the perpetual service of the negro."[78] Though Kent appreciated the English courts' advocacy of slaves, he also recognized that the parent country's law did not always work in the slave's favor. Under common law, a master had no authority over a slave while they resided in England, but Kent pointed out that the same was not true if a slave subsequently returned to a place in which slavery was legal. He cited yet another English case in which a slave from the West Indies accompanied his master to England and then returned to the West Indies. In this case the court held that the slave's temporary residence in England did not fully emancipate him, and he reverted to his former status upon his return to the West Indies.[79] Even in English courts moral considerations did not always trump common law.

When he turned his attention toward slavery in the United States, Kent noted some hardening regional distinctions in the presence and character of the institution. By the 1820s, he observed, slavery was virtually extinct in the North, and Kent tried to deal diplomatically with the increasingly contentious subject of slavery in the Southern states. He began by reminding his audience that the responsibility for the institution did not "rest upon the present generation . . . to whom the institution descended by inheritance, provided they [had] endeavoured, by all reasonable means, to arrest and mitigate the calamity." In other words, Kent believed that Southern slaveholders had to work as best they could with the situation their ancestors had dealt them. He rationalized that Southern slave laws were probably as "just and mild" as those governments deemed "to be compatible with the public safety . . . or with the existence and preservation of that species of property."[80] The former New York chancellor observed that the desire to preserve property manifested itself in a "great jealousy in respect to any external influence or communications," particularly when this interference was directed toward fomenting discontent among the slave population. For example, by the 1820s laws in Georgia, Louisiana, and Virginia restricted assemblies of slaves and other persons of color, prohibited any person from teaching a slave or free black to read or write, and barred anyone from using a public forum to incite discontent among slaves. He speculated that the severity of the penalties against this sort of interference "must have proceeded from the strong and fearful apprehension . . . that the kind of knowledge and instruction" that were conveyed in such forums "would increase greatly the means, capacity, and tendency of slaves to combine for purposes of mischief and insurrection."[81] In other words, Southern slaveholders' experiences with rebellions, both real and rumored, provoked Southern legislators to tighten restrictions on slaves in order to prevent further unrest.

While he speculated that such punitive measures were perhaps necessary to enable the present generation to deal with the transgressions of their ancestors, Kent also assured his Southern counterparts that there was a way out of the dilemma. Southern economies relied far more heavily on slave labor than did New York's, but Kent believed that his home state's example could be useful. Therefore, Kent provided his readers with a blueprint for escape from reliance on slavery in the form of a lengthy history of the origin, progress, and demise of slavery in his home state of New York. He stated that before the Revolution, laws of domestic slavery were as "firmly and rigorously established" in New York "as in any part of this country," and he even claimed that colonial New York's laws of slavery were more severe than those of Massachusetts or Connecticut.[82] After Independence, however, "the principles of natural right and civil liberty were better known and obeyed, and domestic slavery speedily and sensibly felt the genial influence of the revolution." Beginning in 1781, a series of acts gradually gave freedom to slaves in New York, though Kent admitted that the laws providing for gradual abolition and prohibiting importation of more slaves were only partial alleviations of the "great public evil" of slavery. Finally, in 1817, the New York legislature passed a law that provided for the emancipation of all slaves by July 4, 1827. The only exceptions were slaves who accompanied their masters on trips to New York from slave states.[83]

By the time Kent presented the story of the rise and gradual fall of slavery in his home state, most other Northern states were well on their way toward a slow emancipation of their own slaves. Vermont came into the union with a constitution that outlawed slavery. Massachusetts and New Hampshire never even legislated the institution away. It died on its own in true common-law fashion, with local custom and court decisions gradually closing it down. Others, by constitutional amendment or legislation, slowly rid themselves of the legal burden of slavery, but many, plagued by resistance from the slave owners within their borders, did not make the final legislative move until the 1840s.[84] Even in more progressive Northern states, change came slowly.

Kent, like many of his contemporaries, maintained the conviction that people of color were intellectually and socially inferior to whites, and the laws to which he directed his audience were designed with concepts of Africans' inferiority in mind. After lauding New York's erasure of slavery from its law books, he noted that the amended state constitution of 1821 still placed people of color, "the former victims of the slave laws," in an inferior position to whites in terms of rights of citizenship. For example, African Americans had to pass a more stringent property qualification than whites to prove that they possessed the independence of will required for suffrage. Kent pointed out that such restrictions were not unusual, and that in most states there was a distinction between the political privileges of whites and blacks. Blacks could not participate equally with whites because, in Kent's opinion and in the opinion of many of his colleagues, "the African race" was "a degraded caste . . . of inferior rank and condition in society."[85] They should be free, Kent proclaimed, but they could never be equal.

With his discussion of slaves' plight and place in his nation, Kent expressed sentiments held by many of his colleagues. Slavery was, as Blackstone had insisted, repugnant to the common law, whether that common law was English or American. Its presence in the United States was one cultural and social distinction that Americans could do without. On the other hand, Kent and his colleagues could not help but insist that their republican institutions had mitigated the severity of slavery, particularly since the Revolution. Moreover, the institution was beginning to disappear from some parts of the nation, and there was always hope that other regions would eventually follow suit. The question then became, what to do with the slaves once they were free.

None of these arguments for a milder form of slavery or plans for emancipation and removal, however, changed the fact that slavery existed in the new and promising republics of America. Tapping Reeve and St. George Tucker could manipulate their perceptions of the law to accommodate their own social opinions about the place of slavery in their states, but the reality of the law did not always correspond to their perceptions. American legists were perhaps a bit more successful at deflecting some of the guilt of slavery from their own nation and onto the backs of the ancient republics and even England. In order to preserve their nation's reputation, Americans did not want to carry the stigma of slavery on their own. Therefore, they tried to find as many common characteristics as possible among their practices, those of ancient republics, and their parent country. American legal scholars, however, claimed that their nation had remade the institution into a milder form of bondage. As they took credit for implementing a more benign slavery, they hoped that these reforms would improve perceptions of the nation's character.

Legists' discussions of slavery's increasingly diverse regional characteristics took on a divisive tone as the debates over the institution's existence became more heated. Slavery had never been as widespread in the North as in the South but, in the years immediately following the American Revolution, all states equally bore the criticisms leveled at them from inside and out. As the North began to respond to these calls for reform, it reshaped its regional identity into one that did not include the specter of slavery. By the time James Kent published his *Commentaries* in the late 1820s, the two regions had taken very different directions with regard to slavery. For U.S. legal scholars, slavery was not just an undesirable—yet indelible—part of their national identity. It was also one difference among regional identities that they could not celebrate.

5 Public Lands, Expansion, and the Native Americans

In a charge to the Grand Jury in 1783, South Carolina judge John F. Grimké celebrated the new nation's victory and congratulated his audience on their new position as the envy of Europe. He encouraged them to "behold the honor you are held in by them . . . see how they press to your hospitable shores." He charged his fellow citizens to "look forward to the immense Empire, the work of your hands, that you are creating." Expansion and attention from other nations were, according to Judge Grimké, "the rewards" of Americans' "Virtue and Bravery!"[1] Empire was certainly on the minds of the victorious Americans.

The new nation boasted endless potential for expansion on a continent that boundlessly stretched westward. Abundance of land and its ease of acquisition characterized and contributed mightily to the shaping of American identities from within and without. American and European alike recognized the potential for individual and national wealth that land brought.[2] Land and its accompanying natural resources were the new nation's most valuable assets, and after the Revolution, the job of granting land fell to state and federal government officials. What began as a matter for individual colonial charters and grants grew from local to federal in scale as expansion issues and their obstacles became more complicated. Lawmakers encountered challenges such as turf wars between local and federal governments, carelessly made or unrecorded surveys, and corruption of officials who administered land sales.

Many early national legal scholars watched the development of land law with great interest. For some, the concern was economic. For others, it was simply jurisprudential. For all, the distribution of territory—who lost the land and why, who got the land and how they used it—was central to their explanations of American identities. Although legists could use English law as the foundation of their property law, the English had never before dealt with the volume of land that North America boasted. Therefore, even more so than in inheritance law, Americans had to rely on legal innovations to shape their laws governing the transfer of land. In their lectures on land ownership, legists constructed histories of the growth of the American colonies, the abundance of land, and the ease with which settlers could gain title to it, and they pointed to these distinctive elements of their societies as important components of the American character. At some point in their lectures regarding the transfer and acquisition of real property, however, legists had to reconcile their desire for empire and wealth with the presence of the "original lords of the soil," Native Americans. No English precedent existed for such a situation. Indians' insistence on retaining their ancestral lands meant that white Americans had to employ new legal and moral tactics to obtain more territory so that they could satiate settlers' land hunger. Their justifications for displacing the first inhabitants of the land provide a glimpse into Anglo-Americans' sense of entitlement to territory and empire.

Americans of the late eighteenth and early nineteenth centuries looked upon their social, political, and cultural accomplishments as part of the natural course of human progress. They considered themselves more advanced than, hence superior to, Indians, who simply had not progressed as far culturally or socially. Some Americans compared Indians to their own primitive ancestors, believing that someday Native Americans would be as advanced as they. Therefore, it was fashionable in certain circles to exhibit optimism that Indians eventually could be "civilized" and thus assimilated into white society. In yet another example of the innovations possible in America's experimental republican polities, leaders of these new, expansive societies could transform the Indians from primitive, simple savages into "civilized" human beings. The eyes of the world would be upon them as they effected this transformation and proved the virtues of their republics. Men like George Washington's secretary of war Henry Knox, Thomas Jefferson, and other leaders were convinced that such a civilization program would work.[3]

But increasingly in the early nineteenth century, some legal scholars, like many Americans, began to voice the conviction that Indians were not capable of civilization and eventual assimilation into the Western world.

Moreover, they became convinced that Native Americans' rejection of whites' philanthropic efforts to "improve" and civilize them would lead to their eventual destruction. They had to face the fact that many whites not only opposed the assimilation of Indians, but also wanted to destroy Native Americans and snatch their lands by any means, legal or illegal. As they crafted their historical and legal lessons about whites' attempts to civilize Indians and appropriate Indian lands, legists struggled with the challenge of making this part of the American character a positive attribute.

In the early national period, private citizens and public concerns alike took advantage of land's profit potential. Land was a valuable resource, and states sold off millions of acres of their western holdings to wealthy men who could afford to purchase large tracts of land. New York, Virginia, and Pennsylvania, among others, rewarded their Revolutionary War veterans with acreages that land speculators then bought and gathered into large parcels. With the consolidation of western lands under the federal government and the Northwest Ordinances of the 1780s, the U.S. government implemented plans designed to bring in much-needed revenue from the sale of lands. Speculators took advantage of this opportunity as well. They already possessed the social prestige and authority that land brought, and they did not intend to draw wealth from the land as long-term investments. Their goal was to turn quick profits by capitalizing on the added value that rapid post-Revolution population growth and increase in material wealth brought.[4] Many of the nation's legal scholars invested in western lands, with mixed results.

Whether or not they invested in western lands, the states' leading jurists and legal scholars observed the sale and settlement of the new territories with concern.[5] Poorly trained surveyors and careless land officers left many deeds erroneously measured or recorded. Some officials took bribes to record deeds inaccurately or not to record them at all. Overlapping claims due to careless surveying and recording were especially common in the Southern states.[6] Officers conspired with government officials to acquire land in shady deals that benefited both parties. Perhaps the most famous land speculation scandal of the early republic occurred in Georgia, where the legislators voted to sell four speculation companies forty million acres for $500,000. An investigation led to the discovery that all but one of Georgia's legislators had invested in one of the land companies or had taken a bribe to vote in favor of the transactions.[7] America's legal scholars watched these scandals unfold and worried about the integrity of their own states' land practices.

Virginia's inefficient land policy provoked St. George Tucker to call for reform similar to the innovations contained in the federal government's management of expansion. In his edition of Blackstone's *Commentaries*, Tucker criticized Virginia's system of land grants, calling the state's laws an open season for speculators and con artists. In the early 1800s, Virginia land patents—both legitimate and fraudulent—served as currency in the state and beyond it. Unscrupulous speculators took the patents to Europe to sell to unsuspecting investors, and the loopholes allowing this practice had not been closed in subsequent legislation. Virginia's General Assembly required that the governor issue grants after reviewing the claims and comparing them to land surveys. This process, Tucker complained, was flawed, because claims were often not adjacent to each other. Considerable tracts of lands were sometimes interspersed with small parcels that had been claimed and patented separately. Those who claimed the leftover lands sometimes had to cobble together a patchwork of unconnected parcels. Tucker asserted that the law should have required that claim locations be made adjacent to one another, or it should have limited the amount of land to be granted in a single patent "to any reasonable number of acres." He accused "rapacious land-mongers" of preventing productive amendments to the regulation because they did not want to pay for a full survey. Instead, they referred to "some well known natural boundary . . . with a reservation of prior claims, of which there might be an hundred or five hundred, founded upon prior patents." Because Virginia law did not require precise surveys of patents, unsuspecting patentees received "an emmense extent of territory to appearance, whilst perhaps in reality there was not a single acre of arable land within their bounds, which was not comprehended in the reservation of prior claims." Moreover, Virginia law did not require that speculators survey the entire claim, but rather they merely had to survey a few lines, because surveys for prior claims had already been done. Tucker saw in this practice unlimited potential for lawsuits and messy settlements, "endless contention, and controversies between those who may be unfortunate enough to derive their titles from such an impure source." The General Assembly tried to plug this loophole in 1795 by prohibiting the land office from accepting any plat and certificate of survey that conflicted with prior claims. However, according to Tucker, the solution was too late to prevent many people from being swindled.[8] The Old Dominion's land records remained a disorganized mess for years after the law went into effect.

Tucker looked to the Northwest Ordinance of 1787 as an ideal format for parceling out territory. It provided for the orderly division of the territory northwest of the Ohio River in north and south lines, apportioning the land into townships of six square miles, except in those places where natural boundaries or treaty boundaries with Indians prevented straight lines. He admonished his fellow Virginians: "The United States will obtain as much for *one* acre of their land, as Virginia gets for an *hundred*." Moreover, Virginia would lose industrious men to the more efficient system in the Northwest. A settler who wanted "to set down in peaceable possession of his lands; to improve them, and to transmit them to his posterity" would, Tucker concluded, "turn his eyes to the northwest of the Ohio for an establishment." Those who wished "only to deceive and defraud others, who buy, merely to sell; who regard not in what miseries or perplexities they may involve ignorant persons, and foreigners, will, until the *bubble bursts,* continue to traffic in parchment" to the injury of the innocent.[9] Other areas would win the competition of land management, while Virginia lagged behind because of her lawmakers' lack of foresight. The "bubble" continued to move westward for decades, causing Tucker's descendants and others of future generations much consternation and enriching many along the way. Corruption and inefficiency continued to plague expansion, not just in Virginia, but throughout new territories of the United States. But the obstacle that preoccupied legal scholars even more involved conflicting claims to territory from Native Americans.

II

In his *Commentaries on American Law,* James Kent wrote that "the subject of the treatment of the Indians is one which appears to be, in every view, replete with difficulty and danger." Their interaction with whites, Kent observed, seemed to "have had an immoral influence upon Indian manners and habits, and to have destroyed all that was noble and elevated in the Indian character." Because they simply seemed unable—or unwilling—to accept the Anglo-American version of "civilization," Kent predicted that "the Indians of this continent appear to be destined, at no very distant period of time, to disappear with those vast forests which once covered the country."[10] He did not address the Native Americans' condition in his treatise simply because he was concerned about their plight. Because early national legal scholars like Kent considered themselves teachers of much more than the law, they expended considerable energy defending their nation's right to territory, justifying the taking of land and alternately condemning or apologizing for European Americans' treatment of America's First Peoples. Their visions of Indians' place in America's history and in contemporary society provide insight into their self-conceptions, as well as into the meanings that they invested in the images of "America" and "Americans."

Early national legal scholars had to negotiate the "narrow confines" of safe Indian policy and judicial politics.[11] It was difficult for them to find a comfortable spot in their histories for those peoples who held original title to North America. Their explanations of Native American property rights incorporated a variety of ideas about race, civilization, and rights to occupy or possess land.[12] Early national legists espoused Enlightenment-era scientific theories about race and progress. They were, with a few notable exceptions, detached from the frontier struggles between Indians and white settlers, but they expressed dismay over the violent tactics that white migrants adopted to drive Indians from their ancestral lands.

Early Americans were quick to point out the differences between their own modes of land acquisition and possession and Native American practices, but they were less willing to admit to similarities. With regard to differences, European observers consistently noted that Native Americans did not recognize individual ownership and individual right to convey land away from the nation. Similarities were harder for Europeans to see. For example, both Europeans and Indians shared customs of marking boundaries with piles of stones, colored posts placed in the ground, or marks in trees. However, whites refused to recognize the legitimacy of Indians' marks as signs of possession. Additionally, claims to sovereign territory rested on military success for both cultures. Victory in war meant territorial gains. Although English customs of common land use lasted through the sixteenth century, by the seventeenth century the enclosure system had erased English ideas about use of certain lands in common.[13] The transition to enclosure and individual use and possession of land drove a cultural wedge between white and Native American ideas about possession.

Because they had to keep the "big picture" of America's Revolutionary mission intact, legists had to be careful about how they constructed their histories of European-American seizure of Indian lands. Because Blackstone had laid out the argument so neatly in his discussion of *Calvin's Case,* the easiest justification for this appropriation would have been conquest.[14] But Americans could not comfortably characterize their possession of all lands in North America as a result of conquest. Pre-Revolutionary political debates over America's designation as conquered territory threatened the legitimacy of Americans' claims to common-law protections.[15] Legal scholars believed that they had put to rest the argument that British American colonies had originated in conquest. They asserted their claims to the common law under the argument that American colonies were not born of conquest and, therefore, were not inferior to Britain. In his version of colonial history, Wilson depicted a confident and independent group of English citizens who, "permitted and commissioned by the crown, . . . undertook, at their own expense, expeditions to this distant country, took possession of it, planted it, and cultivated it."[16] Of course, Wilson's story of peacefully settled lands omitted the constant struggles between European settlers and Native Americans.

The conquest theory rested on the assumption that a conquered *people* accompanied a conquered land, therefore it was in Americans' interest to portray their land as unpopulated or containing an easily removed people. Indeed, most history lessons about the settlement of colonial America bore a resemblance to St. George Tucker's description of it as settled by "the conquerors themselves, or colonists, settling a vacant territory." Echoing Thomas Jefferson's sentiments, Tucker asserted that status of conquered territory simply did not apply "to any colony, which was settled by English emigrants, after the Indian natives had ceded, or withdrawn themselves from, the territory."[17] Instead, Tucker found "repeated proofs of purchase" of land throughout the South, and he asserted that the northern part of the United States was "acquired altogether by purchases made in the most unexceptionable form."[18] In his version of colonial-era Indian/white relations, the Indians voluntarily disappeared from the picture by ceding their lands to whites. By the time English settlers came in any number, the Indians had already melted into the wilderness, and by the end of the eighteenth century, according to Tucker, Virginia's Indian population was "too small to require particular notice."[19] A history lesson that peacefully erased Native Americans from the landscape supported the notion that Englishmen had no competitors for the land. Thus, Tucker's "disappearing Indian" cleared the way for discussions of conveyance and possession among whites without the complications of conflicting claims.

In Peter DuPonceau's case, the Indian was barely there from the beginning. DuPonceau was fascinated with Native American languages and enamored of their sense of order and logic, but he did not accord Indians a significant role in Pennsylvania's history. In a speech to the American Philosophical Society, DuPonceau gave the Native Americans little notice. When he did mention them, they seemed to be a part of the landscape rather than actors in the drama of discovery or possession. In his narrative of the arrival of the first ship in William Penn's contingent, DuPonceau set the scene of a "gallant ship" sailing up the Delaware River, decks covered with passengers "enjoying the mild temperature of our climate, and the serenity of our autumnal sky." He described the vast forests as nearly vacant wilderness: "No noise is heard around them, save that of the deer rustling through the trees, as she flies from the Indian who pursues her with his bow and arrow. Now and then a strange yell strikes the ear from a distance, which the echoes of the woods reverberate, and forms a strong contrast to the awful stillness of the scene."[20] DuPonceau's history lesson included the Indian only as part of the wildlife. He depicted Native Americans as invisible, but not unheard, predators.

DuPonceau acknowledged one distinctive Indian personality in his history of the Penn settlement, the Lenni Lenape chief Tamanend, whom he described as unequaled in virtue and goodness. His account of Penn's meeting with Tamanend was designed to tell his audience as much about Penn's character, and Tamanend's trust of the English proprietor, as it did about Tamanend himself: "His [Tamanend's] eye is steadily fixed on William Penn! His great mind has already discovered in him a congenial soul; alone among his tribe, he shews by his looks that noble confidence which will not be deceived." DuPonceau contrasts Tamanend's reception of Penn with the other Native Americans who greeted the Englishmen, "a motley group . . . whose anxiety manifests itself on their countenances, and who view the new comers with looks in which suspicion seems as yet to predominate."[21] He characterized the group of Indians as nervous and suspicious of whites, but not threatening. Collectively, DuPonceau's indigenous peoples were barely there, simply a part of nature. However, DuPonceau bestowed redeeming human qualities on Tamanend, whom he depicted as honorable.

Legal scholars, American and European alike, often used William Penn as the ideal man of honor who treated Native Americans well, and DuPonceau echoed other authors' accolades of Pennsylvania's founder by assuring his audience that, in Penn's lifetime, the treaty he signed with Tamanend was not broken. However, DuPonceau admitted, the treaty did not last long after Penn's descendents were out of power. Moreover, he candidly placed the blame for deterioration of Indian relations on the white leaders who succeeded Penn's descendents.[22] DuPonceau carefully protected Penn's heirs from the taint of corruption, but he found subsequent generations of colonial leaders guilty of succumbing to land hunger and, thus, breaking promises to Pennsylvania's first peoples.

III Whether they lived in places where American Indians were disappearing, like Tucker's Virginia, or were barely visible, like DuPonceau's Pennsylvania, or whether they lived in states where Native Americans made their presence known by pressing their land claims in the courts, early national legists used natural law concepts of discovery and occupancy and the notion of consent to justify appropriation of Indian lands. They acknowledged that the law of nature vested rights to land in the first occupant. But in 1814, frontier jurist and Indian-hater Hugh Henry Brackenridge disagreed with the idea that Indians possessed natural rights of occupancy in his *Law Miscellanies.* Brackenridge could look to Vattel's *Law of Nations,* the most popular reference for natural-law concepts of territory possession, to justify his objection. According to Vattel, every nation was bound by natural law to cultivate the land. Those who adopted the lifestyle of hunting occupied more land than they should; therefore other nations that intended to use the land for agriculture had a right to occupy the unused land.[23] He acknowledged that the Indians had, "from earliest times . . . possessed their country." But, Brackenridge complained, "shall a few tribes thinly scattered over an immense continent retain possession of it, while other parts of the globe are overcharged with inhabitants?"[24] Brackenridge took Vattel's ideas about territorial rights and turned the question of rights to property into a question of what was best for the largest number of people—at least for the largest number of white people.

James Kent crafted a more sophisticated answer to the Indian question with his 1823 *Goodell v. Jackson* decision and his masterful explanation of Native Americans' right to territory and whites' right to usurp Indian claims in his *Commentaries.*[25] His interpretation of Native American property rights blended older notions of property ownership as a conservator of traditional social order and more progressive views of property as a commodity. From Kent's point of view, Native Americans' refusal to accept whites' version of civilization disrupted the social order *and* stood in the way of economic progress.[26] Kent claimed that Indians' title to the land "was imperfect" because it was limited to title by occupancy. He offered a more elegantly worded version of Brackenridge's complaint when he argued that the foundation of European claims to North American territory was based on "the sounder claim of agricultural settlers over tribes of hunters; and from the loose and frail, if not absurd title of wandering savages to an immense continent." Thus, Kent concluded, Americans' moral obligation to possess, "subdue, and cultivate" the land created a superior title to the land.[27]

Though Kent flirted with the idea of conquest as historical justification for American land claims, he seemed more comfortable resting claims to American territory on rights of discovery, "immemorial usage of the land," and the Indians' consent to transfer land to whites.[28] Kent borrowed liberally from *Johnson v. M'Intosh*, a Supreme Court case also decided in 1823, which, in his words, confirmed as "historical fact" that discovery of the continent was considered to have given the government of the discoverers "the sole right of acquiring the soil from the natives as against all other European powers."[29] Each nation subsequently regulated the relationship between Indians and its citizens, and the new relationship "necessarily impaired . . . the rights of the original inhabitants" as Europeans asserted a superior title to the land. Europeans' "superior genius . . . founded on civilization and Christianity, and on their superiority in the means, and in the art of war" entitled them to the land, according to Kent.[30] Kent's version of discovery implied that the threat of conquest, because of Europeans' superior military technology, was often enough to bring indigenous peoples and their territory under European control.

After establishing "title to the soil" through discovery, European nations allowed Indians the right of occupancy. St. George Tucker explained that colonial governments became the sole grantors of territory in a colony, and all grants had to be approved by the colonial assembly and governor. The state and federal governments continued that practice after Independence.[31] Kent elaborated on the history of American land claims by explaining that these local governments possessed the "exclusive right to extinguish the Indian title by purchase or conquest, and to grant the soil, and exercise such a degree of sovereignty as circumstances required." In other words, this superior claim to American lands meant that Indians had no permanent right, not even of occupancy, to these lands. Indians' claims to title were "obliged to yield to the combined influence with military, intellectual, and moral power," in the form of European immigrants.[32] But despite local governments' superior claims to Indian lands, officials still tried to negotiate the sale or trade of lands rather than forcing Native American tribes to cede territory. For Kent, as for many of his contemporaries, the peaceful method of consent was preferable to coercion. However, Kent was willing to sanction the use of force to acquire land, if that force was in the form of a "just and necessary war."[33]

Kent claimed that whites had a moral obligation to assert their rights to the soil, because "to leave the Indians in possession of the country was to leave the country a wilderness."[34] To allow land to go to waste without improvement was a grave offense in Anglo-American culture. Until Native Americans adopted American modes of civilization, Kent found it impossible to consider allowing indigenous peoples the same rights and privileges to property that whites enjoyed. He believed that Indians did not have the moral or intellectual capacity to own or convey real property, and he seemed to hold out little hope that they would ever progress beyond a state of "dependence and pupilage." Therefore, according to Kent, not only did governments have to carefully assert their rights to territory, but they also had to offer a certain measure of protection to the Indians. As long as they held fast to their traditional lifestyles, Indians had to be kept "separate, subordinate, and dependent, with a guardian care thrown around them for their protection."[35] To illustrate his points about the benefits of offering protection and peaceful land exchanges to Native Americans, Kent offered the example of New York's relationship with the Six Nations, who "placed their lands under the protection of [the New York] government from the earliest periods of the colony administration." Glossing over a rather bumpy history of Iroquois distrust of the colonists, their preference for neutrality, and their divided sympathies during the Revolution, Kent praised their loyalty to America, even in the face of war "and the artful means which were used from time to time to detach them" from American alliances. He expressed admiration for "the intrepid spirit" of those "generous barbarians."[36]

In a lengthy footnote to his ode to the Iroquois, Kent mourned the Six Nations' disintegration. He explained that, at the close of the seventeenth century, the confederacy contained as many as ten thousand warriors. But by 1747 the number was less than fifteen hundred.[37] Kent added to his description of the Iroquois population decline in his third edition, published in 1836. Because of "their paucity in numbers and insignificance (with the exception perhaps of the Senecas)," Kent claimed that the Six Nations had "ceased to exist in a distinct national capacity as tribes, exercising self-government, with a sufficient competency to protect themselves." He noted that in 1822, the state of New York asserted criminal jurisdiction over the Indians, inside and outside of the reservations.[38] In his fourth edition, published in 1840, Kent explained that in September of 1836, the United States and the "New York Indians," which Kent defined as the remains of the Six Nations, negotiated a treaty by which the Iroquois voluntarily removed to Indian Territory west of Missouri. He assured his audience that the treaty included "liberal provisions for their removal and support."[39] Even in the fourth edition, the last edition that Kent edited, he still praised the Iroquois confederacy as a great empire that had driven out or exterminated many of its rivals. But Kent's version of the confederacy's history only served as a foil for his image of the Six Nations' degraded state by the Revolution, and its continued deterioration in the early nineteenth century. With his story of the rise and fall of the Iroquois Confederation, Kent made his point that even the strongest of Native American nations eventually required the protection of the culturally superior white Americans.

IV Even among those who looked upon them as uncivilized, First Peoples had their advocates. These champions, however, often were the same men who condemned Native Americans for their resistance to white civilization and for stubbornly refusing to abandon their wandering ways. Kent's description of Native American/white conflicts over land combined elements of the two most popular nineteenth-century images of Native Americans: Indian as cruel and inhuman beast and Indian as noble savage.[40] He created his own historical version of conflicts between American Indians and whites in which, conveniently omitting the numerous instances of Indian military victories, he asserted that Native Americans' powers and means of war had never been equal to those of whites. He characterized Native tactics in war as "ferocious and cruel," yet he pointed out that "there was still much in the Indian character, in their earlier and better state, to excite admiration, and in their sufferings, at all times, to excite sympathy."[41] Despite Kent's depiction of Native Americans as shadows of their former selves, indigenous peoples still invoked fear in many Americans, and the New York jurist tried to downplay the image of the savage Indian.

Kent defended American Indians' actions against whites, insisting that although conflicts were "never unjustly provoked by the colonial governments or people, . . . they were, no doubt, stimulated on the part of the Indians, by a deep sense of injury, by a view of impending danger, by the suggestions of patriotism, and by a fierce and lofty spirit of national independence."[42] This notion that Native Americans could harbor nationalistic sentiments may have surprised many of Kent's contemporaries. Kent illustrated Indians' sense of nationhood through their ties to a larger, pan-Indian community, using examples from the distant past: the alliances among New England Natives in the Pequot War of 1637 and the pan-Indian movement attempted by Metacom in 1675. He ignored more recent examples, such as Pontiac's pan-Indian movement of 1763 or, even closer to home, the early nineteenth-century conflicts between whites and Tecumseh's alliance. There was safety in temporal distance, and perhaps more recent examples of patriotism and "fierce and lofty national independence" would have worked against his theory that in recent years the noble spirit of the Indians had degenerated into weakness and dependence. His description of their weakened state offered additional justification for taking their lands and placing Native Americans more firmly under the "pupilage" of the U.S. government.

Kent was not the only early national legal scholar to tell his audience that these noble—and very American—patriotic impulses existed among the savages of North America. In his *Sketches of the Principles of Government*, published in 1793, Nathaniel Chipman used similar language to describe Native American character, though his ideas about how Native Americans demonstrated their patriotism differed from Kent's. For Chipman, ties to place and cultural tradition demonstrated patriotism. He used plenty of fashionable rhetoric about Native Americans in his treatise, describing them as vengeful hunters who treated their women "little better than slaves."[43] But he rejected observations that First People's nomadic ways left them without territorial attachments, and he insisted that their patriotism, which he simply defined as "love of country," was apparent through their ties to the soil. He pointed out that although they occupied "but a small part" of "their country," Native Americans claimed these larger pieces of land as their own. Only extreme circumstances, such as war, famine, "or some more powerful cause," could compel them to relinquish their territory.[44] He illustrated his point with a story in which the French proposed to remove some Canadian Indians from their native soil. He quoted a chief who allegedly responded to the French, "We were born . . . on this ground. Our fathers lie buried in it. Shall we say to the bones of our fathers, Arise, and come with us into a foreign land?" Was this, Chipman asked, "the language of a people . . . [w]ho have no national attachments? No republic? No social state?" He related another story of Logan, a Mingo chief who, for the good of his nation, refused to wage war to avenge the murder of his entire family, a sacrifice that Chipman lauded as the ultimate act of patriotism. The Vermont legist reminded his readers that Americans "who have had frequent occasion to transact business with the American natives, both as individuals, and in their national councils, know the strength of their national attachments."[45] With his version of Native American histories, Chipman tried to find common ground between First Peoples and white Americans.

Chipman did not mean to imply, however, that American Indians possessed "civilized" traits like patriotism. Instead, he pointed out that the "love of country" was a trait that even "uncivilized" people could own. He quoted Abbe Raynal, in his history of the East and West Indies, as saying that patriotism was not a natural passion of man. Raynal used the indigenous peoples of Brazil as examples, asserting that they had "no particular attachment to their native place. The love of country, which is a ruling passion in civilized states; which, in good governments, rises to enthusiasm, and in bad ones grows habitual; *this love of our country* is but a fictitious sentiment arising from society; but unknown in a state of nature."[46] Chipman was not convinced. He stated that though Raynal wrote of indigenous Brazilians' "want of attachment to their native soil," Raynal's evidence refuted this assertion. Chipman pointed out that in the case of the Brazilians, "love of country" was equal to "love of community." According to Chipman, "an attachment to the soil collects, limits, and fixes the passion, and gives a locality to its object; but is not necessary to its existence. Take from the country the community, all its inhabitants, the object ceases." He asserted that in all peoples, an attachment to community was present. He used the "ancient barbarians of the north," ancestors of Europeans, as examples of peoples who possessed this national attachment, but he acknowledged that "their attachment to the soil was not so strong." This attachment, he explained, was "fixed, principally, by the cultivation of the earth for subsistence, which collects the interest and attention to one pot, and gives a locality to conveniences."[47] Therefore, at least in the case of the First Peoples of Brazil, patriotism did not require ties to the soil. Chipman implied that removal from the land would not eliminate a people's ties to community, because their ties were not to a particular place, but rather to one another. However, this assertion did not seem to match the argument he made for North American Indians.

Chipman's self-contradictions tell the reader much about his place and time. Around the time that he wrote his *Sketches*, Chipman's home territory,

Vermont, was applying for admission to the union as a state. Their bid was not warmly received, however. Some of the same questions about Native Americans' abilities to become civilized were being raised about Vermonters, who had a reputation for being a rough and wild bunch. This personal experience could have given Chipman some measure of empathy for the Indians' situation at the hands of the U.S. government. However, shared experience did not offer him enough reason to believe that Indians were cultural equals. Even as he complimented them, Chipman designated American Indians a less-civilized people.

Chipman used the "savages of America" as examples of beings who lived in the state of nature. These peoples, he asserted, "esteem war and hunting almost the only pursuits worthy of a man," while leaving most other labor to their women, "who are little better than slaves." Because men's attention was devoted to hunting and war, Chipman characterized them as exhibiting "an excessive ferocity of manners." He explained that "their resentment is keen, and revenge their most darling gratification." Part of Indians' lack of civility, according to Chipman, stemmed from their lack of a legal or justice system. In Indian society, Chipman stated, "every man is left to judge in his own cause, and to avenge his own wrongs." However, in the next paragraph, he noted that "the injuries of an individual are resented as national," a comment that bestowed a strong sense of community on the Indians. An Anglo-American would have considered property ownership individual, and therefore trespass onto property should have been a matter between individuals, rather than a community problem. However, because Indians' lives were tied to hunting rather than agriculture, their communal property meant more to them than would individual agricultural plots. Chipman projected Anglo-American imperial ambitions onto Native Americans when he claimed that "the possession of a hunting ground is, to them, the possession of an empire." Disputes over hunting grounds were "sources of frequent wars," causing "butchering and scalping of old men, women, and children, of torturing and burning of prisoners, in cold blood, with the most shocking circumstances of cruelty." These acts of violence were public and "under what is to them, the law of nations."[48] With this example, Chipman's own evidence refuted his assertion that Indians had no law or justice system. He attributed to them the potential for great violence and cruelty, yet on the next line, he bestowed upon them a primitive sense of order brought by law.

Chipman's account of the Native American character is full of such contradictions. Even when he laid lavish compliments on them, Chipman somehow found a way to take away the virtues that he briefly bestowed. For example, the Vermonter carried on a rather curious discussion of the American Indians' talent for "hospitality," a characteristic that he believed whites had all but lost in the civilization process and that he considered "the finest trait" in Native Americans' character. But while American Indians' practice of the art of hospitality indicated "some advance in civilization," the absence of further progress in the forms of an increase in population and the establishment of inns and other places of lodging made this trait obsolete. Therefore, Indians' generous hospitality attested to their backward society. Besides, in Chipman's estimation, the "North American natives have never been equally noted for the practice of this virtue, with the ancient Germans, or the more ancient inhabitants of Greece."[49] They did not measure up to the great ancient societies in their practices of primitive forms of hospitality.

In fact, Chipman complained that the simple state of the savage was overrated. He criticized those who saw virtue in natives' simplicity, stating that those writers who looked at Indians with a "romantic eye" saw too much virtue in the uncivilized. He noted Indians' lack of concern about the future, stating that they were "too indolent to think of making an adequate provision against the inclemency of the season, or, indeed, against any future want." Chipman considered this sort of simple life a double-edged sword. While Indians did not have as many vices as "civilized" men, they also possessed "fewer virtues than more civilized nations." He described the Indians as possessing "little curiousity, and no conception of any knowledge which can be of use, beyond that of forming the bow, or some instrument of the chace."[50] Fellow New Englander James Sullivan agreed with Chipman. He laid the blame for Native Americans' decline on their refusal to pursue Western modes of learning and culture. He accused Indians of leading a lifestyle that "excluded all ideas of civilization, and shut up the human mind from cultivation; rejected the arts and sciences, and quite subverted the embellishment and prevented the extension of the rational faculties of man." In a surprising departure from prevailing theories of race, Sullivan elevated Africans' propensity to cultivation over that of Native Americans. He asserted that Africans had "frequently been induced to attend to letters, painting, and some of the finer arts." He also noted their "natural turn to music," but Native Americans, on the other hand, had "no organs suited to a taste for literature, poetry, or music."[51] Ironically, Europeans had leveled similar criticisms about a lack of indigenous culture on the new American nation. Yet, Sullivan suggested that if Native Americans were willing to improve themselves, white Americans would be willing to help.

Sullivan emphasized whites' paternal efforts to help Indians to progress toward civilization, but he also warned that the Native Americans' disappearance might be inevitable. It was possible that Indians were destined not to listen to whites' advice. "Divine Providence" dictated that the New World should be inhabited and used by God's "rational offspring." After "expensive attempts" to teach Indians agriculture, Christianity, and other white ways failed, Sullivan argued that they might not be destined to be a part of the civilized world.[52] The idea that Native Americans' disappearance was an inevitable result of their own intransigence relieved white Americans of any responsibility for the First Peoples' fate.

V

Hugh Henry Brackenridge was not willing to wait on divine providence to rid the United States of Native Americans. His opinions about Indians and their rights to territory were, perhaps, products of his experiences in the backcountry, although he seemed to have been inclined toward a hatred of Native Americans even before he relocated to the frontier hamlet of Pittsburgh. Brackenridge was among the more colorful figures in early American legal history. He was a frontier lawyer and judge, a poet and a literary figure. Some legists questioned Brackenridge's credibility as an expert on the law, but he made a valuable contribution to early American legal literature with his *Law Miscellanies*. Brackenridge's encounters with Indians in western Pennsylvania shaped his attitudes toward Native American wars, treaty negotiations, and removal. While many of his contemporaries lived far from Native American strongholds, Brackenridge settled at the epicenter of contentions between whites and American Indians. Therefore, the frontier legist brought a very different perspective to the table in his discussions about the foundation of title to land. Though his fundamental ideas about treaty negotiations and Native American rights to land were the same regardless of his audience, his rhetoric underwent transformations depending on whether he was building an argument for one of his legal or political treatises, or whether he was writing for a more general audience. Always, his mission was to persuade his audience that Indians had no natural right to the land, and that they could be—and ought to be—relocated or exterminated to make way for the more "civilized" whites.

Brackenridge was practiced in appealing to a myriad of audiences. While a student at Princeton, he composed and read an epic poem, "The Rising Glory of America," at commencement in 1771. From the Revolution onward, he authored patriotic tragedies and political pamphlets. During the Revolution, he founded and edited the *United States Magazine* in Philadelphia. After moving to Pennsylvania's frontier, he founded the *Pittsburgh Gazette.* In 1783, Brackenridge edited and published an Indian captivity narrative entitled *Narratives of a Late Expedition against the Indians with an Account of the Barbarous Execution of Col. Crawford; and the Wonderful Escape of Dr. Knight and John Slover from Captivity, in 1782.*[53] This narrative, Brackenridge hoped, would convince lawmakers to provide more protection for frontier dwellers against the "savage" Indian. He embellished the description of Colonel Crawford's ordeal and execution, providing grisly details of the hours-long torture in order to illustrate even more graphically the Indians' propensity toward cruelty. The story appealed to popular interest in captivity narratives and certainly gained popular support for the eviction or elimination of Native Americans on the Pennsylvania frontier. In the 1790s and early 1800s, Brackenridge published a four-volume comic narrative in the style of Don Quixote, entitled *Modern Chivalry.* And in an effort to provide American lawyers with an "American Blackstone," Brackenridge published *Law Miscellanies* in 1814. Always mindful of his genre and audience, Brackenridge modified his rhetoric for maximum effectiveness.

The rhetoric and tone that Brackenridge used in his *Law Miscellanies* differed from those in "Thoughts on the Present Indian War," and these variations reveal his self-consciousness when it came to audience. His legal treatise called for a more reasoned approach, therefore Brackenridge toned down his descriptions of Indians and concentrated on explaining the theories of discovery and occupancy that justified removal. But, instead of relying on legal precedent to support his points, he resorted to biblical stories and Lockean ideas about labor and property. He first addressed the law of nature and what he considered man's natural right to dominate the earth. Because man cultivated the earth, Brackenridge explained, man's labor gave him the right to possess land and to dominate the earth and "brute animals." He considered "savages who do not cultivate the soil, or sustain themselves to much extent" through agricultural means the same as "the beasts." Like other contemporary legal scholars, he described rights to the soil as founded on discovery, although that right was "limited in its extent, by the right of the natives," as well as the rights of other nations that may have discovered certain lands first. To counter the argument that the rights of Natives excluded others because the right to soil should be vested in its first occupant, he employed an argument around agricultural labor that limited Native American claims. Brackenridge invoked the biblical charge to "be fruitful and multiply and replenish the earth, and subdue it." He noted the crucial differences between natural law, or God's law, and civil policy by pointing out that God's charge did not convey the right of primogeniture, nor any other right by which one man could hold a larger portion of the soil than his neighbor. Those rights, he explained, were not part of God's law, but rather they were civil law, not arising from a state of nature, but rather from a state of society.[54] In other words, he turned Blackstone's arguments about the positive laws of inheritance to his advantage as he asserted whites' right to territory.

Brackenridge applied his definition of the law of nature and equal distribution of property to Indians, asking whether the Indians, who were "inferior in number to perhaps one twentieth of the inhabitants of Europe," should "possess ten times the territory." Their defenders would argue that their "manner of life" made more territory necessary because they lived by hunting, but he asked whether the laws of nature ought to allow every man to live as he pleased, rather than living in a way that would help the largest number of people. He resurrected the biblical story of Adam's "lapse" and banishment from Eden, asserting that "the Lord God sent him forth from the garden of Eden, to till the ground." Therefore, if God's order was to till the ground, then the Indians were not obeying God. Brackenridge asserted that the law of nature, even where God's law was not yet known, dictated that all men should have equal access to land so that all could "pursue that manner of life which is most consistent with the general population of the earth, and the increase of happiness to mankind." Moreover, Brackenridge argued, a life of hunting retarded the progress of the race. When men lived by hunting rather than agriculture and thus were "necessarily scattered" over thinly settled territory, "the powers of genius are inactive, the arts and sciences remain unknown, and man continues to be an animal differing in nothing but in shape from the beasts of prey that roam upon the mountain."[55] They were, in other words, not leading a "human" life if they were not encouraging progress through their chosen lifestyle. Indians, he insisted, did not have a solid claim to a place they had never cultivated. The most they could claim was the place "where their wigwams have been planted, and to so much of the soil around them as may be necessary to produce grain to support them" and their families. If they wanted to move away, however, Brackenridge was perfectly willing to allow them "a right to occupy a different country," where they might be able to continue living as hunters.[56] In this way, two incompatible peoples could continue to live peacefully—and separately.

His comments in the *Gazette* emphasized racial characteristics, but in *Law Miscellanies* Brackenridge was careful to present an argument that was based on what was best for the community. Brackenridge stated that all nations should be judged by the same standards for territorial claims as he set out for the Indians. No nation or nations, he insisted, should "possess a more extensive tract of country, than is necessary for their particular subsistence." Therefore, a nation with more people, "whose numbers overcharge the soil, have a right to demand territory from a nation in possession of a soil equally fertile, and less abounding with inhabitants." Even the right of discovery, according to Brackenridge, did not give any nation a right to take any more territory "than is necessary for subsistence; and not indeed any portion of it, unless the visitant remains to occupy and dwell upon it."[57] This comment applied to other territorial rivals in addition to Indians. He had in mind specific European targets as well, namely the French and Spanish, who had laid claim to parts of North America, yet settled very few of their citizens on the territory that they claimed. European rivals for empire in North America still existed, and Brackenridge was well aware that his arguments worked equally as well against the French, Spanish, and even the English, as they did against the Indians.

Brackenridge used the history of overlapping, conflicting and usurping claims among the European nations as evidence that the mere right of discovery did not give any nation exclusive control over the vast tracts of land in the New World. He accused the Swedes and Dutch of ignoring Britain's claim in North America through explorer Sebastian Cabot's discovery. But Brackenridge actually sanctioned this kind of disregard, because "no expence, enterprize, or labour of a nation, or of any individual, can give a right which in its operation would defeat the end in view by the Creator, which was, that the earth be fully stocked with inhabitants." Therefore, the claims of the first discoverers should have been only to as much of the soil as their settlers were able to inhabit and cultivate. But he admitted that because the nations and their explorers bore the expense and effort of exploration and discovery, they were entitled to reap the profits of that discovery, and they should be given time and opportunity to encourage their countrymen to emigrate. In this way, the earth would "become peopled," according to "the will of the Creator."[58] Even the natural law, according to Brackenridge, did not favor Native Americans having more land than they could cultivate.

Brackenridge did not explicitly advocate the extermination or wholesale removal of the Indians in his *Law Miscellanies.* Instead, he took a milder stance that called for containment of Native Americans on only as much land as they could cultivate, while redistributing their vast hunting grounds so that whites could "subdue and cultivate the earth." Even as he deemed North America to be "a vacant country and liable to become the property of those who should take the trouble to possess it," he was careful to point out that he was not advocating war against the Indians, nor was he pushing for their extermination. However, he encouraged a calculated "encroachment on the territory claimed by them, until they are reduced to smaller bounds, and under the necessity of changing their unpolished and ferocious state of life, for fixed habitations and the arts of agriculture." Brackenridge encouraged purchase of Native American lands, "if it may be done conveniently." He reasoned that it was more humane not to take property by force, because that tactic could involve "the shedding of the blood of those, who though sunk beneath the dignity of human nature, yet bear the name and are seen in the shape of men."[59] When writing for an audience of lawyers, Brackenridge carefully asserted that even those who barely qualified as human beings should only be treated with violence as a last resort.

When writing for a broader audience, Brackenridge cast the same argument in more emotional language. He used the legal lingo of "occupancy" and "discovery" in his popular publications, but with more dramatic illustrations and examples. In an afterword to his edition of the *Narratives of a Late Expedition against the Indians,* Brackenridge elaborated on an essay that he wrote for the *United States Magazine* in 1779, in which he argued that Indians had no right to the soil. Using vivid imagery to illustrate the defense of Indian rights to the soil on occupancy, he wrote: "A wild Indian with his skin painted red, and a feather through his nose, has set his foot on the broad continent of North and South America" and claimed it as his own, bidding all other comers "take his foot off the continent, for he being first upon it, had occupied the whole, to kill buffaloes, and tall elks with long horns." Brackenridge admitted that some believed the claim to be just.[60] In his *Gazette Publications,* Brackenridge spared the reader his savage image of the claimant, but he used the same image of the Indian "having his foot first on the continent." He considered the claim unreasonable because of the uncertainty over the number of claimants there must be to uphold such a right.

Equally uncertain was how much territory they could claim. He insisted on a fixed principle on which the right to soil depended. Under the law of nature, he argued, a person only had right to enough land as would provide subsistence. Moreover, the amount of land should be measured by agriculture, rather than by "pasturage and hunting." If a society used that criteria, then more people could subsist off the land.[61] Because Native Americans had not followed God's charge to till the ground, they had not made proper use of the soil, and therefore, "not having made a better use of it for many hundred years," he concluded that "they have forfeited all pretence to claim, and ought to be driven from it."[62]

The frontier legist reminded his readers that, according to the Bible, all of the earth was given to man, and all descendants of Adam should have an equal share. To those who argued that, in a state of society, some men could hold more land than others and, therefore, Indians had a right to own large tracts of land, Brackenridge responded that these unequal holdings were because of civil law, the laws to which citizens of a society had consented. Men living under a state of society were protected by laws that secured property in that unequal manner. However, while wealthy men or large families might lay a civil claim to more space on which to live or garden, "an agile, nimble runner, like an Indian," should not expect more land than his neighbors "because he has traversed a greater space."[63] In other words, exceptional physical strength should not trump intellectual and moral superiority.

Brackenridge was not among those white Americans who believed that Indians could eventually be civilized and assimilated into white society. He related examples of instances when "several of these creatures" were taken from their homes and placed in American schools to learn trades and "civilization." He claimed that he did not know of "one who has even by these means been rendered a useful member of society: they retain the temper of their race." He held up John Montour, son of mixed-blood cultural intermediary Andrew Montour, as an example of the uncivilizable Indian who was educated "at one of the northern seminaries, [was] taught Greek and Latin, and in [the Revolution] dignified with a commission of captain. No greater savage ever existed." Brackenridge accused Montour of killing many of his own people and being forced to flee his people's vengeance because of his actions. This breach of honor, according to Brackenridge, was unforgivable. To punctuate his description of Montour, he told his audience that he saw "this man with the bloody scalp of an Indian in his hand, which he had just taken off, having first tomahawked the creature, though submitting and praying for his life." Brackenridge was convinced "that for a keg of whiskey you might induce any Indian to murder his wife, child, or best friend."[64] Persons of this character, Brackenridge insisted, were not to be defended, nor should their rights be protected.

Brackenridge leveled harsh criticism at those whites who defended Native American rights to territory. In his "Thoughts on the Present Indian War," published in the *Pittsburgh Gazette*, Brackenridge responded to congressional debates over Native American rights to territory. He characterized defenders of Native American territorial rights as "philosophers," an occupation that did not garner much respect on the frontier, where men valued action more than reflection. He accused those who were "soft" on the Indian territorial question of being ignorant of the situation. He compared defenders of Native American character and rights to "young women who have read romances, and have as improper an idea of the Indian character in the one case, as the female mind has of real life in the other." In other words, Brackenridge characterized his opponents in this debate as soft, effeminate, of little resolution, misinformed, and romantic. These traits simply did not sit well with the frontier-dwelling readers of the *Gazette*. Using a popularized version of the anti-natural rights argument, Brackenridge accused defenders of Indian territorial rights of trying to "affect the public mind by holding up *the original right* of these aborigines to the soil." He described their defense as "the claim of the children: it is mine, for I first saw it." He then paraphrased Vattel's ideas about natural right to the soil by asserting that the earth was given to man in common, and each man should only use as much as he needed, so that all may have their share. He wrote that the land should be used in a way that would sustain the greatest number of people and provide "the greatest sum of happiness; that is, the cultivation of the soil." Any right not housed in "agricultural occupancy," according to Brackenridge, was not valid.[65] Improvement of land brought progress, which, for Brackenridge, represented a greater good.

Brackenridge derided the ideas of those who believed in the virtues of "the unimproved state." The misguided "philosopher," according to the frontier jurist, saw "green fields and meadows in the customs and virtues of the savages." He assured his audience that only experience could correct this image. Brackenridge was a firm believer that "all that is good and great in a man, results from education; an uncivilized Indian is but a little way removed from a beast who, when incensed, can only tear and devour, but the savage applies the ingenuity of man to torture and inflict anguish." He used as an example the story of a French botanist and "philosopher" who claimed "the man of nature" as his "darling favourite." Unarmed and with only two other men, the botanist undertook an expedition on the Ohio River, confident that any Indians he encountered "could wish him no harm." But while on his expedition, he met a party of Indians who, he thought, approached to "pay their respects to him; but the first circumstance of ceremony when they came on board, was to impress the tomahack [*sic*] and take off the scalp of the philosopher."[66] According to Brackenridge, whites held no moral obligation to protect those who did not feel a reciprocal obligation of protection.

Brackenridge saw no reason to treat with Native Americans, because, from his perspective, they would only break the treaty when it was in their interest. He laid the blame for tensions between Anglo-Americans and Native Americans squarely on Indians' failure to honor treaties. In his "Thoughts on the Present Indian War," Brackenridge provided colonial-era examples of treaties that Indians broke with the British in order to ally with the French in Canada. Because it was not in the Indians' interest to have Britain and France at peace, they instigated war at the expense of treaties. The United States was, Brackenridge asserted, still in the same situation, now that Canada was a British possession. Native Americans in Canada had already shown that they would not honor treaty terms; therefore, he argued, the U.S. government should not negotiate with them at all.[67] He even blamed the Indians for the U.S. government's need to sell, rather than give away, land in the Old Northwest to white settlers, because "they have been at expence in combating the false claim of the savages, and ought to be paid for it."[68] Their claims to territory not only cost lives, Brackenridge complained, but such claims also cost the money of settlers who were willing to populate the western lands. The roadblocks that Indians threw in the way of America's progress toward empire enraged the Pennsylvania jurist.

Brackenridge refused to acknowledge that whites may have instigated some conflicts with Indians. He claimed that he knew of only three instances in which an Indian had been hurt by a white since the Revolution, yet Native Americans became more dangerous and less trustworthy by the day. His stories about Indian chiefs "driven out of a kitchen by a maid with a broomstick, lest [they] should steal a tin cup or a table spoon" supported his claim that Indians' dishonesty extended to their word. They respected no treaty.[69] The only recourses, Brackenridge insisted, were "war and reduction," doing away with the government's system of agents and interpreters and making the Native Americans "stay in their woods and negotiate an equal trade" for their land. Better relations could be achieved only when "the line of savages that are at present hostile, is removed," because he believed that other Indian nations further west were more open to negotiation with the United States for trade and territory.[70] In a poem published in the *Pittsburgh Gazette,* Brackenridge pleaded with government officials, especially secretary of war "General [Henry] Knox" to

> stick to war; at least,
> until they're properly repress'd
> And if they will treat, why then treat
> But give them neither strouds nor meat
> But leave to live as they do us,
> Nor dare again to be our foes.[71]

The captivity narratives that Brackenridge edited provided even more graphic evidence for his assertions that Native Americans could not be trusted. Indians may have "the shapes of men and may be of the human species," he wrote, "but certainly in their present state they approach nearer the character of devils: take an Indian; is there any faith in him? . . . Can you trust his word or confide in his promise?" Brackenridge further exploited the emotion of the narratives by asking his reader, fresh from the gory tale of Colonel Crawford's agony and death, that when an Indian "makes war upon you, when he takes you prisoner and has you in his power[,] will he spare you?" According to Brackenridge, the merciless Indian "departs from the law of nature, by which . . . it is unjustifiable to take away the life of him who submits; the conqueror in doing otherwise becomes a murderer, who ought to be put to death." In Brackenridge's eyes, the Indians violated the law of nature; therefore, there should be no debate over their right to land. According to Brackenridge, "The tortures which they exercise on the bodies of their prisoners" justified their extermination.[72] Because of the duplicitous character of the Indians, he concluded that the United States' "best defense is *offence.* Instead of warding off blows, give one." Instead of "watching beasts of prey," he suggested that American troops should "penetrate the forests where they haunt, and extirpat[e] the race."[73] The frontier judge proposed to

> dispossess them of the goodly lands, springs and rivers to the westward, which they have so long made a scene of horror by their practices. . . .

> Instead of forming treaties, and sending any other talk to them, and prophaning ourselves by calling them brothers, I would simply let them know that they are no longer to show themselves below the heads of the great rivers that fall from the westward into the Ohio and Mississippi waters.

Brackenridge wished for them to be driven further north and west into the cold, "where darkness reigns six months in the year," where "their practices shall be obscured, and the tribes gradually abolished."[74]

The language of violence against American Indians did not appear in Brackenridge's *Law Miscellanies.* He reserved such unabashedly hateful prose for popular audiences. However, even in his legal treatise, Brackenridge's argument departed from those of many of his colleagues. His reliance on biblical history and active advocacy of dispossession contrasted with Kent's explorations of legal precedent and Tucker's dismissal of the Indians as already gone. While Brackenridge advocated dispossession and extermination in his popular publications, his contemporaries took a more passive approach, generally answering the fate of the Indians with embarrassed efforts to erase them from American histories—or, at least, from the present and future of early national America.

VI As legal scholars built their opposing images of Native Americans, James Kent simultaneously crafted a dual image of whites. Kent developed his thinking on this subject more fully, and over a longer span of years, than any other legal scholar. In his first edition, Kent depicted the government's treatment of Native Americans as benign and paternal while acknowledging a few individuals' cruelty toward the Indians. He insisted that whites had acquired Indian lands with "as little violence and aggression . . . as were compatible with the fact of the entry of a race of civilized men into the territory of savages." He echoed Vattel's and DuPonceau's words of praise for men like William Penn, who purchased land from the "Indian proprietors." He acknowledged, however, that not all lands had been acquired peacefully, and he blamed the wars on "the fact of the presence and location of white people" and the Indians' realization "that the destruction of their race must be the consequence of the settlements of the English colonists, and their extension over the country."[75] The New York jurist chose language that characterized as passively as possible whites' contributions to Native

Americans' eviction. For Kent, it was whites' "presence and location," not their aggressive migrations into Indian territories, that provoked Native Americans to violence.

Again, Kent emphasized U.S. government officials' good intentions when he described their efforts to protect Indians "from wars with each other, from their own propensity to intemperance, from the frauds and injustice of the whites." These philanthropic and paternal efforts, Kent claimed, reflected "the luster" of America's "national character."[76] Kent did, however, differentiate between the American government's "uniformly just and benevolent" intent with regard to First Peoples and the practice of certain individuals whose negotiations with the American Indians were "attended with much abuse . . . and with very injurious effects upon the moral and civil condition of the Indian tribes."[77]

Kent's ideas about the place of indigenous peoples in America followed the same lines of logic as one of his more prominent contemporaries. In the first edition of his American *Commentaries*, he echoed Chief Justice John Marshall's opinion that the discovery doctrine had "necessarily impaired" Native Americans' rights to territory, and it privileged European claims to land over those of the Indians.[78] However, when Marshall retreated from his position on the discovery doctrine, Kent followed suit. The case *The Cherokee Nation v. The State of Georgia* (1831) appeared in Kent's second edition, with the majority opinion that the Cherokee nation was not a foreign state as defined by use of the term in the Constitution. Instead, the Cherokees "were *a state*, or distinct political society, capable of managing its own affairs, and governing itself." The difference, then, was in their "peculiar" relation to the United States, in that they were "domestic dependent nations, and their relation to us resembled that of a ward and guardian; and they had an unquestionable right to the lands they occupied, until that right should be extinguished by a voluntary cession to our government."[79] He went on to discuss *Worcester v. The State of Georgia* (1832), in which Georgia claimed sovereignty over the Cherokee nation and proclaimed that the Cherokee government could not be sovereign within the boundaries of an established state. Writing for the majority, Chief Justice Marshall declared that the right of discovery gave the discovering nation exclusive right to purchase, but that nation had to procure the consent of the Indian possessor to sell. The Court upheld the Cherokee nation's status as a "distinct community, occupying its own territory . . . in which the laws of Georgia cannot rightfully have any force."[80] Kent's reaction to *Worcester* was fresh in the second edition of the *Commentaries*, which also came off the press in 1832. He pointed out that the Supreme Court's decision did not represent "the promulgation of any new doctrine." The principles of discovery and sovereignty outlined in the decision had been the custom for generations. Without explicitly pointing out the reversal, Kent implied that Marshall had departed from custom in his *Johnson* opinion, and that *Worcester* had restored the common-law understanding of Native Americans' legal relationship to their ancestral lands.[81] Unfortunately, subsequent court decisions ignored Marshall's revision of the discovery doctrine's meaning and continued to use Marshall's *Johnson v. M'Intosh* definition.

Kent expanded his own definition of the nature of Native Americans' dependence on the U.S. government by adding some local descriptions of how American Indians' dependent status affected their relationships with the states and the federal government. Kent referred to his own opinion in *Goodell v. Jackson* and an 1810 case in Tennessee, *Jackson v. Wood,* which "explicitly recognized the historical fact" that Indians were governed by their own laws, "under their own chiefs, and competent to act in a national character, and exercise self-government . . . owing no allegiance to the municipal laws of the whites." Indian nations had, as Kent pointed out with his example of the Iroquois, "placed themselves under the protection of the whites, and they were cherished as dependent allies, but subject to such restraints and qualified control in their national capacity, as were considered by the whites to be indispensable to their own safety."[82] Kent's descriptions of Indians' dependent status emphasized the U.S. government's moral obligation to protect Native Americans from predatory whites as well as from one another. Moreover, Kent implied that the federal government had fulfilled its obligation, at least up until President Andrew Jackson took office.

Kent still emphasized Indians' dependent status in editions of his *Commentaries* published during and after efforts to remove Indian nations from their ancestral lands in Georgia, Tennessee, and Alabama. In the third edition published in 1836, the *Worcester v. Georgia* decision and state legislation hedging the legal rights of Native Americans, particularly the Cherokee, became the centerpiece of his chapter on the foundation of title to land. Emboldened by the Georgia court's successful refusal to abide by the Supreme Court's *Worcester* decision, the Alabama and Tennessee legislatures quickly extended civil and criminal jurisdiction over all of the Indian territories within their limits. However, Kent defended these actions by insisting that the extension of their laws over Indian territory "was made with mild and reasonable qualifications, in respect to the Cherokees, compared with similar acts in some other states." The laws prohibited confiscation of Native American property and encroachment on Indian lands by whites. Kent compared Alabama and Tennessee's laws to a New York law of 1822, which asserted jurisdiction over any crimes committed in the Indian territories within the boundaries of that state. He also claimed that the Tennessee act was necessary, given the reduced numbers of Cherokee in that state "and the too great imbecility of their organization and authority to preserve order, and protect themselves from atrocious crimes."[83] Again, Kent justified laws that hedged Native Americans' rights by invoking whites' moral obligation to protect inferior beings. Unfortunately, white authorities rarely enforced the provisions prohibiting white encroachment on Indian lands.

Beginning with his second edition, Kent paid more attention to colonial and state legislation regarding diplomatic exchanges between Europeans and Native Americans. He seemed to have two objectives for these history lessons. First, he supported the popular argument that most Europeans tried to maintain peaceful relations with the Indians and tried to use peaceful means to conduct land transactions with them. With these examples he also implied Native American sovereignty. European negotiations of land sales with Native Americans helped to prove sovereignty of Indian nations. He argued that from the beginning of English, French, and Spanish settlement, most European nations tried to maintain peaceful relations and to use peaceful means to conduct land transactions with the Native Americans. They established regulations that restricted dealings with First Peoples to transactions between authorized members of tribes and the colonial governments. Individuals could not contract with Indians for land.[84] He also added a footnote with examples of a North Carolina law of 1783 and an 1830 ruling of the Tennessee Supreme Court that upheld Native American national sovereignty and affirmed that indigenous people's lands were held under the "right of exclusive occupancy and enjoyment." He noted an 1813 New York law authorizing the governor to pay the Oneida Nation for lands ceded to the state under a treaty.[85] With these examples, Kent tried to help Marshall to set the record straight on America's obligation to uphold Indian sovereignty and to protect Indians' rights to their territory.

Kent edited four editions of his *Commentaries*, and with each iteration the footnote explaining the fate of America's remaining Indian nations lengthened. As treaties and coercion pushed the Native Americans further westward, Kent added to his commentary on the fate of the Indians who remained under the "pupilage" of the United States. He alternated between defending and condemning the government's actions, although he continued to assert that, while government officials in general tried to treat Indians fairly and equitably, certain individuals were not so inclined. Unfortunately, starting in 1828, one of the individuals was the nation's president, Andrew Jackson.

As part of his defense of the U.S. government, Kent pointed out the money and effort that the government put forth to help the nations with removal and rebuilding. He listed over forty Indian nations that benefited from a congressional act of March 3, 1835, that granted $1,830,000 in appropriations to those tribes. He continued to defend "the intentions of the government of the United States" as "uniformly just and benevolent"—until 1829, when President Jackson's administration "essentially changed" the policy and course of conduct toward the Indians. Kent claimed that Jackson's administration withdrew protections afforded Indians under treaties and legislation negotiated in previous administrations. The Cherokees in particular, Kent stated, were "left in a defenceless state, to the penal laws of the state of Georgia." Kent quoted from Jackson's 1832 messages to Congress regarding his continued insistence that the "entire and speedy migration" of Indians westward must continue, and his threat that any Indians that did not remove from the settled portions of the nation would be left with "such privileges and disabilities as the respective states within whose jurisdiction they be may prescribe."[86]

The 1840 edition gave his audience the end of the Cherokees' struggle to maintain their territory in the east. Kent wrote that since his previous edition in 1838, "those Indians have been expelled, by military force, from the southern states, and transported across the Mississippi." He described President Martin Van Buren's "elaborate vindication" of the government's actions, in which Van Buren held that "a mixed occupancy of the same territory by the white and red man, was incompatible with the safety and happiness of either, and that their removal was dictated by necessity." Kent also related Van Buren's assurance that the "upwards of one hundred and sixteen millions of acres of land," the removal to which the federal government had paid "upwards of seventy-two millions of dollars to and on behalf of the Indians, in permanent annuities, lands, reservations, and the necessary expense of removal and settlement of them," was now "guarantied" to the Indians as their own, for their "exclusive and peaceful possession."[87] Kent used the language of law, not the language of emotion, to describe the Indians' fate at the hands of American settlers and their polities. But he appeared to be deeply saddened by the First Peoples' situation.

In his lecture "Of the Foundation of Title to Land," Kent admitted that, all too frequently, whites only dwelled on "the darkest traits in [Indians'] character." Because Native Americans were, according to Kent, "ignorant of letters" and had no historians of their own, they had no one to "transmit to posterity the specimens of their genius, to portray their feelings, to record their grievances, to vindicate their character, or to perpetuate the memory of their daring achievements."[88] Kent's sympathetic, ethnocentric remarks about the shortcomings of Native American culture illustrated the kind of "help" that Indians could expect from whites who were sympathetic to their cause. Kent and a few other policy makers and legal scholars felt obligated to defend Native American character with descriptions and histories that were ambivalent mixes of compliments and affronts. They were motivated by the obligation to justify their states' and nation's policies toward expansion, land possession, and dispossession, issues in which Indians figured prominently.

With his histories of a once-noble culture of "generous barbarians," Kent managed to balance his own patriotic impulse to justify the U.S. appropriation of Native American territory with his perceived obligation to protect the only thing that he believed many Indians had left—their noble and honorable pasts. Kent did not, however, harbor any optimism for the Indians' fate. He carefully situated his admiration of the Native American character in his colonial history lessons and reserved his sympathetic rendering of their "poverty and misery" for more recent times. Their interaction with whites, Kent observed, seemed to "have had an immoral influence upon Indian manners and habits, and to have destroyed all that was noble and elevated in the Indian character." While Kent condemned the frontiersmen for their "fierce and lawless manners," he could not lose sight of America's expansionist vision. The new waves of white settlers, Kent insisted, "must have" these Indian territories.[89] Kent predicted that America's Indians were "destined, at no very distant period of time, to disappear with those vast forests which once covered the country," because they simply seemed unable—or unwilling—to accept the Anglo-American version of "civilization."[90] This tone of inevitability, combined with enthusiasm for territorial expansion, helped give the next generation of legal practitioners the intellectual tools to participate in, and justify, imperial expansion.

6 Custom, the Written Law, and American Legal Treatises

In an 1823 address, Philadelphia attorney Charles Jared Ingersoll boasted that America's mechanical arts—its ships, houses, carriages, and other items of construction—were certainly Great Britain's equal. The nation was also gaining on Europe in the quality of its education and science. By far, Ingersoll proclaimed, America's crowning point of superiority was the creation of a model form of representative democracy, the principles of which could be found not just in the state and federal legislatures but also in its Bible societies and civic organizations. Free speech and the right to assembly, according to Ingersoll, had made everyone a representative. But although these forms of self-government had made America's governing bodies the finest in the world, he complained that American judges and lawyers still stubbornly insisted on adhering "with professional tenacity to the laws of the mother country." English adjudications were "received with a respect too much bordering on submission." Americans readily adopted British commercial law, which Ingersoll believed was inferior to that of continental Europe. Even more frustrating for Ingersoll was his impression that English legists were ignoring important American legal innovations in favor of inferior European legal authority. He complained that America's statesmen were turning out principles of international law that he considered far superior to those of British admiralty courts, yet English lawyers, "while silently availing" themselves of European law, had "seldom if ever made use of an American law book." The English committed this slight despite the fact that American law was of the "same language, system, and subject matter." The Philadelphia attorney deplored the "colonial acquiescence" under which Americans adopted English legal principles and insisted that "the use and respect of

American jurisprudence in Great Britain" would begin only when Americans "ceased to prefer English adjudications" to their own.[1]

As Ingersoll pointed out, in the decades since Independence, America had made great social, economic, and political strides. Through a war and occasional economic setbacks, the new nation pressed hard to establish itself as a political and economic contender in the Atlantic world. The Louisiana Purchase of 1803 and acquisition of additional territory along the Gulf Coast and west of the Rocky Mountains quickly turned the young nation into an empire. These territorial gains gave America's citizens even more easily accessible land and more opportunity for social and economic success. As new territories gained population, residents quickly organized and joined the union as new states. Territorial expansion meant internal commercial growth. At the same time, Americans' efforts to break into international markets gave them ample and varied opportunities to realize their economic potentials externally as well.[2] Although many American visions remained locally oriented, even the most isolated sections of the nation had some ties to networks that led into the next state or territory and eventually across the sea.

A vocal minority echoed Ingersoll's fears that America's law was not keeping pace with the changes occurring in other parts of its society, and some raised questions about whether the common law was compatible with their expanding societies. To be sure, the courts had been busy, particularly after 1815, creating indigenous precedent. By the 1820s, this precedent was also being recorded and published in law reports on the state and federal levels, but a growing body of more accessible American legal precedent still did not provide a separate American legal identity to some legists' satisfaction. American lawyers still had to rely far more on English precedent and treatises than some would have preferred. Blackstone's *Commentaries* was still the preeminent text with which they learned the fundamentals of common law, and American legists had to rely on English and continental European treatises for their foundations in the growing field of commercial law. Demands for a distinctive American form of law, combined with a strengthened desire to treat the law as a rational science, produced a resurgence of calls for law reform, particularly through codification.

The frustration that Ingersoll expressed represented that same tension between custom and innovation that had plagued legists during initial debates over common law's usefulness in America. The codification movement of the 1820s and 1830s engendered far broader debates than the more tentative suggestions for reform made around the Revolution. Like the earlier deliberations over change in American legal foundations, the move to codify American law in the manner of the civilian systems of continental Europe grew out of Enlightenment ideas of rational and scientific order. Lawmakers saw a variety of advantages to simplifying their law. Creating a comprehensive body of statutes with which to decide cases would, they believed, take the subjectivity out of judicial decisions. Codification would also place lawmaking more firmly under the control of the legislators. Proponents of reform argued that codes represented a more progressive form of governance, because they created order and tangible evidence of the law.[3] Most American legists, however, believed that their common law already was an orderly and scientific system and was by far the best form of jurisprudence for their societies. While they recognized that there was room for improvement in their states' and nation's common law, they believed that these improvements could be accomplished by building upon the "republican" foundations of the English common law and then borrowing from other law traditions or inventing other techniques when necessary.

Once again, American legists faced choices about the place of custom in their polities, and in this case most favored custom over innovations like codes that reduced law to stiff principles. The Anglo-American common law could change with societal needs and therefore was a better fit within America's rapidly changing republics. Colonization continued after state formation, and the U.S. empire grew as a set of decentralized entities. If anything, the individual states' needs varied even more with the opening of western territories and the admission of immature and economically distinct new polities. This diversity within the union, and the potential for even more differences as new states joined the nation, required a law that not only could accommodate individual states' needs, but could also provide a unified federal legal system. The common law seemed to them to be the best accommodation for this distinctive American combination of political and cultural unity and diversity. As customs evolved within societies, the common law could change too, with the help of the courts and the legislatures.

Although their works may not have been direct responses to codifiers' efforts to replace the common-law system, legal scholars at least indirectly responded to law reformers' concerns about the capacity of the common law to meet the needs of America's growing and changing republics and the changing legal climate within them. In the dynamic legal culture of the

1820s, Tapping Reeve, Henry St. George Tucker, and James Kent produced treatises that exemplified the trends of legal writing emerging in the nineteenth century. In their works, these legists still described many similarities between American and English law, but they also frequently highlighted the distinctions between the two legal systems and the reforms that continued to move their legal culture away from Britain and toward distinctly American forms of law and society.

I

The first third of the nineteenth century had seen significant escalation in the number and complexity of laws and court cases. As the nation grew, so did its laws, in number and sophistication. This growth not only generated an increase in law reports and law schools, but it also re-energized the conviction that the law should be treated as an ordered, scientific discipline. Visions of law as science were not new, but rather they were born of the Enlightenment. Seventeenth-century English jurist Matthew Hale conceived of the law reduced to a system, and according to Nathaniel Chipman, Blackstone's *Commentaries* perfected the Enlightenment-era vision.[4] David Hoffman's writings and teachings reflected the efforts to treat the law as a science. In 1817 Hoffman published an extensive course of legal study that was an impressively methodical annotated syllabus of recommended reading for aspiring lawyers. He complained that many young men who wished to study the law became mired in disorganized, immethodical reading. Hoffman's course of study professed to take care of that problem. He stated that his goal was to create a true science of jurisprudence, beginning with a syllabus that included not only law but moral philosophy, history, economics, and literature. For example, along with cases like *Marbury v. Madison*, Hoffman included portions of the *Federalist*, John Adams's *Defence of the Constitutions of the Government of the United States*, Justinian's *Institutes*, and works by Montesquieu, Grotius, Pufendorf, and the like.[5] This broader curriculum would serve as a more solid foundation for a generation of lawyers who would have to cope with even more economic, social, and demographic growth.

Tapping Reeve was one of the American originators of a methodical study of the law at his school in Litchfield, Connecticut. By the 1820s, under the proprietorship of James Gould, the law school placed even more emphasis on a systematic legal education. In an 1822 advertisement for the school, Gould explained to his readers that the object of his plan of instruction at

Litchfield was to teach the law "not as a collection of *insulated positive rules,*" but "as a *system of connected, rational principles.*" Gould explained that he regarded most of the texts on the law as "extremely defective," because they treated the law as a "code of arbitrary, but authoritative rules and dogmas" rather than "as a *science.*" If a student were to read and attend his lectures, Gould asserted, he could prepare himself both technically and intellectually for a prominent career in the law.[6]

Treating the law as a science held various meanings among law professionals. While some believed that the science of jurisprudence should include a generous helping of classical works and the legal and political thought of men like Grotius and Pufendorf, others tended to believe that a scientific law required more focused, technical discipline. In some places the stripping away of the "art" of the law became a point of worry for the older, classically trained lawyers who had been educated in the "philosophical" manner of the eighteenth century. In Virginia, for example, some of the proprietary law schools, and even the new program at the University of Virginia, drew fire from the old guard by catering to the desire of young men to get a quick legal education. These law schools often left students to their own devices, assigning a few "well selected text books" and keeping lectures to a minimum. To attract young men who wanted a fast education in the law while still catering to those who preferred the more thorough mode of schooling, Virginia offered students the option of attending law school for only one session, during which they could learn the fundamental principles of the municipal law.[7] Virginia's "philosophically trained" lawyers, however, worried that these shortcuts in education would hurt the law profession as well as Virginia's legal and political reputation among the other republics. They believed that the law required a rigorous course of study that included not just legal works but also a selection of classical works and other important treatises. The old guard criticized this new generation of lawyers for being lazy and poorly read, and lawyers trained in the old methods feared that the fast-track legal education that the younger set demanded would turn their profession into nothing more than a trade. Moreover, they were concerned that these young men would not be equal to the task of preserving and improving on the republican governments and laws that the Revolutionary generation had so carefully built.[8]

Efforts to make the law more "scientific" became entangled with a push to "Americanize" the law through codification. Decisions to retain the fundamentals of the common law during the Revolution had not permanently buried the issue of codification. In the 1820s and 1830s, one camp of law reformers grounded its arguments for codification within the ongoing American struggle to form its own national identity separate from that of England. William Sampson, one of the movement's leaders, claimed that the only way America ever would gain full independence from England would be to adopt its own distinctive American legal codes. He praised American legists for pruning "the exorbitances and strange peculiarities of the English jurisprudence" from American law, and he counseled American lawyers to move even further away from English legal authority by using the decisions of American judges, because they stood "so far above" the decisions imported from England. Sampson insisted that Americans "should import no more; for with every deference due to the learning, wisdom, and integrity of English judges," he asserted, they were not "fit persons to legislate" for Americans. Dependence, Sampson insisted, could "never cease if one nation [was] always to teach, and the other always to learn." The common law, he claimed, would only keep America in England's shadow. Sampson urged the states and the nation to follow Louisiana's admirable venture into codification. At the time of Sampson's speech, legislators in this new state planned to draw from their French and Spanish legal traditions to craft a code closely following the continental model of codification.[9] After Louisiana's leaders set the tone, Americans no longer needed to look across the Atlantic for innovative approaches to the law.

Although lawmakers and legal scholars believed that instituting rigid legal codes in their polities would take science a bit too far, they were not against creating what one historian has called "partial codes." In the first third of the nineteenth century, state legislatures began to authorize the publication of the statutes in force at the time. Certain states undertook extensive statute consolidations that in essence partially codified specific areas of their laws. For example, the New York legislature formed its real-property law into a systematic statute in 1828. This comprehensive statute met with such success that several years later New Yorkers compiled a new Code of Civil Procedure that over twenty other states and territories eventually used as a model for similar codes.[10] This model was not new to New Yorkers, whose Dutch roots may have made them more receptive to the continental model of codes.[11] Many state legislatures had passed similar consolidated statutes during the Revolution to designate formally those parts of the common law they had adopted into their state laws. These subsequent "partial codifications" were convenient modes of collecting all of the laws governing a particular area of jurisprudence for ease of reference and to clear up any confusion as to what laws were still valid.

The American law treatises that appeared from the Revolution to the 1820s also contributed to this "partial codification" movement. America's legal scholars possessed the model for such works in Blackstone's *Commentaries*, which in essence had codified the general principles of the common law. Using Blackstone's work as his template, St. George Tucker took partial codification into Virginia law with his edition of Blackstone, and Zephaniah Swift followed suit for his home state when he published his *System of the Laws of the State of Connecticut*.[12] As we have seen, others followed suit with their own legal and constitutional contributions in the 1790s and early 1800s. The same point about codification can be made even more strongly for the American legal works that appeared in the 1820s. In the mid-1820s, Nathan Dane published his important nine-volume *General Abridgement and Digest of American Law*. Most states by this time were producing their courts' reports as well, and Louisiana's Edward Livingston strengthened the codifiers' arguments when he spearheaded the publication of a code of laws for that state.[13]

The authors of the treatises produced in the 1820s and into the 1830s were responding to the needs of their changing societies. Tapping Reeve, James Kent, and Henry St. George Tucker observed the nation's territorial and economic expansions and their effects on the nation's societies and legal cultures. They were part of the move toward professionalization in the law, the drive for a more scientific study of the law, and agitation for Americanization of the law through codification. In different combinations, and with very different results, each legist answered the needs of his legal community by producing a treatise that he believed would be of use to his colleagues. Within their works, these men also expressed pride and confidence in the American common law as a unique creation of their American culture as well as a part of the character of the individual polities that comprised the nation.

II

Tapping Reeve was well aware of the benefits that improved transportation and growth of commercial networks could bring to Americans. Reeve himself was a direct beneficiary, as his law school attracted increasing numbers of students from across the nation. Because of his national perspective, Reeve also recognized that increased interstate networks required more knowledge of other states' laws. Therefore, to contribute to this need, Reeve produced two treatises based on his Litchfield Law School lectures, *The Law of Baron and Femme* (1816) and *The Law of Descents* (1825). Both of his publications reflected his devotion to a scientific study of the law, as Reeve systematically compiled all relevant statutes, common-law references, and available reports on his chosen subjects.

Reeve's *Law of Baron and Femme* showed the nation's lawyers and law students that many parts of English common law required very little modification in order to meet the needs of American societies. Although different states had adopted slight variations on the laws governing household relations, most general principles were still derived from the English common law. Reeve's motivation for publishing the work was to provide law practitioners with an easy reference manual for regulations governing domestic relations. To accomplish this task, Reeve drew from Blackstone, Sir Edward Coke, and English precedents on this topic to compile all common-law principles regarding the legal relationship between husband and wife, parent and child, and master and servant. Reeve left out most mention of state laws except in those rare cases when they differed from the common law or provided some level of illumination on the meaning of a particular regulation of English origin. Thus, Reeve believed, he could make his book "equally valuable to all parts of our country."[14]

Tapping Reeve's second work, *The Law of Descents,* published in 1825, was perhaps an even more valuable tool for finding one's way through the confusing variety of inheritance laws. The federal government had no jurisdiction over the laws of inheritance and descent. Therefore, Reeve explained, the "distinct, separate sovereignties" that comprised the American nation each maintained the power to enact appropriate laws "affecting the property within its own jurisdiction." This arrangement may have been convenient for each state, but it made for considerable confusion among the states. No matter how well acquainted a lawyer was with the laws of descent within his own polity, Reeve claimed that such knowledge afforded him "not the smallest assistance in ascertaining the law of any other state."[15] To aid the confused practitioner, the Connecticut legist gathered the various state laws of descent into one comprehensive and coherent work that exemplified the law as science.

Reeve's work made the nation's confusing inheritance laws accessible to educated Americans. He first summarized the laws relating to the descent of property for each state. Then, using the fictional estates of "Black

Acre" and "White Acre," he provided his readers with every conceivable inheritance scenario that could originate under that particular state's law. He made it clear that he was not providing a study of the case law in each state, but rather that his purpose was to identify the "principles which govern[ed] . . . and the result" in each of his imaginary permutations of that state's laws of descent. First Reeve reviewed the laws of descent in each of fifteen of the twenty-four states in the union in 1825.[16] He then examined the general differences among certain states with regard to the principles of inheritance of whole-blooded and half-blooded relatives, inheritance of collateral relatives, and the extent to which seisin was regarded in each of the states.[17] Reeve then provided an extensive review of the "peculiarities of the states" in each of their laws of descent. Finally, the Connecticut legist created elaborate case studies involving the descent of an ancestral estate and the descent of an estate by purchase under the various permutations of kinship in the different states. Reeve's undertaking required an enormous amount of analysis and application, and his work saved many lawyers and subsequent treatise writers considerable labor. A reader of *The Commentaries on American Law* could almost hear James Kent's sighs of relief as he repeatedly referred his audience to Reeve's *Laws of Descent* instead of providing his own explanations of the many and varied modes of descent in America. In fact, in his introduction to his chapter on the law of descents, Kent referred his readers to Reeve's work to "explain all the variations and shades of difference between the regulations of descent" among the states.[18]

The significance of Reeve's work to the analysis of a growing body of distinctively American law should not be underestimated. Reeve's objective and "scientific" examination of American laws of descent contained little political discussion and very few statements about America's government or legal systems, nor did it include Reeve's visions of the collective American character. But the treatise provided an important representation of the simultaneous nationalization and localization of American law. Reeve recognized the diversity of locally oriented laws of descent, and he noted that local regulation of such matters would naturally, and rightfully, lead to such diversity. At the same time, Reeve had recognized and responded to the need for a text that would help each state's lawyers function in a collection of legal systems that increasingly crossed political borders in order to carry on the business of a growing nation. As the business of America became more nationally oriented, lawyers, merchants, and others needed legal treatises like Reeve's to unravel the mysteries of each state's legal diversity.

III After retiring as New York's chancellor in 1823 at a still-vigorous sixty years of age, James Kent returned to teaching the law at Columbia College. Very soon thereafter, publishers and colleagues began to urge Kent to publish his lectures. He agreed to do so, perhaps in part to show those in favor of codification that the common law was already a coherent, scientific system of law and did not need to be replaced by codes. Indeed, Kent warned that the "new and dazzling theory of codification" harbored the dangerous potential for too much reduction of legal subtleties into overly abbreviated generalizations. In some instances, Kent cautioned, "brevity" could become "obscurity," and many subtleties of the law could be lost.[19] Kent's work was, in many ways, a defense of the common law as the best legal system for America, but it was also an even-handed assessment of those areas of American law that needed improvement. To realize the common law's full potential in America, Kent asserted that lawmakers could not ignore other legal sources, particularly civil and natural law principles, that would help to shape an American version of the common law. He still used numerous examples of New York statute and case law, but Kent extended his work beyond his own state's borders into every other state's laws as well. Moreover, he concentrated much energy on highlighting the rapidly growing body of federal judicial decisions from the previous thirty years, making his work the first comprehensive national survey of the major principles of American law.

Although Kent did not consider a strict codification of laws to be beneficial to American societies, he recognized that certain elements of codification on the civilian model could be useful in the reshaping of the common law to republican specifications. Kent devoted a significant amount of space to the history and merits of the civil law and Justinian's code. In his view, the sudden increase in law reports and state and federal statutes created a lot of confusion. Kent believed that it was time to remedy this increasingly complicated body of law through a digest of "the whole body of the American common law." This work would, in Kent's opinion, make the laws more manageable by "retaining what [was] applicable . . . and rejecting every thing that [was] obsolete and inapplicable" to American institutions.[20] In effect, Kent advocated a partial codification that would simplify the law while maintaining a flexible common-law foundation.

Kent understood that the common- and civil-law systems shared far more qualities than jurists on either side cared to admit, and he carefully crafted his description of the civil law to highlight their similarities. He explained that the civil law was in force in most European nations, in most of Spanish America, in the province of Lower Canada, and in the state of Louisiana. Kent tried to relate the civil code as closely as possible to the common law by defining the civil code as constituting "the principal basis" of these polities' "unwritten or common law."[21] He accused previous generations of English lawyers of forming and cultivating a prejudice against the civil law, but he assured his readers that in modern times this prejudice was beginning to wane, and that by the 1820s some jurists were even willing to admit that the civil- and common-law systems "were grounded on the same reason." Regardless of the qualities that civil and common law shared, Kent concluded that the common law was more compatible with the identities that Americans had shaped for themselves, because "in everything which concern[ed] civil and political liberty," the civil law could not "be compared with the free spirit of the English and American common law."[22] The common law's flexibility allowed local customs to flourish, thus cultivating diverse American identities rather than narrowing the scope of identities to one national vision.

While Kent believed that the common law was the best system for American society, he took great pains to distinguish American common law from English common law. One of the ways in which he set American common law apart was in his interpretation of the place of custom in American law. By the time Kent published his *Commentaries*, it seemed to be a foregone conclusion that in America, immemorial custom was not the preeminent protector of common-law rights. Earlier treatise writers had already untied American common law from English law's feudal origins by removing the necessity for an immemorial common law and bestowing on the people the right to choose and consent to the laws they needed. The people had become their own protectors under American common law. Following their lead, Kent built a new premise derived from the universal source of "natural justice" to justify American common-law principles. The essence of Kent's argument was that if a practice met with universal consent and application, then that universality was "pretty good evidence" that the rule or obligation had "its foundation in natural law."[23] This justification of America's common-law practices through the lens of universality and natural justice was far more compatible with American notions of social equality and equal access to the law than were English notions of an immemorial common law.

Kent also transformed custom in his treatment of the laws of commerce. By the early nineteenth century, America enjoyed growing prominence in the commercial world. Kent's attention to commerce and its laws sharply distinguished his work from Blackstone's work, as well as that of earlier American legal scholars. Though commerce was an important part of the English economy in the eighteenth century, Blackstone barely touched upon the law merchant, calling it a "system of customs used only among one set of the king's subjects," those who were involved in trade and commerce. The English legist set it aside as a separate part of the law, a part that was not truly immemorial, because it grew up around modern needs for a law regulating commercial transactions.[24] Early national professors and treatise writers generally followed Blackstone's lead and did not dwell on laws regulating commerce in their lectures and writings. Not until after 1810, for example, did the Litchfield professors begin to lecture extensively on topics such as contracts, arbitration, insurance, and other issues of commercial interest. The volume of Litchfield students' notes on topics dealing with personal property and commercial issues dramatically increased after 1800. Litchfield student Timothy Follett took almost seven hundred pages of notes on personal property and commercial issues in 1812 and 1813. Compare this, for example, to Seth Staples's notebook of 1798, in which he covered the law of merchants in about forty pages and the law of contracts in about eighty pages.[25]

Kent, on the other hand, responded to growing commercial interests in much of the nation by placing the law of nations at the beginning of his volumes on American law. He impressed upon his readers the importance of this branch of jurisprudence, and he noted that many questions arose "in the course of commercial transactions" that required an acquaintance with the conventional law of Europe as well as the doctrines of tribunals that governed international law. A "comprehensive and scientific knowledge of international law," Kent posited, was necessary, not only for lawyers practicing in commercial ports, but also for "every gentleman who [was] animated by liberal views" and who possessed "a generous ambition to assume stations of high public trust." Kent observed that by the 1820s the nation's courts were experiencing a "constant growth and accumulation of cases on commercial law generally" and an increase in cases particularly relating to "policies of insurance, negotiable paper, mercantile partnerships, and the various customs of the law merchant."[26] For that reason, Kent invested considerable energy on descriptions of the changes in these commercial laws.

These areas of commercial law also represented a significant body of law within which English, continental European, and American statute law and judicial precedent mingled freely. While some jurists complained about slavish American devotion to English precedent, Kent borrowed liberally from English and other sources to explain the intricacies of the law merchant. For example, in his description of the law regarding the ability of a ship's captain to contract on behalf of the vessel's owners, Kent cited New York statutes, cases from U.S. admiralty courts, Supreme Court decisions, British admiralty precedent, and two British treatises, George Bell's *Commentaries on the Laws of Scotland* and Lord Tenterden's *Treatise of the Law Relative to Merchant Ships and Seamen.*[27] In other discussions on commercial and admiralty law, Kent recommended treatises from the civilian tradition such as Simon van Leeuwen's *Commentaries on the Roman Dutch Law* and the French *Cours de Droit Commercial Maritime*, and he made frequent reference to France's *Code de Commerce.*[28]

Kent filled his volumes with expansive language about commercial law's central place in contemporary American society. He expressed the desire to "awaken" in the law student's "breast a generous zeal to become familiar with the leading judicial decisions . . . of those great masters of maritime law," in order to help the student complete a "faithful summary of the doctrines of commercial jurisprudence."[29] The chancellor observed that particularly after 1810, the Supreme Court "constantly" dealt with "great questions . . . embracing the rights and the policy of nations." During this period, Kent proudly stated, the prize and maritime law, "not of England only, but of all the commercial nations of Europe . . . was suddenly introduced . . . and deeply and permanently interwoven with the municipal law of the United States."[30] Kent not only found nothing wrong with the American practice of borrowing this law from other nations, but he was pleased that American lawmakers exercised their right to choose from among so many different kinds of commercial law. This freedom to choose allowed legists to blend many different kinds of law into the best mix for a distinctively American commercial law.

In addition to his praise of the nation's commercial growth, Kent also boasted of the nation's progress toward creating a body of indigenous federal precedent. While the "scanty decisions of the Supreme Court" from 1790 to 1801 were almost all located in one volume of Dallas's *Reports*, Kent informed his readers that between 1801 and 1815 the Court had experienced a tremendous expansion in its case load. The reports for that "very active period" consumed nine volumes. Kent announced that by 1816 the decisions of the Supreme Court "had embraced so many topics of public and municipal law . . . that, for the first time in the history of this country," Americans could "perceive the broad foundations and rapid growth of a code of national jurisprudence." That code, Kent proclaimed, had been growing and improving ever since, and had "become a solid and magnificent structure" that represented a growing American independence from English precedent.[31] In fact, although he did not refer to a code in the civilian model, even Kent's use of the word "code" seemed to set American law apart from English common law.

This expanding body of federal court decisions held even more significance for Kent, who was in favor of a strong federal court system. He predicted that the federal judiciary was "destined, at no very distant period of time, to cast a shade over the less elevated, and perhaps . . . the less attractive and ambitious systems of justice in the several states." Kent believed that the federal judiciary would eventually eclipse the state courts for several reasons. First, the federal government held the advantage in tenure of office and salary of judges; therefore they could "command better talents" and more learned men than could the states. Second, the federal administration of justice held more prestige than state courts, because their decisions applied uniformly to all states. Moreover, every state court was "naturally disposed to borrow light and aid" from their federal counterparts rather than borrowing from other states' courts.[32]

Despite his Federalist sensibilities, this last reason caused Kent some concern. He wanted the states to look to federal courts for precedent, but Kent feared that the individual states would look only to the federal courts and not to sister states for legal authority. States were multiplying so rapidly, and judicial reports were becoming so numerous, that Kent predicted soon few lawyers would be able to master the case law of any other state besides their own. Kent feared that because of the rapid growth of the nation and the daunting accumulation of legal precedent, students would not "have the courage to enter the complicated labyrinth of so many systems." He worried that aspiring lawyers would neglect other states' law in favor of their own local law and the law of the United States, and that they would then "resort for further assistance to the never failing fountains of European wisdom."[33] While European sources were acceptable alternatives when there was no American precedent, Kent strongly believed that all American resources should be exhausted before the lawyer searched outside the nation for answers.

After enthusiastically predicting that the federal courts' authority would soon eclipse that of the state, Kent quickly added his conviction that the states' roles as protectors of certain rights were crucial to maintaining the balance of powers between state and federal governments. He assured his readers that he supported the preservation of state and local courts' identities as guardians of individual property and civil rights. Although the federal courts took care of national issues, Kent posited that the laws of property, equity jurisdiction, and civil and domestic relations were the natural provinces of local courts. He looked to state governments to continue to protect those internal interests. States' judicial duties were all-important, Kent insisted, because they touched "every cord of human sympathy" and controlled the nation's "best destinies." Kent believed that the jurisprudence of the individual states should be "cultivated, cherished, and exalted" and that each state court should "in their subordinate relation to the United States . . . endeavour to discharge the duty which they owe[d] to the latter, without forgetting the respect which they owe[d] to themselves." The New York legist summarized his vision of the state courts' place within the federal republic by quoting Sir William Blackstone's instructions to "the people of his own country," that "they should be 'loyal, yet free; obedient, and yet independent.'"[34] Preserving the hierarchy of federal courts over state courts was, according to Kent, the key to order in American law.

With his descriptions of America's place in the commercial world and the federal and state courts' roles in American society, Kent was revealing part of his vision of the directions that America's republics should take in the future. Kent believed that American freedom to move away from England's immemorial common law gave its polities the opportunity to experiment with laws that would provide the appropriate measure of universal acceptance and natural justice for their own individual needs. Commercial law was the perfect venue for such experiments in borrowing and blending various legal principles to create a distinctly American body of law based on unique economic and social needs. Finally, the nation's judiciary, assisted by independent, yet subordinate, state courts, churned out indigenous precedent that made America less reliant on outside legal authority. All of these developments, he thought, led to a common law that still shared its heritage and some fundamental characteristics with English law but was uniquely fit for American republics.

IV Even after Kent published the *Commentaries*, there was still a place for local legal treatises. St. George Tucker had provided a great service to his colleagues in and outside of his home state when he published his edition of Blackstone's *Commentaries* in 1803. While St. George Tucker concentrated on Virginia law in his treatise, he also included many points of federal law and constitutional principles. His son Henry St. George Tucker, however, concentrated almost exclusively on the municipal laws of his home state in order to give Virginia lawyers as comprehensive a text as possible for local use.

Henry Tucker, eldest son of St. George Tucker, was born into the independent republics of Virginia and America in 1780. He was educated at the College of William and Mary and received his law degree from that school in 1801, under his father's tutelage. The younger Tucker started his practice in Winchester in 1802, briefly served in the Virginia House of Delegates, and from 1815 to 1819 represented the Commonwealth in Congress. Finding that he preferred state politics to national, Henry Tucker returned to Virginia in 1819 to serve in the state senate. In 1824 he was elected to a district equity judgeship and returned to Winchester, where he also opened a proprietary law school. At the height of the school's popularity, it housed thirty-four students, among them young men from Georgia, Louisiana, South Carolina, Alabama, Ohio, and Massachusetts. His school still enjoyed a strong reputation when he closed it in 1831 to move to Richmond and take a position on the Virginia Court of Appeals.[35]

Henry Tucker's career spanned a time of great spatial and economic expansion in the nation. While Virginia saw some of that prosperity and expansion, its economy remained predominantly agrarian. Neither Virginia's socioeconomic circumstances nor its legal system in the 1820s fit the commercially oriented character of states to its north.[36] Tobacco cultivation and other forms of agriculture were still the most important sectors of the Virginia economy, and although they had to participate in the larger commercial market in order to sell their agricultural goods, most of Virginians' economic transactions were still local.[37] This locally based agrarian economy did not require complicated forms of law and government. Even as lawyers in other parts of the nation handled greater quantities of commercial and international law, Virginia lawyers still dealt primarily with cases of debt and, as Henry Tucker put it, "private oeconomical relations."[38]

Because the bulk of his students would be dealing with cases of a local nature, Henry Tucker wanted to provide the tools that would allow them to practice effectively in their communities. By the late 1820s, Henry Tucker's students had James Kent's *Commentaries on American Law* with which to study any federal legal principles they might need to know, and he frequently referred them to this text when questions arose. His students did not, however, have an updated text on Virginia law. Henry Tucker noted that between 1803, when his father's edition of Blackstone's *Commentaries* appeared, and the mid-1820s, twenty-one volumes of Virginia court reports had been printed.[39] To give his own students an updated picture of the developments in Virginia law, Henry Tucker first published a guide entitled *Notes on Blackstone's Commentaries* (1826). In 1831, the year that his law school closed, Henry Tucker produced an expanded edition of his lectures entitled *Commentaries on the Laws of Virginia*.[40]

In the introduction to his *Commentaries,* Henry Tucker asserted that his objective in publishing the work was "*to be useful.*"[41] He explained that he hoped his work would fill the void that contemporary treatises left in terms of educating law students on the fundamental principles of his state's law. Contemporary publications focused on the needs of the bar and not of the student, therefore necessitating the publication of his own lectures for law students. A law school text, Tucker explained, should not only investigate every case that bore upon a particular legal issue, but it should also provide its reader with the general principle behind each matter, so that the student would not be confused by "the innumerable modifications with which [each principle was] clogged and qualified" during its journey through the courts.[42]

As his father had done, Henry Tucker used Blackstone's *Commentaries* as a template for his work. The elder Tucker had kept Blackstone's work intact and embellished the treatise with his own comments and appendixes. Henry Tucker, however, did not show quite so much deference toward the English master's work. While he believed that he could not "do better than to make the *Commentaries* of Blackstone [his] ground-work," Henry Tucker also knew that the time had come to prune the unnecessary and obsolete parts of the English work away from those parts of the *Commentaries* that were still of use to the American student. The younger Tucker obviously felt a certain measure of guilt for dismembering Blackstone's classic work. In the introductory lecture for his *Commentaries,* he apologetically explained that the length of Blackstone's original volumes, plus Virginia's own increasing body of statute and case law and, added to that, related federal cases and statutes, would have made for a cumbersome work indeed. Therefore, he chose to lead "the mind of the student to those subjects which [were] most important" and to relieve his reader "from unnecessary trouble in the pursuit of what [was] obsolete . . . or forgotten . . . or repealed." He extracted from Blackstone's *Commentaries* "whatever was appropriate" to Virginia's laws and customs and eliminated "what was obviously obsolete and irrelevant." Tucker then added extracts from any other elementary essays he thought might be of value to his students, along with "such explanations and illustrations as . . . occurred" to him, as well as important state and federal laws and court cases as he thought appropriate. He pointed out that he excluded Blackstone's "political part" and the portion that was devoted to criminal law because he thought that his students could study these topics on their own.[43]

Henry Tucker left more than just Blackstone's criminal law and political and constitutional thought on the cutting room floor. Like Blackstone and St. George Tucker, the younger Tucker concentrated on the general principles of the law rather than dwelling on the minutiae of numerous court case citations. These details, he asserted, one could find in the more complicated treatises that were designed not for the student but for the experienced practitioner. Unlike his two esteemed predecessors, Henry Tucker pared his work down even to the barest principles having to do only with Virginia's municipal law. At the beginning of his lecture on municipal law, he warned his students that there would not be much discussion about divine or revealed law, the law of nature, or the law of nations. These "philosophical" principles, Tucker opined, did not have much to do with the fundamental principles that his students would need to master before proceeding to the technical details of Virginia law. Therefore, he confined the bulk of his discussion to "the subject of municipal law alone: and chiefly to that municipal law which form[ed] the rule of action in Virginia."[44] By creating such a narrow definition of municipal law in his classroom, Henry Tucker may have been one of the educators who drew fire from his father's cohort for providing a narrow and one-dimensional legal education to Virginia's aspiring lawyers.

Beyond the anatomical changes that eradicated some of the purely English elements of Blackstone's work, Tucker's volumes on Virginia law revealed other distinctive components of an American common law. For example, as it was for Kent by the 1820s, Henry Tucker considered it a foregone conclusion that America rightfully possessed its own forms of common law, despite the fact that the nation was not old enough to possess its own "immemorial" custom. In fact, the younger Tucker insisted that while in England the common law's foundations rested on immemorial custom, in Virginia there were, "properly speaking, no customs." By the English definition, the essence of every custom was "that it should have been used so long as the memory of man runneth not to the contrary," which, under English law, meant prior to the reign of Richard I. Obviously, Henry Tucker admitted, because there was no settlement of America until long after Richard I's reign, the English version of custom could not exist anywhere in the New World.[45] This revelation did not seem to bother the younger Tucker, however, and he certainly did not see the country's lack of immemorial custom as a threat to America's adoption and adaptation of the common law.

Instead of dwelling on English definitions of custom, Henry Tucker applied essentially the same natural law concept of universality that James Kent had used in his *Commentaries*. The younger Tucker noted that there were cases in which "the general *practice* of the country [had] been permitted to control the strict principles of the law." Thus, he explained, Virginia courts had recently decided that such general usages and understandings of the community, though they were not immemorial, were "important circumstance[s] to be considered" even when these usages were contrary to established law. In Virginia's western counties, for example, it was a "universal practice" that land leases that typically commenced in April would include the right to sow in the preceding fall and reap in the following harvest. Reason dictated this practice, Henry Tucker explained, because "it would be a hardship and fraud on the tenant if he were to pay his full rent for only a summer crop." In other parts of Virginia, Henry Tucker noted, this custom was not valid and was even contrary to established law, but he concluded that Virginia courts had established that "general usage even of a neighborhood may be justly considered as having an important bearing on the construction of a contract."[46] Thus, the younger Tucker's version of common law privileged local exigencies over long-standing and less-practical general mandates.

Henry Tucker's view of the place of custom in the law extended beyond the confirmation of general use in the courts and into the occasional necessity to use statutes to confirm common-law regulations. In America, veneration of the unwritten customary law was gradually going the way of the unwritten constitution. While Henry Tucker and many of his counterparts believed that the common law's mutability was the best way to accommodate changes in their society, they also understood that there were limitations to the usefulness of English concepts of custom and the common law's immemorial nature. The younger Tucker resurrected a theory about the origins of the common law that James Wilson had suggested—and that Henry's father St. George had rejected—a few decades earlier. Henry Tucker asserted that England's common law was simply "statutes worn out by time." In other words, at one time the law had been written, but the written legal texts had faded through the centuries. He pointed out that this idea did not receive "the unqualified assent of a former editor of the commentaries," namely his father, but "upon reflection" Henry chose to believe "its perfect correctness." Henry Tucker argued that certainly there must have been some law enacted during the time of Alfred, who had ordained that England's legislature should meet at least twice each year. Surely, he continued, Alfred's successors would have written something down as well, and if the king and legislature passed laws during these sessions, what was more natural than the idea that a "great part" of the unwritten law was "founded upon the memory of some positive statute?" Henry's differences with his father may have been more of degree than absolute, however.[47] In his extensive footnote on that page of *Blackstone's Commentaries*, St. George Tucker argued against the idea that "all the unwritten rules of law" were "founded upon some positive Statute, the memory of which" had been lost. The elder Tucker claimed that the evidence was simply too faint to determine the origins of immemorial law.[48]

By 1830, it was already more difficult for Henry St. George Tucker, a generation removed from the Revolution, to accept the authority of an ancient and unwritten law than it had been for his father, who had been born a Briton. Henry Tucker could not fathom the existence of anything like a regular government without a written "*law* or rule of government for the people." This written law, even if it had been lost in time, was, for Henry Tucker, still statutory in character, provided it was the command of the "*de facto* . . . supreme authority in the state."[49] Although this theory had been expressed before, Henry Tucker's emphatic declaration in favor of a written law as the foundation of the common law was still a telling illustration of the shift in mentality from the custom-oriented, unwritten-law society of Henry St. George Tucker's father to a society that saw considerable merit in statute law. Only a few decades after the Revolution, Americans were adopting the written law rather than retaining the English custom of unwritten law as part of their American legal character.

Although Henry Tucker, in many places, still drew directly from the English master's work, his Virginia treatise was very much an "American" law treatise. Henry Tucker's lectures reflected a greater regard for statute law and written regulation and a greater separation from the outmoded English notion of immemorial custom that had become impractical for American polities. Tucker did not reject the notion of custom altogether. He still held to the common-law belief that custom was an important part of allowing the law to accommodate changes in place and time. With his transition to the idea that common law confirmed a general practice, he merely shortened the time within which a custom had to exist before it was accepted by law and introduced natural law concepts of universal acceptance as the authority by which a practice was confirmed as law. In these ways Tucker showed his readers the changes and improvements that common-law principles had undergone to accommodate his polity's individual needs.

Each treatise author created his own version of law as a science. Reeve contributed to the science of the law by compiling sets of laws on specific projects into rational codes that students and practitioners could use as ready references. For Henry Tucker, scientific study of his state's law meant stripping away the "political" and "philosophical" parts of the law and dealing with only the bare technical aspects of Virginia's municipal law. James Kent, however, took a very different direction, as he created the first comprehensive treatise on the main principles of American law. Kent seemed to believe that if the law truly was a science, then legal scholars were obliged to investigate principles from all available legal sources and then choose and apply those principles that were most appropriate to their needs, regardless of origin. In Kent's opinion, this mixing of legal traditions and ideas was also an ideal way to create a distinctly American blending of the common law.

Reeve and Kent's treatises also indicated a trend toward nationally oriented treatise writing that would grow in the following decades, as more legists wrote treatises that dealt with federal law and legal issues. This trend could lead one to think that perhaps the law was moving toward a more nationally focused identity and away from the local identities that had been more prevalent in those legal works of the late eighteenth and early nineteenth centuries. This was not entirely the case, however. Henry Tucker's Virginia treatise indicated that legists were still concerned with local law and a local legal identity, and in the coming decades many more treatises on local legal forms, principles, and procedures would appear. These same indications of enduring local identities existed within Reeve's and Kent's works as well. Reeve directed his collection of state laws of descent toward a national audience, but the work obviously also featured a part of American law that hinged on local traditions and needs. Even Kent, a proponent of a strong federal government, believed that states should retain their roles as guardians of individual rights, and that they should do so in ways tailored to the individual customs and needs of each state. The American science of the law, a science increasingly concerned with national and international issues, still seemed to have plenty of room for local identities and concerns. National identities grew out of local identities, therefore the centrality of local law in American law provided the foundations for the U.S. national character.

Conclusion

In the mid-1820s, while studying with Henry St. George Tucker in Winchester, Virginia, Charles James Faulkner penned an essay on the distinctiveness of American law. "The peculiar situation of this country," Faulkner wrote, "has given a very peculiar cast to our legal institutions." Emigrating "from a nation whose body of civil regulations had already acquired a perfection & intensity and at a period when the knowledge of human rights & remedies had grown into a science," Virginia's first colonists, he announced, left the parent country, "not as infants without ideas & [not] without a conception of these rights" that were their inheritance, but rather with solidly formed beliefs about their own rights as English people. Although they settled far from their homeland, Virginians did not stop thinking of themselves as Englishmen who were entitled to the same rights and laws as those who remained in England. "By a kind of fiction," therefore, they "merely extended the bounds of that Empire where this law was to exercise its full influence & operation."[1]

It seemed very simple, the way that young Faulkner described it. English migrations to the New World extended the bounds of the British Empire. The colonists carried with them an Anglo-American cultural identity that was tied to custom and an immemorial Constitution and law. But they did not require all the trappings of the English legal process. Considering themselves part of an extended British jurisdiction, American colonists molded their legal institutions in the familiar image of those of the parent state. But the result was not as simple as Faulkner implied. The first settlers chose to import only those parts of the common law that were compatible with their societies. Each group of colonists formulated customs that were suited to their peculiar social circumstances, thus producing their own unique local law traditions.[2] By the time Faulkner began his law studies, America had won independence, the Louisiana Purchase had doubled the size of the United States, and new waves of colonists were heading westward, extending the imperial boundaries for their nation. Once again, their laws and governments traveled with them, adapting to the changing social and economic circumstances of the frontier.

The early republic's legal scholars were well aware of America's potential for expansion when they wrote their treatises and lectures. They had helped to create and interpret legal cultures that could adapt to the individual circumstances of place, while maintaining a core of principles that were common to all parts of the nation. Because they lived in places as culturally diverse as New England, the Mid-Atlantic, and the South, it was only natural that legists' visions of American identity differed, and even clashed, over certain issues. Local identity remained central, and law lectures and treatises were not devoid of regional sniping. But, more often, legal scholars expressed appreciation for local diversity, and they recognized the common law's role in preserving difference. Although there were issues that caused division among legal scholars, they were more interested in emphasizing the places where national and local laws differed from England. With only a few exceptions, they chalked up differences among state laws and government to the common law's malleable nature.

From the first settlements, the abundance of land and the ease with which people could acquire it set America apart from England, and every legal scholar identified it as a key element in American identities. The Louisiana Purchase opened even greater opportunity for expansion, and the American impulse to extend the bounds of their own empire westward became further engrained in the national character. Extension of empire meant that Americans transported local identities into the frontier as they established new communities.[3] Now it was the Americanized versions of the common law that, "by a kind of fiction," accompanied these new colonists westward, and American common law again changed to accommodate new places and circumstances.

While broader landownership and ability to dispose freely of property was a common experience in all of the United States, property law was one place where local variances were preserved as well. Legists from Virginia to New York to Connecticut recognized the importance of these property protections to the distinctive U.S. character. America's more fluid property exchange necessitated flexibility that could only be realized on the local level. Property had always been regulated on the colonial level in British America; therefore, the new polities merely upheld custom when states retained control over property law. Legists approved of this local control. It was far more important to them to compare the nation's more liberal property and inheritance laws to those of England than to quibble over local differences. In fact, because of the complex variations in state property laws, legal scholars rarely ventured beyond descriptions of their own states' laws until Tapping Reeve published his *Treatise on the Law of Descents* in 1825, which made the states' diverse laws accessible to law practitioners.

While placing the ultimate sovereignty in the people had been a tremendous philosophical break with England, by the 1820s the idea of consent and political authority protected by written constitutions was second nature to Americans, and an attribute on which all legists agreed. They recognized that Americans enjoyed the common experience of a federal government that relied on written constitutions to protect citizens' rights. As new states, carved out of western territories, submitted their own written constitutions, Americans extended the bounds of their empire and preserved local differences in governance.

Some of the points of agreement among legal scholars did not sit well with all American citizens. Women, particularly married women, still had not gained much more legal latitude in America by the 1820s. American legists generally did not even try to find points of improvement over English law when they discussed women's freedoms and rights. The only objections to limitations placed on women came from Connecticut's Tapping Reeve. Although he lodged vocal protests against the hedging of married women's ability to manage their property, Reeve was the only legal scholar from this group who recorded such sentiments in this period. His colleagues contented themselves with providing descriptions of widows' property rights and women's legal personhood that closely resembled English common law.

As one might expect, legal scholars' sharpest disagreements came over slavery. But even over this controversial issue, the arguments were not as divisive as they would become later, and they did not always run along sectional lines. Slavery was an uncomfortable point of distinction between America and England that ran contrary to boasts of a superior American society and law. All American legists, even Virginian St. George Tucker, echoed Blackstone's condemnation of the institution and tried to find ways to rid their polities of it. Both New York's James Kent and St. George Tucker sought historical and legal ties to similar practices in the ancient Greek and Roman republics, as well as to England's extinct legal status of villenage, to show their audience that their society was not alone in the practice of this abominable institution. Legal scholars also tried to downplay the severity of American slavery by explaining to their audience that America's republican societies had at least partially reformed the institution and had made it into a milder form of bondage than slavery of the past or in other parts of the world.

While legists agreed that slavery had existed in all parts of British North America, some emphasized local distinctions in severity and enforcement of slave law. Slavery was still legal in all states until well into the nineteenth century, but scholars in New England and the mid-Atlantic, where they had begun the gradual emancipation process, could at least argue that slavery in their polities was going away. They also claimed that because of their more compassionate laws, slavery existed in a milder form in their states. Slaves could sometimes own property and had a few other tightly hedged freedoms in Northern states. Even Tucker recognized that slavery and its legal constructions occupied a central role in the shaping of Southern identities. His justifications for retention of human property, though tempered with articulations of his own doubts over the morality of slavery, still signified a widening sectional divide that in a few decades would harden into two drastically different national identities.

The question of what to do with the continent's indigenous peoples met with regional clashes of a different nature. Some legal scholars—those whose polities did not include large concentrations of Native Americans—tended to ignore the issue altogether. Those legists who still regularly encountered the continent's first peoples, either in courtrooms or in their frontier communities, dealt extensively with laws governing treatment of Indians in their treatises. Competing convictions about their rights to the soil revealed complicated local differences. Moreover, differences over Native American issues tended to break along frontier lines rather than along state boundaries. Legists and others who lived on the frontier called stridently for Indians' removal, as Hugh Henry Brackenridge's works illustrate. On the other hand, Peter DuPonceau, Brackenridge's colleague in Philadelphia, dismissed indigenous peoples as part of a distant time and place. New York's James Kent had encountered Native American property claims in his courts and therefore had more opportunity than many of his colleagues to ponder the legal and moral questions surrounding their plight. While his treatment of Indian removal became lengthier and more sympathetic over the years, Kent's discussions conveyed a sense of inevitability, that the Indian was destined to disappear. American legal scholars' visions of empire would not allow Indians to get in the way.

One final difference worth noting is some legists' emphasis on commercial concerns especially after 1820. America's claim to empire extended across the Atlantic as well, in the form of economic influence. James Kent recognized that in order for the United States to grow its commercial empire, some law practitioners had to understand international, commercial, and maritime law. But this discussion of commercial law revealed yet another local variation. Kent's recognition of the importance of commercial and international law sources in his *Commentaries* contrasted with Henry Tucker's treatment of Virginia law and his concentration on Virginia's locally based, agrarian economy. Once again a national, even international, focus coexisted comfortably with strong local identities.

Charles James Faulkner would practice law in a world that was very different from that of the first generation of U.S. lawyers. The technological advances that made territorial expansion easier would also facilitate colonization of American legal culture. In 1830, Tapping Reeve, James Kent, and Henry St. George Tucker were on the leading edge of a mini-explosion in the publication of American law reports and legal authority that continued to increase in the following decades. Advances in transportation and printing technology would make published works far more accessible to people living outside major cities along the East Coast. These advances allowed James Kent to provide frequent revised editions of his *Commentaries* and also allowed more treatises and digests of state laws to appear. In the late 1830s, Supreme Court justice Joseph Story added his own prestigious commentaries on equity, the Constitution, and other subjects. Many other American legal scholars published important works that expanded the scope and accessibility of American legal authorities, to the delight of American students and practitioners.

New technology and a proliferation of American law sources did not, however, eradicate all things English from American law after 1830. American law students and practitioners still used Blackstone as a general reference for common-law principles. Other English legal authority, including old and new precedent, law reports, and legal treatises, still appeared in American lawyers' citations. And some American legists still anxiously warned that continued reliance on English legal principles and forms was destroying America's ability to formulate its own independent identity.

Many more American legal scholars, however, did not seem to share this anxiety about the remaining continuities between English and American common law. In fact, like Kent, they agreed with Peter DuPonceau that taking the common law out of American law would have been like taking the English language away from Americans.

But in order for the common law to function in America's republics, the language had to undergo some subtle changes. Americans altered definitions and shifted the accents on the language of the common law. The American Revolution *was* a transformative experience, but not in the sense that it gave birth to brand-new legal and governmental systems. Rather, the Revolution gave U.S. lawyers a new vocabulary devoid of monarchy and full of republican words and sentiments. These legal scholars combined the best of change and continuity. They acknowledged the value of English legal foundations, while also recognizing the common law's ability to change with republican transformations. From the Revolution onward, men like Reeve, Kent, the Tuckers, and their colleagues could comfortably argue that their common law was not *English*, but *American*, law, built on England's common-law foundations but containing many elements that were purely American inventions and adaptations. They had collected the republican parts of common law, added a few outstanding elements of civil law, combined that mixture with natural law principles and many innovations of their own, and had created a common-law system that remained an integral part of their American identities.

Notes

Abbreviations

UVA	Alderman Library, University of Virginia
EGS	Earl Gregg Swem Library, College of William and Mary
LHS	Litchfield Historical Society
LOC	Library of Congress
UCSC	University of Connecticut Special Collections
VHS	Virginia Historical Society
YLS	Yale Law School

Introduction

1. Kent, *Commentaries on American Law,* 3:125n (italics in original). All citations are to the first edition of Kent's *Commentaries* unless otherwise indicated.

2. For more information on the development of law education in the colonial, Revolutionary, and early national periods, see Chroust, *The Rise of the Legal Profession in America.* See also Bryson, *Legal Education in Virginia;* Carrington, "The Revolutionary Idea of University Legal Education"; Reed, *Training for the Public Profession of the Law;* McKirdy, "The Lawyer as Apprentice."

3. Blackstone, *Commentaries on the Laws of England.* For a discussion of Blackstone's importance to English and Anglo-American law, see Boorstin, *The Mysterious Science of the Law;* Lieberman, *The Province of Legislation Determined;* Kennedy, "The Structure of Blackstone's Commentaries"; Lockmiller, *Sir William Blackstone;* Warden, *The Life of Blackstone;* Doolittle, "Sir William Blackstone and His *Commentaries on the Laws of England*"; and Watson, "The Structure of Blackstone's Commentaries."

4. "Of the Study of the Law," in *The Works of James Wilson,* 80; Hugh Blair Grigsby Diary, October 6, 1828, Grigsby Papers, VHS; Hoffman, *A Lecture Introductory to a Course of Lectures,* 27.

5. Kent to Thomas Washington, October 6, 1828, James Kent Papers, LOC.

6. James Iredell to Francis Iredell Sr., July 31, 1771, *The Papers of James Iredell,* 1:74.

7. For more on Tucker's life and career, see Hamilton, *The Making and Unmaking of a*

Revolutionary Family; and Cullen, *St. George Tucker and the Discipline of Law in Jeffersonian Virginia.*

8. St. George Tucker, *Blackstone's Commentaries.*

9. Conrad, "Metaphor and Imagination in James Wilson's Theory of the Federal Union"; Kermit L. Hall, *The Oxford Companion to the Supreme Court of the United States,* 932–33; McCloskey, Introduction to Wilson, in *The Works of James Wilson,* 59–65.

10. Tapping Reeve, *The Law of Baron and Femme;* Reeve, *A Treatise on the Law of Descents in the Several States of America.* Little has been written about Reeve, his protégé and partner James Gould, or the Litchfield Law School. The most comprehensive work is McKenna, *Tapping Reeve and the Litchfield Law School.* See also Fisher, "The Litchfield Law School"; Goetsch, "The Litchfield Law School"; Herbert S. Jones, "America's First Law School," 2–7.

11. Swift, *A System of the Laws of the State of Connecticut;* Henry St. George Tucker, *Commentaries on the Laws of Virginia.*

12. Brackenridge, *Law Miscellanies;* Brackenridge, *Considerations on the Jurisprudence of the State of Pennsylvania;* DuPonceau, *A Discourse on the Early History of Pennsylvania;* DuPonceau, *A Dissertation on the Nature and Extent of the Jurisdiction of the Courts of the United States.*

13. Chipman, *Sketches of the Principles of Government;* Chipman, *Reports and Dissertations in Two Parts.*

14. Grimké, *The Duties of Executors and Administrators;* Grimké, *The Public Laws of the State of South Carolina.*

15. Sullivan, *History of Land Titles in Massachusetts.*

16. Hoffman, *A Course of Legal Study;* Hoffman, *A Lecture Introductory to a Course of Lectures;* Hoffman, *An Address to Students of Law;* Hoffman, *A Syllabus of a Course of Lectures on Law;* Hoffman, *A Lecture Being the Second of a Series.*

17. The only full-length biography of Kent is Horton, *James Kent.* Perry Miller pays considerable attention to Kent in his *The Life of the Mind in America,* especially 105–55. More recent work on Kent includes Raack, "'To Preserve the Best Fruits'"; and Stychin, "The Commentaries of Chancellor James Kent."

18. St. George Tucker refers to his correspondence with Jeremy Belknap and Zephaniah Swift in "On the State of Slavery in Virginia" (see St. George Tucker, *Blackstone's Commentaries,* 2:A54). Tucker's five-volume edition entitled *Blackstone's Commentaries* reproduces Blackstone's original *Commentaries* in the main text and includes Tucker's "notes" on Blackstone in the extensive appendixes, which are designated using letters, as in "Note A," "Note B," etc. The appendixes are through-numbered, beginning with page 1. In order to distinguish page numbers in the main text from those in Tucker's appendixes, here and elsewhere I have used the prefix "A," to indicate that the page cited is an appendix page number.

19. *Davis's Executors v. Fulton et. als.,* 2 Tenn. 111 (1805). In his remarks, the judge noted that many nonresidents of Tennessee owned property in the state. He commented, "It is probably the case in every state, in some degree," and he cited Swift's *A System of the Laws of the State of Connecticut* (no page number) to support this speculation.

20. See, e.g., *Glasgow's Lessee v. Smith and Blackwell,* 2 Tenn. 144 (1805); *Noland v.*

Cromwell, 4 Munford (Va.) 161 (1814). Tucker's discussion of Virginia's colonial laws governing Indian slavery were cited in cases such as *Hudgins v. Wright*, 1 Hening & Munford (Va.) 134 (1806); *Butt v. Rachel and others*, 4 Munford (Va.) 213 (1813); and a Missouri case that eventually rose to the U.S. Supreme Court, *Marguerite v. Choteau*. 37 U.S. 507 (1825).

21. Citations to Kent's *Commentaries on American Law* are numerous. A sampling of U.S. Supreme Court cases in which Kent's treatise is cited as authority includes *Ogden v. Saunders*, 37 U.S. (1828); *The American Insurance Company and the Ocean Insurance Company (of New York) v. 356 Bales of Cotton, David Canter*, 26 U.S. 511 (1828); *William Robinson, Jr. v. William Noble's Administrators*, 33 U.S. 88 (1834); and *Henry Wheaton and Robert Donaldson v. Richard Peters and John Grigg*, 33 U.S. 591 (1834).

22. Kent, *An Introductory Lecture to a Course of Law Lectures*, 3–6. See also Blackstone, *Commentaries on the Laws of England*, 1:4–5.

23. St. George Tucker, *Blackstone's Commentaries*, 1:xvii.

24. Grimké, *The Duty of Executors and Administrators*, iii.

25. Swift, *An Oration on Domestic Slavery;* Brackenridge, *Narratives of a Late Expedition against the Indians;* Brackenridge, "Thoughts on the Present Indian War."

26. For works on the transmission of English law to its colonies, see Brown, *British Statutes in American Law*, especially 1–22; Greene, *Negotiated Authorities*, especially chaps. 1–3, 8; and Katz, "The Problem of a Colonial Legal History."

27. Two important books on law and American transformations are Horwitz, *The Transformation of American Law;* and Nelson, *Americanization of the Common Law*. For recent works on colonial law and regionalism, see Bilder, *The Transatlantic Constitution;* Billings, *A Little Parliament;* Fernandez, *From Chaos to Continuity;* Greene, "Colonial History and National History"; Greene, "Elaborations"; Hulsebosch, *Constituting Empire;* Konig, "Regionalism in Early American Law"; F. Thornton Miller, *Juries and Judges versus the Law;* and Roeber, *Faithful Magistrates and Republican Lawyers*.

28. "Of the Study of the Law," in *The Works of James Wilson*, 76–77.

1. America's Common Law

1. Some of the best work on colonial and Revolutionary-era legal culture includes Brown, *British Statutes in American Law*, especially 1–22; Pole, "Reflections on American Law and the American Revolution"; Greene, *Negotiated Authorities*, especially chaps. 1–3 and 8; and Katz, "The Problem of a Colonial Legal History."

2. For more on personal and national honor in the early republic, see Freeman, *Affairs of Honor*.

3. For the best and most thorough interpretations of Americans' unfavorable self-comparisons with England and the "culture of emulation" those feelings cultivated, see Bushman, *The Refinement of America*, especially 181–203, 402–47; and Greene, "Search for Identity."

4. On the constitutional development of Anglo-America and appropriation of English laws from the late seventeenth century through the promulgation of the U.S. Constitution, see Greene, *Peripheries and Center*. John Philip Reid has also written extensively on this subject; see his *In Defiance of the Law*.

5. "Of the Study of the Law," in *The Works of James Wilson*, 79–80.

6. Lieberman, *The Province of Legislation Determined,* 88–121.

7. Perry Miller, *The Life of the Mind in America,* especially 156–204, 239–68.

8. See, e.g., the Litchfield Law School student notebooks of Asa Bacon (1794), 6; Daniel Sheldon Jr. (1798), 5; Aaron Burr Reeve (1802–3), 1:11; and Ely Warner (1808–9), 1:10, all at the LHS. See also unknown author, Litchfield Law School student notebook (1813), 1:8–17, YLS.

9. Jefferson, "Autobiography," 1:50.

10. Ibid., 1:48–63.

11. For recent scholarly debates on the evolution of American law, see Brewer, "Entailing Aristocracy in Colonial Virginia"; Bruce H. Mann, "Legal Reform and the Revolution"; and Mann, "The Evolutionary Revolution in American Law."

12. Blackstone, *Commentaries on the Laws of England,* 1:63–64.

13. Ibid., 1:85–86.

14. "Letter to the Speaker," in *The Works of James Wilson,* 60–61. See also Brackenridge, *Law Miscellanies,* 70.

15. Ely Warner, Litchfield Law School student notebook (1808–9), 1:21, LHS.

16. Charles James Faulkner, "Winchester Law School Notes," Faulkner Law Practice/Winchester Law School Materials, 1825–26, Faulkner Family Papers, VHS.

17. For the strength of English reliance on custom and its importance in governing themselves and one another, see such works as Pocock, *Ancient Constitution;* and Thompson, *Customs in Common.* There are numerous works that document the translation of these values to Anglo-America. Among the most prominent are Greene, *Pursuits of Happiness;* Horn, *Adapting to a New World;* Allen, *In English Ways;* and Billings, "The Transfer of English Law to Virginia." J. R. Pole gives an admirably succinct assessment of the relationship between community custom and the common law in "Reflections on American Law and the American Revolution," 142.

18. DuPonceau, *A Dissertation on the Nature and Extent of the Jurisdiction of the Courts of the United States,* 91.

19. "Comparison of the Constitution of the United States, With That of Great Britain," 311; "Of the Common Law," *The Works of James Wilson,* 335.

20. St. George Tucker, *Blackstone's Commentaries,* 1:iv. For more on St. George Tucker's attitudes toward the maturation of American law, see Hamilton, *The Making and Unmaking of a Revolutionary Family,* 89–90.

21. Hoffman, *A Lecture Introductory to a Course of Lectures,* 27.

22. Blackstone, *Commentaries on the Laws of England,* 1:76–79. American legists closely followed Blackstone's criteria for valid custom in their lectures and writings. See, e.g., St. George Tucker, *Blackstone's Commentaries,* 1:A74–79; James D. Riddle, Litchfield Law School student notebook (1815), VHS; and the Litchfield Law School student notebooks of Asa Bacon (1794), 1; Daniel Sheldon Jr. (1798), 2; and Aaron Burr Reeve (1802–3), 1:5, all at the LHS.

23. St. George Tucker, *Blackstone's Commentaries,* 1:76n, 3:A30. Tucker's definition of custom was taken from Blackstone, *Commentaries on the Laws of England,* 1:74–79.

24. Ely Warner, Litchfield Law School student notebook (1808–9), 1:9, LHS (my italics).

25. Quotations are taken from Asa Bacon, Litchfield Law School student notebook (1794), 3, LHS. Every Litchfield notebook I examined had nearly identical passages with regard to the argument about common law extending from the time of Richard I.

26. Origen Storrs Seymour, Litchfield Law School student notebook (1824–25), 1:4, UCSC (italics in original).

27. This argument is first found in Aaron Burr Reeve, Litchfield Law School student notebook (1802–3), 1:22, LHS. This argument is also found in all subsequent notebooks examined, through George Flagg Mann's Litchfield notebook of 1825–26.

28. William Stith, *The History of the First Discovery and Settlement of Virginia: Being an Essay Towards a General History of this Colony* (Williamsburg, Va., 1747), 4, 8, quoted in St. George Tucker, *Blackstone's Commentaries,* 1:A383–84.

29. St. George Tucker, *Blackstone's Commentaries,* 1:A383–84.

30. Blackstone, *Commentaries on the Laws of England* (7th ed., 1775), 1:106. See also *Calvin v. Smith,* also known as *Calvin's Case,* 7 Rep. 17 (1608). James Wilson refers to this edition of Blackstone's *Commentaries* in "Of Legislative Authority," in *The Works of James Wilson,* 739–40.

31. For a discussion of New Yorkers' reactions to *Calvin's Case,* see Hulsebosch, *Constituting Empire,* 24–28.

32. St. George Tucker, *Blackstone's Commentaries,* 1:A382.

33. "Of Legislative Authority," in *The Works of James Wilson,* 739–40.

34. Black, "The Constitution of Empire," 1199–1200. In this article, Black offers an innovative analysis of *Calvin's Case* and its importance to legal arguments about the Revolution. For colonial and Revolutionary-era debates over the question of whether America was a conquered territory, see Greene, *Peripheries and Center,* 24–28; and Reid, *In Defiance of the Law,* 79–80.

35. Blackstone, *Commentaries on the Laws of England,* 1:44–46.

36. Swift, *A System of the Laws of the State of Connecticut,* 1:37.

37. St. George Tucker, lecture notebook, vol. [3], appendix note G, p. 28, Tucker-Coleman Papers, EGS. (N.b.: St. George Tucker based his lectures on Sir William Blackstone's *Commentaries on the Laws of England.* In his lecture notebooks, Tucker interleaved his own comments with Blackstone's text. He also added appendixes, which he called "Notes," to the back of each lecture volume, designating each note by letter—e.g., "Note A," "Note B," etc.—and numbering each note's pages separately, beginning with page 1. Tucker assigned numbers to ten of his notebook volumes, but an additional nine notebooks were unnumbered. The Special Collections Department at the Earl G. Swem Library has assigned catalog numbers to the unnumbered volumes. I use brackets to indicate that a particular notebook's volume number was assigned by EGS; volume numbers without brackets are the ones Tucker himself assigned.) This passage was taken, verbatim, from "Query 13: Constitutions," in Thomas Jefferson's *Notes on the State of Virginia.* Jefferson borrowed the passage from Richard Bland's writings (see Gutzman, "Jefferson's Draft Declaration of Independence, Richard Bland, and the Revolutionary Legacy").

38. Blackstone, *Commentaries on the Laws of England,* 1:74.

39. St. George Tucker, lecture notebook, vol. [3], appendix note G, p. 25, Tucker-Coleman Papers, EGS.

40. "Of Municipal," and "On Law and Obligation," in *The Works of James Wilson,* 182, 102.

41. Ely Warner, Litchfield Law School student notebook (1808–9), 1:2, LHS. See also Aaron Burr Reeve, Litchfield Law School student notebook (1802–3), 1:5, LHS.

42. Brackenridge, *Law Miscellanies,* 32, 40–43 (italics in original).

43. Swift, *A System of the Laws of the State of Connecticut,* 1:42.

44. Seth Staples, Litchfield Law School student notebook (1798), 5, LHS.

45. Asa Bacon, Litchfield Law School student notebook (1794), 6, LHS. See also the Litchfield notebooks of Daniel Sheldon Jr. (1798), 5; Aaron Burr Reeve (1802–3), 1:13; Ely Warner (1808–9), 1:11, all at the LHS; and Origen Storrs Seymour (1824–25), 1:12, UCSC.

46. "Of the Common Law," in *The Works of James Wilson,* 356.

47. Ibid., 362.

48. DuPonceau, *A Dissertation on the Nature and Extent of the Jurisdiction of the Courts of the United States,* xvii (italics in original).

49. James Wilson's charge to the grand jury, trial of John Singleterry and Gideon Henfield, July 22, 1793, as quoted in ibid., xvii.

50. Hoffman, *A Lecture Introductory to a Course of Lectures,* 33 (italics in original).

51. "Of the Common Law," in *The Works of James Wilson,* 345, 348.

52. For more on the debates over federal common-law jurisdiction, see Cornell and Leonard, "The Consolidation of the Early Federal System," 520–21, 545–52; and Jay, "Origins of Federal Common Law," pts. 1 and 2. See also Preyer, "Jurisdiction to Punish."

53. St. George Tucker, *Blackstone's Commentaries,* 1:A394–401.

54. Ibid., 1:A406–7.

55. Ibid., 1:A411–12.

56. "Of the Common Law," in *The Works of James Wilson,* 1:348.

57. "Of the Study of Law," ibid., 1:77.

58. DuPonceau, *A Dissertation on the Nature and Extent of the Jurisdiction of the Courts of the United States,* x.

2. American Constitutions and American Character

1. Blackstone, *Commentaries on the Laws of England,* 1:123.

2. Among the most important works on these ideas are Bailyn, *Ideological Origins of the American Revolution;* and Wood, *The Creation of the American Republic.*

3. St. George Tucker, *Blackstone's Commentaries,* 1:A1.

4. Ibid., 1:A20–21; St. George Tucker, lecture notebook, vol. [3], p. 40–42, Tucker-Coleman Papers, EGS. Here, Tucker seems to be drawing his ideas about the importance of a written constitution from a number of sources, including Thomas Paine's *Common Sense* and *Rights of Man,* and political pamphleteers who wrote such works as *Four Letters on Interesting Subjects* (Philadelphia, 1776), as well as Charles Inglis's *The True Interest of America Impartially Stated* (Philadelphia, 1776). See also Bailyn, *Ideological Origins of the American Revolution,* 182–83; and Wood, *The Creation of the American Republic,* 259–68.

5. St. George Tucker, *Blackstone's Commentaries,* 1:79.

6. Chipman, *Sketches of the Principles of Government,* 242.

7. "Of the Legislative Department," in *The Works of James Wilson*, 406–8; and "Of Legislative Authority," ibid., 725.

8. Blackstone, *Commentaries on the Laws of England*, 1:165.

9. Chipman, *Sketches of the Principles of Government*, 242.

10. "Of the Legislative Department," in *The Works of James Wilson*, 407.

11. Ibid., 407–8.

12. St. George Tucker, *Blackstone's Commentaries*, 1:A210.

13. Brackenridge, *Law Miscellanies*, 110.

14. Ibid., 99–101.

15. Chipman, *Sketches of the Principles of Government*, 146.

16. For an examination of early national convictions about the importance of a well-informed citizenry to the survival of republican government, see Brown, *The Strength of a People*, 65–118.

17. Blackstone, *Commentaries on the Laws of England*, 1:178.

18. St. George Tucker, *Blackstone's Commentaries*, 1:A45–46.

19. St. George Tucker, lecture notebook, vol. 1, p. 23, Tucker-Coleman Papers, EGS.

20. Blackstone, *Commentaries on the Laws of England*, 1:172, quoted in "Comparison of the Constitution of the United States, With That of Great Britain," in *The Works of James Wilson*, 311, 313.

21. "Of Citizens and Aliens," in *The Works of James Wilson*, 2:576.

22. St. George Tucker, *Blackstone's Commentaries*, 1:A212–13.

23. Brackenridge, *Law Miscellanies*, 110.

24. "Of the Legislative Department," in *The Works of James Wilson*, 412.

25. St. George Tucker, *Blackstone's Commentaries*, 1:A193, quoted in Brackenridge, *Law Miscellanies*, 96 (Brackenridge's italics).

26. Brackenridge, *Law Miscellanies*, 96–99 (italics in original).

27. Ibid., 102 (italics in original). For Brackenridge's debate with his constituency over the nature of representation and his behavior in the Pennsylvania legislature, see Marder, *Hugh Henry Brackenridge*, 178–81.

28. Swift, *A System of the Laws of the State of Connecticut*, 1:35.

29. Blackstone, *Commentaries on the Laws of England*, 1:47–49, 91.

30. For more on the views regarding parliamentary sovereignty, see Grey, "Origins of the Unwritten Constitution."

31. St. George Tucker, *Blackstone's Commentaries*, 1:52n.

32. Ibid., 1:48–49n.

33. "Comparison of the Constitution of the United States, With That of Great Britain," in *The Works of James Wilson*, 309.

34. "Of Municipal Law," ibid., 177–78 (italics in original quotation); Jezierski, "Parliament or People," 102.

35. St. George Tucker, *Blackstone's Commentaries*, 1:A207.

36. Ibid., 1:A128.

37. St. George Tucker, lecture notebook, vol. 4, p. 157, Tucker-Coleman Papers, EGS. For a similar but shorter discussion of dual state and federal legislative jurisdiction, see Swift, *A System of the Laws of the State of Connecticut*, 1:21.

38. "Of Municipal Law," in *The Works of James Wilson,* 86.

39. St. George Tucker, lecture notebook, vol. 3, p. 83, Tucker-Coleman Papers, EGS. For more about American frustration with English taxation policies, see Bailyn, *Ideological Origins of the American Revolution;* Greene, "Political Mimesis"; and Christie and Labaree, *Empire or Independence.*

40. "Of the Legislative Department," in *The Works of James Wilson,* 419.

41. Paine, *Rights of Man,* pt. 1, 56, quoted in St. George Tucker, *Blackstone's Commentaries,* 2:A227. (Bracketed reference is Tucker's).

42. St. George Tucker, *Blackstone's Commentaries,* 1:A215.

43. Swift, *A System of the Laws of the State of Connecticut,* 1:29. Here he cites Adams, *A Defense of the Constitutions of Government of the United States.*

44. "Of the Legislative Department," in *The Works of James Wilson,* 414–15.

45. Blackstone, *Commentaries on the Laws of England,* 1:183.

46. St. George Tucker, *Blackstone's Commentaries,* 2:245n.

47. Ibid., 1:A348.

48. Blackstone, *Commentaries on the Laws of England,* 1:236–37.

49. St. George Tucker, *Blackstone's Commentaries,* 1:A316–17.

50. Blackstone, *Commentaries on the Laws of England,* 1:183–89.

51. St. George Tucker, *Blackstone's Commentaries,* 1:A316–17, 2:A192–93 St. George Tucker, lecture notebook, vol. [4], pp. 161–63, Tucker-Coleman Papers, EGS.

52. St. George Tucker, *Blackstone's Commentaries,* 1:A319.

53. Ibid., 2:A123.

54. "Comparison of the Constitution of the United States, With That of Great Britain," in *The Works of James Wilson,* 317.

55. St. George Tucker, *Blackstone's Commentaries,* 2:A238.

56. Blackstone, *Commentaries on the Laws of England,* 1:183, 236.

57. St. George Tucker, *Blackstone's Commentaries,* 2:A241.

58. Ibid., 2:281n, 283n, 286n, 289–90n, 291–94n.

59. Blackstone, *Commentaries on the Laws of England,* 1:271.

60. St. George Tucker, *Blackstone's Commentaries,* 2:335n.

61. "Of the Legislative Department," in *The Works of James Wilson,* 433–34. On the president's position as commander-in-chief and Congress's ability to declare war, see also Tucker, *Blackstone's Commentaries,* 2:A261–63.

62. St. George Tucker, *Blackstone's Commentaries,* 1:A324–25.

63. Ibid., 1:A225.

64. Kent, *Commentaries on American Law,* 1:240.

65. St. George Tucker, *Blackstone's Commentaries,* 1:356–57.

66. Blackstone, *Commentaries on the Laws of England,* 1:257 (italics in original).

67. Ibid., 1:260.

68. Blackstone uses the Latin term for "during good pleasure," *durante bene placito* (see Henry Campbell Black, *Black's Law Dictionary,* 503).

69. Blackstone uses the Latin term for "during good behavior," *quamdiu se bene gesserit* (see ibid., 1241).

70. Blackstone, *Commentaries on the Laws of England,* 1:257–58.

71. Ibid., 1:259–60.

72. For details on the colonies' fights for an independent judiciary, see Bailyn, *Ideological Origins of the American Revolution,* 105–8; Milton M. Klein, "Prelude to Revolution in New York," 452; Roeber, *Faithful Magistrates and Republican Lawyers,* 62–63; and Wood, *The Creation of the American Republic,* 160–61.

73. St. George Tucker, lecture notebook, vol. [5], pp. 201–2, Tucker-Coleman Papers, EGS.

74. Kent, *An Introductory Lecture to a Course of Law Lectures,* 12–13; Lutz, *The Origins of American Constitutionalism,* 108–9, 157; Lutz, *Popular Consent and Popular Control;* Wood, *The Creation of the American Republic,* 408, 452.

75. St. George Tucker, *Blackstone's Commentaries,* 1:A356–57.

76. Ibid., 1:A353–54 (Blackstone's italics).

77. Wood, *The Creation of the American Republic,* 151–53; Adams, *The First American Constitutions.*

78. Grimké, "Charge to Camden District," *South Carolina State Gazette,* December 27 and 30, 1790.

79. Tucker to John Coalter, November 22, 1811, Grinnan Family Papers, VHS; copy of Tucker's letter of resignation from the Bench to James Monroe, Governor of Virginia, April 2, 1811, in St. George Tucker, case notebook, vol. 3, no. 33, p. 762, Tucker-Coleman Papers, EGS. For more details on Tucker's career on the Virginia Superior Court and his complaints about financial compensation for the work, see Hamilton, *The Making and Unmaking of a Revolutionary Family.*

80. St. George Tucker, *Blackstone's Commentaries,* 1:A356. For another discussion of the advantages of an independent judiciary, see "Comparison of the Constitution of the United States, With That of Great Britain," in *The Works of James Wilson,* 331.

81. Chipman, *Sketches of the Principles of Government,* 160–62.

82. Blackstone's general descriptions and histories of England's courts are found in *Commentaries on the Laws of England,* 3:30–85.

83. St. George Tucker, *Blackstone's Commentaries,* 4:83. Blackstone's section on special jurisdiction courts is in his *Commentaries on the Laws of England,* 3:71–85.

84. For more details on the structure of each state's court systems, see, for Virginia, St. George Tucker, *Blackstone's Commentaries,* 4:A3–23; for Connecticut, Swift, *A System of the Laws of the State of Connecticut,* 1:93–110; and for Pennsylvania, "Of the Judicial Department," in *The Works of James Wilson,* 446–93; and Brackenridge, *Law Miscellanies,* 162–71.

85. Brackenridge, *Law Miscellanies,* 163–64, 166.

86. Grimké, "Charge to Camden District."

87. Ibid. South Carolina citizens were particularly sensitive to the issue of judicial inaccessibility in frontier areas. This issue had been a point of contention in the Regulator movements in the years prior to the Revolution (see Brown, *The South Carolina Regulators;* and Klein, *Unification of a Slave State.*

88. St. George Tucker, *Blackstone's Commentaries,* 4:17.

89. For a description of the House of Lords' duties as an appellate court, see Blackstone, *Commentaries on the Laws of England,* 3:56–57.

90. Unknown author, Litchfield Law School student notebook (1794), 38, LHS; George Flagg Mann, Litchfield Law School student notebook (1826–27), 2:126, UCSC.

91. Swift, *A System of the Laws of the State of Connecticut,* 1:93–94.

92. George Flagg Mann, Litchfield Law School student notebook (1826–27), 2:126, UCSC.

93. Blackstone, *Commentaries on the Laws of England*, 3:46–49.

94. Ibid., 3:46–49.

95. Ibid., 3:49–55.

96. Hoffman, *A Course of Legal Study*, 205–6.

97. St. George Tucker, *Blackstone's Commentaries*, 4:A18–19; Kent, *Commentaries on American Law*, 4:163.

98. Brackenridge, *Law Miscellanies*, 166 (italics in original).

99. "Of the Judicial Department," in *The Works of James Wilson*, 2:478. Wilson extracted Aristotle's quote from Hugo Grotius, *On the Law of War and Peace*, 366.

100. "Of the Judicial Department," in *The Works of James Wilson*, 2:478.

101. Ibid., 2:483–84.

102. Kent, *Commentaries on American Law*, 2:163.

103. Story, *Commentaries on Equity Jurisprudence*. Peter Hoffer argues that the concept of equity was absorbed into the fundamental law of the Constitution, calling the American version of this absorption "a confederation of trusteeship republics." This is probably partially true, in that the written constitutions became protectors of citizens' rights. But this is not where men like Brackenridge and Wilson saw the softening influence of equity going (see Hoffer, *The Law's Conscience*, 23, passim).

104. Two recent interpretations of the role of precedent in early national and nineteenth-century law are Karsten, *Heart versus Head;* and Klafter, *Reason over Precedents*.

105. Blackstone, *Commentaries on the Laws of England*, 1:69.

106. Ibid., 1:70.

107. "Of the Judges," in *The Works of James Wilson*, 2:500–502.

108. Asa Bacon, Litchfield Law School student notebook (1794), 1, 3, LHS.

109. Daniel Sheldon Jr., Litchfield Law School student notebook (1798), 430, LHS (italics in original).

110. Swift, *A System of the Laws of the State of Connecticut*, 1:43–44.

111. Ibid., 1:45–46.

112. DuPonceau, *A Dissertation on the Nature and Extent of the Jurisdiction of the Courts of the United States*, xxii, 124.

113. Sullivan, *History of Land Titles in Massachusetts*, 337.

114. Ibid., xxii.

115. Chipman, *Reports and Dissertations, in Two Parts*, 123–25.

116. "Of the Judges," in *The Works of James Wilson*, 501–2.

117. Brackenridge, *Law Miscellanies*, 467–69.

118. Ibid., 52.

119. Blackstone, *Commentaries on the Laws of England*, 3:410.

120. Daniel Sheldon Jr., Litchfield Law School student notebook (1798), 3, LHS. He cites Blackstone, *Commentaries on the Laws of England*, 1:69–71.

121. Daniel Sheldon Jr., Litchfield Law School student notebook (1798), 3, LHS.

122. Seth Staples, Litchfield Law School student notebook (1798), 2, LHS. For similar observations from Litchfield students, see the Litchfield Law School student notebooks

for Aaron Burr Reeve (1802–3), 1:3, LHS; unknown author (1794), 3–4, LHS; and George Flagg Mann (1826–27), 1:6, UCSC (Mann cites Blackstone, *Commentaries on the Laws of England*, 1:63, 70, 71).

123. St. George Tucker, *Blackstone's Commentaries*, 1:5, 4:A4.

124. Blackstone, *Commentaries on the Laws of England*, 4:342.

125. Ibid., 3:349–51.

126. Baker, "Criminal Courts and Procedure," 269; Ferguson, *Law and Letters in American Culture*, 8, 69; Pole, "Reflections on American Law and the American Revolution," 129; Roeber, *Faithful Magistrates and Republican Lawyers*, 73–111; Stimson, *The American Revolution in the Law*, 60–66.

127. On the representative nature of juries, see Amar, *The Bill of Rights*, 81–118; and Pole, "Reflections on American Law and the American Revolution," 123–59.

128. St. George Tucker, *Blackstone's Commentaries*, 4:349–50, 5:348n.

129. "Comparison of the Constitution of the United States, With That of Great Britain," in *The Works of James Wilson*, 332.

130. "Of Juries," ibid., 541.

131. Chipman, *Sketches of the Principles of Government*, 164–65.

132. Grimké, *Charges by Hon. Judge Grimké at the Courts of General Sessions of the Peace for Districts of Cheraw and Camden.*

133. Chipman, *Sketches of the Principles of Government*, 164, 166–67.

134. Ibid., 166.

135. "Of Juries," in *The Works of James Wilson*, 547–48.

136. Grimké, "Charge to Camden," *South Carolina State Gazette*, December 30, 1790.

137. St. George Tucker, *Blackstone's Commentaries*, 4:A65. For more details on Tucker's beliefs regarding the capacity of "the masses" to govern and participate in the judicial system, see Hamilton, "The Tucker Family and the Dynamics of Generational Change in Jeffersonian Virginia," 381, passim.

138. Blackstone, *Commentaries on the Laws of England*, 4:277–78. For details on these kinds of trials—for example, trials by certificate, by record, by witness without the intervention of a jury (a rare occurrence in England), and others—see ibid., 3:325–48. For instances in which juries were not used for English criminal trials, see ibid., 4:277–85.

139. St. George Tucker, *Blackstone's Commentaries*, 4:A56–57.

140. Ibid., 4:347n (Tucker's italics).

141. "Of the Legislative Department," in *The Works of James Wilson*, 399 (italics in original).

3. Property Acquisition and Inheritance

1. "Comparison of the Constitution of the United States, With That of Great Britain," in *The Works of James Wilson*, 331.

2. Much work has been done on the evolution of property and inheritance laws in British colonial America. Examples of this scholarship include Crowley, "Family Relations and Inheritance in Early South Carolina"; Ditz, *Property and Kinship*; Greven, *Four Generations*; Mann, *Neighbors and Strangers*; Pole, "Property and Law in the American Republic"; and Salmon, *Women and the Law of Property in Early America*.

3. Blackstone, *Commentaries on the Laws of England,* 2:4–8.

4. "Collateral" referred to kin who were not lineally descended from the first owner and thus, in England, were not in the direct line of inheritance. For example, siblings and cousins are collateral relations (see *Black's Law Dictionary,* 262).

5. Aaron Burr Reeve, Litchfield Law School student notebook (1802–3), 2:4, LHS. See also the Litchfield Law School student notebooks of Ely Warner (1808–9), vol. 2, s.v. "Real Property—Reeve," LHS; and George Flagg Mann, vol. 5, s.v. "Real Property," UCSC. The Mann notes are from lectures given by James Gould, but the content is almost identical to Reeve's lectures of two decades earlier. Reeve took his lectures on property theory from Blackstone, *Commentaries on the Laws of England,* 2:1–19, 44–58. The term "blood of the first purchaser" is defined as "one who is directly descended from the person who first claimed the land as his own" (*Black's Law Dictionary,* 172).

6. "On the History of Property," in *The Works of James Wilson,* 2:718.

7. Kent, *Commentaries on American Law,* 2:328–29n. Wilson and Kent cited Stith's *History of Virginia;* Morton's *New-England Memorial,* 93; and Baylie's *Historical Memoir,* 1:120, 158. For an analysis of the role that private property ownership plays in American constitutional thought, see Nedelsky, *Private Property and the Limits of American Constitutionalism.*

8. "On the History of Property," in *The Works of James Wilson,* 2:719.

9. Kent, *Commentaries on American Law,* 2:319.

10. Ibid., 2:319–20, 328–29n.

11. Blackstone, *Commentaries on the Laws of England,* 2:2. See Kent, *Commentaries on American Law,* 2:341–54, for an almost identical description of the kinds of personal property.

12. Blackstone, *Commentaries on the Laws of England,* 2:16–18.

13. St. George Tucker, *Blackstone's Commentaries,* 3:35n.

14. Ibid., 3:36n; Kent, *Commentaries on American Law,* 3:402.

15. Blackstone, *Commentaries on the Laws of England,* 2:105, 112–19.

16. Henry St. George Tucker, *Notes on Blackstone's Commentaries, for the Use of Students,* bk. 2, 246.

17. Sullivan, *History of Land Titles in Massachusetts,* 42.

18. Kent, *Commentaries on American Law,* 3:501. He cites Blackstone, *Commentaries on the Laws of England,* 2:50, along with *Wright on Tenures.*

19. Kent, *Commentaries on American Law,* 4:3–4. He refers to Blackstone, *Commentaries on the Laws of England,* 2:259. Kent wrote a chapter on the history of the law of tenure, with particular emphasis on tenure in England and its transfer to America, at least in the language of the law. He then concluded that in America the terms "fee simple" and "allodium" were interchangeable (Kent, *Commentaries on American Law,* 3:487–515, 4:2).

20. Daniel Sheldon Jr., Litchfield Law School student notebook (1798), s.v. "Property," LHS (italics in original).

21. Chipman, *Reports and Dissertations, in Two Parts,* 125–26.

22. St. George Tucker, *Blackstone's Commentaries,* 3:A104–5.

23. Swift, *A System of the Laws of the State of Connecticut,* 1:239.

24. Blackstone, *Commentaries on the Laws of England,* 2:241–42.

25. Ibid., 2:244–57.

26. Ibid., 2:258–62.

27. Ibid., 2:263–66.

28. Ibid., 2:267–86.

29. Ibid., 2:287.

30. Timothy Follett, Litchfield Law School student notebook (1812–13), vol. 5, s.v. "Things Real," YLS.

31. Blackstone, *Commentaries on the Laws of England*, 2:244–49, quote on 246.

32. Ibid., 2:257.

33. St. George Tucker, *Blackstone's Commentaries*, 3:254n.

34. Timothy Follett, Litchfield Law School student notebook (1812–13), vol. 5, s.v. "Things Real," YLS, in which he cites Connecticut Statute C.434.Ib.8.

35. Kent, *Commentaries on American Law*, 2:385–87. See also Reeve, *The Law of Baron and Femme*, 52.

36. Here Kent also refers to the practices of the ancient Germans, and he cites Tacitus (Kent, *Commentaries on American Law*, 4:424–25).

37. The term "ultimate haeres" means the ultimate, or most remote, heir (*Black's Law Dictionary*, 1522). See also St. George Tucker, *Blackstone's Commentaries*, 1:299–300n. St. George Tucker's son, Henry St. George Tucker, made the identical point in his *Notes on Blackstone's Commentaries, for the Use of Students*, bk. 2, 246.

38. St. George Tucker, *Blackstone's Commentaries*, 1:299–300n, 303n; see also ibid., 3:276n. There is a similar notation about the abolition of the "practice of the common law . . . not in force in this country," of forfeiting goods and chattels when convicted of a felony, in Charles James Faulkner, "Winchester Law School Notes," Faulkner Law Practice/Winchester Law School Materials, 1825–26, Faulkner Family Papers, VHS.

39. St. George Tucker, *Blackstone's Commentaries*, 3:A22. Tucker's discussion of Blackstone refers to Blackstone's *Commentaries on the Laws of England*, 2:208–12. The practice of lineal ascent in America is discussed later in this chapter.

40. Asa Bacon, Litchfield Law School student notebook (1794), 61, LHS.

41. Brackenridge, *Law Miscellanies*, 424–25. See also similar remarks in Kent, *Commentaries on American Law*, 2:287.

42. St. George Tucker, *Blackstone's Commentaries*, 4:A31–34.

43. Ibid., 3:A53–65.

44. Swift, *A System of the Laws of the State of Connecticut*, 1:340.

45. St. George Tucker, case notebook, vol. 1, no. 3, pp. 39–50, Tucker-Coleman Papers, EGS; *Hunter v. Fairfax District Court at Winchester, Va.* (1794); *Fairfax's Devisee v. Hunter's Lessee*, 11 U.S. 603 (1813); *Martin v. Hunter's Lessee*, 14 U.S. 304 (1816). These cases brought to the fore the issue of the Supreme Court's authority over decisions of state supreme courts under the Judiciary Act of 1789, among other things. For a more detailed explanation of these cases and their roles in the nationalist movement of the federal courts, see Miller, *Juries and Judges versus the Law*, 74–86.

46. Henry St. George Tucker, *Notes on Blackstone's Commentaries, for the Use of Students*, bk. 2, 248n.

47. Kent, *Commentaries on American Law*, 2:62 (italics in original). Brackenridge made similar comments about Pennsylvania laws regarding aliens and property ownership in *Law Miscellanies*, 424–25.

48. St. George Tucker, *Blackstone's Commentaries*, 3:A53–65.

49. Swift, *A System of the Laws of the State of Connecticut*, 1:332.

50. St. George Tucker, *Blackstone's Commentaries*, 3:280n.

51. *Black's Law Dictionary*, 1589–90.

52. St. George Tucker, *Blackstone's Commentaries*, 3:A3–10.

53. Ibid., 3:A3–10.

54. Ibid., 3:A66–72. For other explanations of modes of purchase, see unknown author, Litchfield Law School student notebook (1794), 139, VHS; Seth Staples, Litchfield Law School student notebook (1798), s.v. "Real Estate—Manner Acquired," LHS; and Daniel Sheldon Jr., Litchfield Law School student notebook (1798), s.v. "Of Devises," LHS.

55. Swift, *A System of the Laws of the State of Connecticut*, 1:298–99.

56. Kent, *Commentaries on American Law*, 4:446.

57. Blackstone, *Commentaries on the Laws of England*, 2:2.

58. St. George Tucker, *Blackstone's Commentaries*, 3:A28.

59. Ibid., 3:A19.

60. Katz, "Republicanism and the Law of Inheritance in the American Revolutionary Era." For a broader look at property theory and the Constitution in the early republic, see Nedelsky, *Private Property and the Limits of American Constitutionalism*.

61. Blackstone, *Commentaries on the Laws of England*, 2:2.

62. Ibid., 2:10–11.

63. Ibid., 2:11–12.

64. Kent, *Commentaries on American Law*, 2:326.

65. Ibid., 2:326.

66. Blackstone, *Commentaries on the Laws of England*, 2:241–42; Kent, *Commentaries on American Law*, 2:327, 4:501.

67. Kent, *Commentaries on American Law*, 4:503–4.

68. Blackstone, *Commentaries on the Laws of England*, 2:208–11.

69. Ibid., 2:208–11.

70. For more on colonial inheritance practices, see Brewer, *By Birth or Consent;* Haskins, "The Beginnings of Partible Inheritance in the American Colonies"; Walsh, "'Till Death Us Do Part'"; and Walsh and Menard, "Death in the Chesapeake."

71. Kent, *Commentaries on American Law*, 4:395. Kent called the admission of the father to the inheritance of his children dying intestate and without lineal descendants "a very great improvement . . . upon the English common law doctrine of descents." See also Brackenridge, *Law Miscellanies*, 138–39.

72. Swift, *A System of the Laws of the State of Connecticut*, 1:289.

73. St. George Tucker, *Blackstone's Commentaries*, 3:A28–39.

74. Tapping Reeve listed similar restrictions on the mother inheriting from a deceased minor child in New Jersey (Reeve, *A Treatise on the Law of Descents in the Several States of America*, 381).

75. Kent, *Commentaries on American Law*, 2:423.

76. Ibid., 4:398.

77. Blackstone, *Commentaries on the Laws of England*, 2:227, 231–32.

78. Kent, *Commentaries on American Law*, 4:403–4.

79. Reeve, *A Treatise on the Law of Descents in the Several States of America*, 364–74. See also Daniel Sheldon Jr., Litchfield Law School student notebook (1798), s.v. "Distribution

of Property of Deceased Intestate," LHS; and St. George Tucker, *Blackstone's Commentaries*, 2:A223. Tucker notes later laws in 1790 and 1792 that further defined inheritance and heirs of the half and whole blood (see St. George Tucker, case notebook, vol. 1, no. 5, p. 8, regarding *Marshall v. Marshall* [Accomack District Court, May 19, 1795]).

80. Blackstone, *Commentaries on the Laws of England*, 2:213–14, 216.

81. Ibid., 2:234–36.

82. Ibid., 2:215–16.

83. Philip Greven and others have shown that the first New England settlers preferred to distribute their property among all sons, and sometimes to their daughters as well. In the Southern colonies, primogeniture was more common, although not mandated by law (Greven, *Four Generations*, 130–31). There is some debate as to the prevalence of primogeniture and entail in some colonies, and the degree to which the Revolution affected change in that area of the law (see Brewer, "Entailing Aristocracy in Colonial Virginia"; Brewer, *By Birth or Consent*, 87–108, 245–47; Ditz, *Property and Kinship*, 46–81; Keim, "Primogeniture and Entail in Colonial Virginia"; Morris, "Primogeniture and Entailed Estates in America"; and Shammas, *A History of Household Government in America*, 56–60).

84. Kent, *Commentaries on American Law*, 4:376n (Kent quoted the *Massachusetts Historical Collections*, 5:178).

85. Sullivan, *History of Land Titles in Massachusetts*, 147.

86. Swift, *A System of the Laws of the State of Connecticut*, 1:282.

87. Sullivan, *History of Land Titles in Massachusetts*, 75, 149.

88. Swift, *A System of the Laws of the State of Connecticut*, 1:282.

89. Grimké, *The Duty of Executors and Administrators*, v.

90. St. George Tucker, *Blackstone's Commentaries*, 3:212n, 214n, 217n.

91. St. George Tucker, lecture notebook, vol. 2, p. 70, Tucker-Coleman Papers, EGS; Tucker, *Blackstone's Commentaries*, vol. 1, appendix pp. 222–25 (Blackstone's italics).

92. St. George Tucker, lecture notebook, vol. 2, p. 71 (Tucker's italics).

93. Brackenridge, *Law Miscellanies*, 123–24, 143–44.

94. Kent, *Commentaries on American Law*, 4:383–85.

95. Aaron Burr Reeve, Litchfield Law School student notebook (1802–3), vol. 2, s.v. "Real Property—Reeve," LHS.

96. Ditz, *Property and Kinship*, 61–81.

97. James Kent to Moss Kent Jr., March 5, 1792, Kent Family Papers, LOC.

98. St. George Tucker, *Blackstone's Commentaries*, 2:212n.

99. Kent, *Commentaries on American Law*, 2:520–26.

100. For two differing opinions on the validity of a woman's will made while *feme sole* after her husband's death, see Kent, *Commentaries on American Law*, 4:527; and George Flagg Mann, Litchfield Law School student notebook (1808–9), 1:41, UCSC.

101. Blackstone, *Commentaries on the Laws of England*, 2:115.

102. For English laws and attitudes toward property as a trust for subsequent generations, see Bonfield, "Marriage, Property, and the 'Affective Family,'"; Cooper, "Ideas of Gentility in Early-Modern England"; Cooper, "Patterns of Inheritance and Settlement by Great Landowners from the Fifteenth to the Seventeenth Centuries"; and Stone, *The Family, Sex, and Marriage in England*.

103. Aaron Burr Reeve, Litchfield Law School student notebook (1802–3), vol. 2, s.v.

"Real Property—Reeve," LHS. English owners of entailed estates had to petition Parliament for relief from the burden of their estates (Blackstone, *Commentaries on the Laws of England,* 2:116).

104. Swift, *A System of the Laws of the State of Connecticut,* 1:246.

105. Asa Bacon, Litchfield Law School student notebook (1794), pt. 3, 9–11, LHS; and Timothy Follett, Litchfield Law School student notebook (1812–13), vol. 5, s.v. "Things Real—Gould," YLS, in which Follett cites the *Statutes of Connecticut,* 43. For other references to the same Connecticut statutes relating to entail, see the Litchfield Law School student notebooks of Daniel Sheldon Jr. (1798), s.v. "Estates Tail," LHS; and George Flagg Mann (1826–27), 5:6, UCSC. Tapping Reeve also notes this law as being peculiar to Connecticut, in his *Treatise on the Law of Descents in the Several States of America,* 381.

106. Swift, *A System of the Laws of the State of Connecticut,* 1:247.

107. St. George Tucker, *Blackstone's Commentaries,* 3:112n, A11–12. For examples of the law of entail with regard to slaves and real property in Virginia, see also *Bates v. Fuquay,* April 13, 1787, in St. George Tucker, case notebook, vol. 1, no. 1, pp. 38–39, Tucker-Coleman Papers, EGS; and *Gleesons v. Scott & als.,* Court of Appeals, appeal from Accomack, March 15, 1809, in St. George Tucker, case notebook, vol. 3, no. 26, p. 741, ibid. For lingering problems that the courts experienced following the act of 1776 sorting out the different types of estates in post-Revolutionary Virginia, see Henry St. George Tucker, *Notes on Blackstone's Commentaries, for the Use of Students,* bk. 2, 175.

108. St. George Tucker, *Blackstone's Commentaries,* 3:A11–12.

109. Brackenridge, *Law Miscellanies,* 139–40.

110. Kent, *Commentaries on American Law,* 4:14–15.

111. Ibid., 4:19–20.

112. Ibid., 4:19–20.

113. Chipman, *Reports and Dissertations, in Two Parts,* 149.

114. Blackstone, *Commentaries on the Laws of England,* 1:430.

115. Some of the best recent scholarship on American women, property, and the law includes Dayton, *Women before the Bar;* Salmon, *Women and the Law of Property in Early America;* Shammas, *A History of Household Government in America;* and Speth, "More Than Her 'Thirds.'"

116. Chipman, *Reports and Dissertations, in Two Parts,* 149.

117. Shammas, *A History of Household Government in America,* 33.

118. Tapping Reeve, lecture notes, vol. 1, pp. 51, Litchfield Law School Papers, LHS.

119. Swift, *A System of the Laws of the State of Connecticut,* 1:194–95.

120. For examples of what Carole Shammas calls "parental dismay" that resulted in prenuptial contracts, see Shammas, *A History of Household Government in America,* 96–97.

121. Tapping Reeve, lecture notes, vol. 1, pp. 4–5, Litchfield Law School Papers, LHS.

122. Ibid., pp. 9–12. These relaxations in Connecticut law regarding the woman's right to hold separate property were first noted in Timothy Follett, Litchfield Law School student notebook (1812–13), vol. 1, s.v. "Husband and Wife," YLS.

123. Tapping Reeve, lecture notes, vol. 1, p. 56, Litchfield Law School Papers, LHS; Reeve, *The Law of Baron and Femme,* 60.

124. George Flagg Mann, Litchfield Law School student notebook (1826–27), 1:12. For

property reforms with regard to women and inheritance in a neighboring state, see Basch, *In the Eyes of the Law.*

125. Tapping Reeve, *The Law of Baron and Femme,* 140.

126. George Flagg Mann, Litchfield Law School student notebook (1826–27), 1:41.

127. Kent, *Commentaries on American Law,* 4:527–28. Although he does not cite any of those court cases to which he refers, Kent notes the Revised Statute as vol. II, 64, sec. 44.

128. In addition to Blackstone's *Commentaries on the Laws of England,* 2:129, Kent also cited the works of Brackton; Coke on Littleton; and Spelman, *Stuart's View of Society,* and *Observations upon the Ancient Statutes.*

129. Sullivan, *History of Land Titles in Massachusetts,* 182–83.

130. Kent, *Commentaries on American Law,* 4:35–36.

131. St. George Tucker, case notebook, vol. 2, no. 14, p. 187, Tucker-Coleman Papers, EGS; Tucker is paraphrasing Blackstone, *Commentaries on the Laws of England,* 2:493. Blackstone goes on to note that although this was the general practice, there were pockets of England, such as York, that still protected the wife from losing her dower. Custom, Blackstone noted, differed from locality to locality.

132. St. George Tucker, case notebook, vol. 2, no. 14, p. 188, Tucker-Coleman Papers, EGS.

133. St. George Tucker, *Blackstone's Commentaries,* 3:308n.

134. Ibid., 3:493n.

135. Brackenridge, *Law Miscellanies,* 128; Reeve, *The Law of Baron and Femme,* 47.

136. Origen Storrs Seymour, Litchfield Law School student notebook (1824–25), vol. 1, s.v. "Husband and wife," UCSC (italics in original).

137. Aaron Burr Reeve, Litchfield Law School student notebook (1802–3), vol. 2, s.v. "Real Property—Reeve," LHS. See also Daniel Sheldon Jr., Litchfield Law School student notebook (1798), s.v. "Life Estates" and "Husband and Wife," LHS; and Ely Warner, Litchfield Law School student notebook (1808–9), vol. 1, s.v. "Baron & Feme—Reeve," LHS.

138. Aaron Burr Reeve, Litchfield Law School student notebook (1802–3), vol. 2, s.v. "Real Property—Reeve," LHS. See also Reeve, *The Law of Baron and Femme,* 56.

139. Reeve, *The Law of Baron and Femme,* 41.

140. Sullivan, *History of Land Titles in Massachusetts,* 53.

141. St. George Tucker, *Blackstone's Commentaries,* 3:A19; Reeve, *A Treatise on the Law of Descents in the Several States of America,* i.

4. The Question of Slavery in the New Republic

1. Swift, *An Oration on Domestic Slavery,* 1.

2. Some of the best works on the question of slavery during the Revolution include Davis, *The Problem of Slavery in the Age of Revolution;* Ellis, *American Sphinx;* and Freehling, *The Road to Disunion.* For an account of one family's journey through this process of Revolution to rationalization, see Hamilton, "Revolutionary Principles and Family Loyalties."

3. For the best account of gradual emancipation in New England, see Melish, *Disowning Slavery.* See also Greene, *The Negro in Colonial New England;* and Zilversmit, *The First Emancipation.*

4. Blackstone, *Commentaries on the Laws of England,* 1:411.

5. Ibid., 1:411, as quoted in Swift, *An Oration on Domestic Slavery*, 4–5. Blackstone quotes Justinian's *Institutes*, 1.3.4.

6. Swift, *An Oration on Domestic Slavery*, 4–5.

7. Kent, *Commentaries on American Law*, 2:250. Kent cites Gibbon's *History of Rome*, 66–68; Taylor's *Elements of the Civil Law*, 433–35; and Hume's *Essay on the Populousness of Ancient Nations* as sources for his historical interpretations of Roman slavery.

8. Kent, *Commentaries on American Law*, 2:249. Kent cites Potter's *Antiquities of Greece*, 57, 67, and 72, as his authority on Grecian slavery.

9. Swift, *An Oration on Domestic Slavery*, 7. For a similar interpretation of the history of slavery, see Kent, *Commentaries on American Law*, 2:250–51.

10. Swift, *An Oration on Domestic Slavery*, 10.

11. Ibid., 10.

12. For more on race and slavery, see Fields, "Slavery, Race, and Ideology in the United States of America"; and Melish, *Disowning Slavery*.

13. Blackstone, *Commentaries on the Laws of England*, 2:93–96.

14. St. George Tucker, lecture notebook, vol. 9, p. 18, Tucker-Coleman Papers, EGS. Here Tucker cites the Somerset case, *Hargraves Case of Negroe Somerset*, 26–27 (see St. George Tucker, *Blackstone's Commentaries*, 2:A43–44n).

15. Kent was referring to praedial servitude, a right granted for the advantage of one piece of land over another. The possessor(s) of the dominant land could exercise this right over possessor(s) of the servient land at will. The practice presupposes two pieces of land belonging to different proprietors, one burdened with servitude and one given dominance (*Black's Law Dictionary*, 1173).

16. Kent, *Commentaries on American Law*, 2:250–51.

17. Ibid., 2:249.

18. Tucker noted that Blackstone borrowed these arguments from Montesquieu, *Spirit of the Laws*, bk. 15, chap. 2 (see St. George Tucker, *Blackstone's Commentaries*, 2:A40).

19. Blackstone, *Commentaries on the Laws of England*, 1:411–12.

20. St. George Tucker, *Blackstone's Commentaries*, 2:A40 (Tucker's italics).

21. Ely Warner, Litchfield Law School student notebook (1808–9), vol. 1, s.v. "Master and Servant—Gould," LHS.

22. Aaron Burr Reeve, Litchfield Law School student notebook (1802–3), 1:123, LHS.

23. Swift, *An Oration on Domestic Slavery*, 17.

24. Asa Bacon, Litchfield Law School student notebook (1794), 41.

25. Ibid., 42.

26. Ely Warner, Litchfield Law School student notebook (1808–9), vol. 1, s.v. "Master and Servant—Gould." For similar statements, see also Timothy Follett, Litchfield Law School student notebook (1812–13), vol. 1, s.v. "Master and Slave"; Origen Storrs Seymour, Litchfield Law School student notebook (1824–25), vol. 6, s.v. "Master and Slave"; George Flagg Mann, Litchfield Law School student notebook (1826–27), 1:137–39.

27. Ely Warner, Litchfield Law School student notebook (1808–9), vol. 1, s.v. "Master and Servant—Gould." For similar statements, see also Timothy Follett, Litchfield Law School student notebook (1812–13), vol. 1, s.v. "Master and Slave"; Origen Storrs Seymour, Litchfield Law School student notebook (1824–25), vol. 6, s.v. "Master and Slave"; George

Flagg Mann, Litchfield Law School student notebook (1826–27), 1:137–39. See also Swift, *An Oration on Domestic Slavery*, 17–18, for his outline of the gradual emancipation law.

28. Patterson used the term "legal personality" in *Slavery and Social Death*, 22. Thomas Morris structures his detailed study, *Southern Slavery and the Law*, around concepts of slaves as property and slaves as persons.

29. Greene, *The Negro in Colonial New England*, 169–72; Melish, *Disowning Slavery*, 25; Morris, *Southern Slavery and the Law*, 172. Although it was not legal for slaves to own property in the South, there were some instances in which local custom allowed ownership of certain kinds of personal property (see Morgan, "Work and Culture").

30. St. George Tucker, *Blackstone's Commentaries*, 3:A73, in which he cites Blackstone, *Commentaries on the Laws of England*, 2:16.

31. St. George Tucker, *Blackstone's Commentaries*, 3:A73.

32. Ibid., 3A:85–86, 92–93.

33. Asa Bacon, Litchfield Law School student notebook (1794), 41, LHS.

34. Ely Warner, Litchfield Law School student notebook (1808–9), 1:99, LHS.

35. Asa Bacon, Litchfield Law School student notebook (1794), 93, LHS.

36. Blackstone, *Commentaries on the Laws of England*, 3:151–52.

37. Daniel Sheldon Jr., Litchfield Law School student notebook (1798), s.v. "Master and Servant," LHS (italics in original).

38. Ibid.; Seth Staples, Litchfield Law School student notebook (1798), s.v. "Master and Servant," LHS.

39. Origen Storrs Seymour, Litchfield Law School student notebook (1824–25), vol. 6, s.v. "Master and Servant," in which he cites Blackstone, *Commentaries on the Laws of England*, 2:411.

40. Daniel Sheldon Jr., Litchfield Law School student notebook (1798), s.v. "Master and Servant," LHS; Blackstone, *Commentaries on the Laws of England*, 1:417–18.

41. Daniel Sheldon Jr., Litchfield Law School student notebook, s.v. "Master and Servant," LHS; George Flagg Mann, Litchfield Law School student notebook (1826–27), 1:137, UCSC.

42. James Gould, lecture notebook, vol. 1, p. 35, James Gould Papers, LHS.

43. "In the place of a parent," *Black's Law Dictionary*, 787; Kent, *Commentaries on American Law*, 2:260–61.

44. St. George Tucker, *Blackstone's Commentaries*, 2:428n, A58.

45. Blackstone, *Commentaries on the Laws of England*, 1:411–12.

46. "Of the Natural Rights of Individuals," in *The Works of James Wilson*, 605.

47. Nash and Soderlund, *Freedom by Degrees*, 115.

48. Swift, *An Oration on Domestic Slavery*, 11.

49. Ibid., 17.

50. Ibid., 16–17.

51. St. George Tucker, lecture notebook, vol. 9, p. 39, Tucker-Coleman Papers, EGS; St. George Tucker, *Blackstone's Commentaries*, 2:A31–35, 51–52n, 51.

52. Jordan, *White over Black*, 301.

53. St. George Tucker, lecture notebook, vol. 9, p. 56, Tucker-Coleman Papers, EGS; St. George Tucker, *Blackstone's Commentaries*, 2:A65.

54. St. George Tucker, *Blackstone's Commentaries,* 2:A54. For an excellent account of the Tucker family's feelings on slavery and emancipation, see Hamilton, "Revolutionary Principles and Family Loyalties." See also Hamilton, *The Making and Unmaking of a Revolutionary Family,* 81–83, 149–50.

55. Tucker and Belknap, "Queries Respecting the Slavery and Emancipation of Negroes in Massachusetts," 191–211.

56. St. George Tucker, *Blackstone's Commentaries,* 2:A68.

57. Ibid., 2:A54 (Tucker's italics).

58. Ibid., 2:A68.

59. "Sketch of a Letter to Reverend William Bentley," June 30, 1797, St. George Tucker, lecture notebook, vol. [1], Tucker-Coleman Papers, EGS.

60. St. George Tucker, *Reflections on the Cession of Louisiana to the United States,* 20; Hamilton, "Revolutionary Principles and Family Loyalties," 543; Hamilton, *The Making and Unmaking of a Revolutionary Family,* 149–55.

61. St. George Tucker manuscript revisions to his edition of *Blackstone's Commentaries,* ca. 1804 and ca. 1821, 84–85, Tucker-Coleman Papers, EGS.

62. The "benefit of clergy" was an ancient common-law custom that originally exempted clergymen from the jurisdiction of secular courts or exempted them from capital punishment. In the eighteenth and nineteenth centuries, a large number of offenses in English common law carried a penalty of death, and the custom evolved that anyone convicted of a crime could request mitigation of the extreme rigor of criminal laws through benefit of clergy. By an act of Congress passed in 1790, the only crime for which a person could not request benefit of clergy was treason (*Black's Law Dictionary,* 158).

63. St. George Tucker, lecture notebook, vol. 9, p. 39, Tucker-Coleman Papers, EGS.

64. Ibid., vol. 9, p. 50, Tucker-Coleman Papers, EGS; St. George Tucker, *Blackstone's Commentaries,* 2:A66, A66n.

65. St. George Tucker, *Blackstone's Commentaries,* 2:A54.

66. Ibid., 2:A35–38.

67. Ibid., 2:A54.

68. St. George Tucker, lecture notebook, vol. 7, pp. 64–65, Tucker-Coleman Papers, EGS.

69. "Copy of a letter to Robert Pleasants on the Abolition of Slavery," June 29, 1797, in St. George Tucker, lecture notebook, vol. 1, pp. 39–40, Tucker-Coleman Papers, EGS.

70. St. George Tucker manuscript revisions to his edition of *Blackstone's Commentaries,* ca. 1804 and ca. 1821, 84–85, Tucker-Coleman Papers, EGS.

71. St. George Tucker manuscript revisions to his edition of *Blackstone's Commentaries,* ca. 1804 and ca. 1821, 84–86, Tucker-Coleman Papers, EGS.

72. Bryman, "St. George Tucker and the Complexities of Antislavery Advocacy in Jeffersonian Virginia," 73–74; Hamilton, "Revolutionary Principles and Family Loyalties," 556.

73. Berlin, *Many Thousands Gone,* 237.

74. Moss Kent Sr. to James Kent, April 14, 1792, James Kent Papers, LOC; and James Kent journal, July 21, 1801, ibid.

75. John Cotton Smith to James Kent, July 22, 1785, James Kent Papers, LOC; and James Kent journal, July 1, 4, and 23, 1785, ibid.

76. Blackstone, *Commentaries on the Laws of England,* 1:411–12.

77. For more on the Somerset case, see Wiecek, "*Somerset.*"

78. Kent, *Commentaries on American Law,* 2:248.

79. Ibid., 2:249. Kent cites a case from England's High Court of Admiralty (2 *Haggard's Admiralty Reports,* 94).

80. Kent, *Commentaries on American Law,* 2:252–53.

81. Ibid., 2:253–54.

82. Ibid., 2:254.

83. Ibid., 2:254–55.

84. Berlin, *Many Thousands Gone,* 229–55; Zilversmit, *The First Emancipation;* Zilversmit, "Quok Walker, Mumbet, and the Abolition of Slavery in Massachusetts," 614–24.

85. Kent, *Commentaries on American Law,* 2:257–58.

5. Public Lands, Expansion, and the Native Americans

1. Grimké, *State of South Carolina. At the Courts of General Sessions . . . November, 1783,* 2.

2. For more on land and the new nation, see Abernethy, *Western Lands and the American Revolution;* Berkhofer, *The White Man's Indian;* and Sakolski, *The Great American Land Bubble.*

3. Berkhofer, *The White Man's Indian,* 44–49; Horsman, *Race and Manifest Destiny,* 104–8; Sheehan, *Seeds of Extinction,* 89–116.

4. Sakolski, *The Great American Land Bubble,* 32–46. For interpretations of changing ideas about property in the early national period, see Alexander, *Commodity and Property;* and Horwitz, *The Transformation of American Law,* 31–62.

5. For more on early national political and legal leaders' investments in land, see Grimké, *The Petition and Memorial of the Subscriber;* Royster, *The Fabulous History of the Great Dismal Swamp Company;* and Sakolski, *The Great American Land Bubble,* 2–12, 20.

6. For more on early speculation, see Abernethy, *Western Lands and the American Revolution;* and Sakolski, *The Great American Land Bubble.*

7. Sakolski, *The Great American Land Bubble,* 124–41.

8. St. George Tucker, *Blackstone's Commentaries,* 3:A69–70.

9. Ibid., 3:A70–71 (Blackstone's italics).

10. Kent, *Commentaries on American Law,* 3:319n.

11. Lerner, *The Thinking Revolutionary,* 142.

12. Some of the more prominent works on the connections between early modern theories of race and progress and American attitudes toward Native Americans are Horsman, *Race and Manifest Destiny;* Pearce, *The Savages of America;* and Sheehan, *Seeds of Extinction.*

13. Blackstone, *Commentaries on the Laws of England,* 2:32–34. For an innovative look at cultural similarities between whites and Native Americans, see Shoemaker, *A Strange Likeness,* especially 2–31.

14. Blackstone, *Commentaries on the Laws of England,* 1:106; Berkhofer, *The White Man's Indian,* 122.

15. For colonial and Revolutionary-era debates over the question of whether America was a conquered territory, see Black, "The Constitution of Empire," 1199–1200; Greene, *Peripheries and Center,* 24–28; and Reid, *In Defiance of the Law,* 79–80.

16. "Of Legislative Authority," in *The Works of James Wilson,* 2:739–40.

17. St. George Tucker, *Blackstone's Commentaries*, 1:A382. For Adams's arguments, see Adams and Leonard, *The American Colonial Crisis;* and Adams, *Works*, 4:126.

18. St. George Tucker, *Blackstone's Commentaries*, 2:A4.

19. Ibid., 2:66.

20. DuPonceau, *A Discourse on the Early History of Pennsylvania*, 21, 24.

21. Ibid., 24–25.

22. Ibid., 26.

23. Vattel, *Droit des gens*, bk. 3, chap. 2, pp. 37–38. For information on Americans' use of these rights with regard to possession of territory, see Green and Dickason, *The Law of Nations;* Horsman, *Race and Manifest Destiny;* Jones, *License for Empire;* Pearce, *The Savages of America;* and Sheehan, *Seeds of Extinction.*

24. Brackenridge, *Law Miscellanies*, 122.

25. *Goodell v. Jackson*, 20 Johnson's Reports [N.Y.] 693 (1823).

26. For a detailed discussion of Kent's blending of proprietarian and commercial purposes of property, see Alexander, *Commodity and Property*, 127–57.

27. Kent, *Commentaries on American Law*, 3:310.

28. Ibid., 3:309; see also White, "Symposium."

29. *Johnson v. M'Intosh*, 21 U.S. 543, 550–51 (1823); Kent, *Commentaries on American Law*, 3:309. The most detailed interpretations of *Johnson v. M'Intosh* are Robertson, *Conquest by Law;* and Williams, *The American Indian in Western Legal Thought.*

30. Kent, *Commentaries on American Law*, 3:309.

31. St. George Tucker, *Blackstone's Commentaries*, 2:A5.

32. Kent, *Commentaries on American Law*, 3:309.

33. Ibid., 3:310.

34. Kent lifted this passage verbatim from Chief Justice John Marshall's opinion in *Johnson v. M'Intosh*, 21 U.S. 590 (1823).

35. Kent, *Commentaries on American Law*, 3:309.

36. Ibid., 3:317.

37. Ibid., 3:317n. Kent does not cite his source for numbers of warriors.

38. Ibid., 3d ed., 3:394n.

39. Ibid., 4th ed., 3:395n.

40. Horsman, *Race and Manifest Destiny*, 103; Sheehan, *Seeds of Extinction*, 89–116.

41. Kent, *Commentaries on American Law*, 3:315.

42. Ibid., 3:315.

43. Chipman, *Sketches of the Principles of Government*, 23.

44. Ibid., 59.

45. Ibid., 62.

46. Raynal, *A Philosophical and Political History of the Settlements and Trade of the Europeans in the East and West Indies* (1776), as quoted in Chipman, *Sketches of the Principles of Government*, 56 (italics in Chipman).

47. Chipman, *Sketches of the Principles of Government*, 56, 58–59.

48. Ibid., 24.

49. Ibid., 25–26.

50. Ibid., 26.

51. Sullivan, *History of Land Titles in Massachusetts,* 29–30.

52. Ibid., 29–30.

53. Brackenridge, *Narratives of a Late Expedition against the Indians.*

54. Brackenridge, *Law Miscellanies,* 122–23.

55. Ibid., 123.

56. Ibid., 124.

57. Ibid., 125–26.

58. Ibid., 126.

59. Ibid., 125.

60. Brackenridge, *Narratives of a Late Expedition against the Indians,* 32.

61. Brackenridge, *Gazette Publications,* 102–3.

62. Brackenridge, *Narratives of a Late Expedition against the Indians,* 35.

63. Ibid., 33–34.

64. Ibid., 37–38.

65. Brackenridge, "Thoughts on the Present Indian War," 94.

66. Brackenridge, *Gazette Publications,* 99–100.

67. Ibid., 95.

68. Ibid., 103.

69. Ibid., 99–100.

70. Ibid., 101.

71. Ibid., 106. Knox opposed removal of Native Americans; instead, he advocated a strategy that combined "civilization" with assimilation.

72. Brackenridge, *Narratives of a Late Expedition against the Indians,* 26.

73. Brackenridge, *Gazette Publications,* 98.

74. Brackenridge, *Narratives of a Late Expedition against the Indians,* 38.

75. Kent, *Commentaries on American Law,* 3:318.

76. Ibid., 3:318.

77. Ibid., 3:318n.

78. *Johnson v. M'Intosh,* 21 U.S. 543, 550–51 (1823); Kent, *Commentaries on American Law,* 3:309.

79. Kent, *Commentaries on American Law,* 2nd ed., 3:382; *The Cherokee Nation v. The State of Georgia,* 30 U.S. 1 (1831). For a discussion of Chief Justice John Marshall's reconsideration of the discovery doctrine, see Robertson, *Conquest by Law,* 117–44.

80. *Worcester v. The State of Georgia,* 31 U.S. 515 (1832).

81. Kent, *Commentaries on American Law,* 2nd ed., 3:383; Robertson, *Conquest by Law,* 133–35.

82. Kent, *Commentaries on American Law,* 2nd ed., 3:385–86; *Goodell v. Jackson,* 20 Johnsons Reports [N.Y.] 693 (1823); *Jackson v. Wood,* 5 Tenn. Reports 348 (1824).

83. Kent, *Commentaries on American Law,* 3rd ed., 3:381–82.

84. Ibid. See also Kent's footnotes, in the 2nd edition of this work, on pp. 390, 392, and 393; in the 3rd edition, on pp. 377, 379, 388–89, and 392; and in the 4th edition, on pp. 376, 378, 379, 385, 387–89, 390, and 392.

85. Kent, *Commentaries on American Law,* 3rd ed., 3:385.

86. Ibid., 3:399n.

87. Kent, *Commentaries on American Law*, 4th ed., 3:399.

88. Ibid., 3:318.

89. Ibid., 3:318n.

90. Ibid., 3:319n.

6. Custom, the Written Law, and American Legal Treatises

1. Ingersoll, *A Discourse concerning the Influence of America on the Mind*, 39–40.

2. For more on the widening influence of America in the early nineteenth century, see Wiebe, *The Opening of American Society*. For the law's response to that economic and social opening of society, see Hurst, *Law and the Conditions of Freedom;* and Horwitz, *The Transformation of American Law.*

3. For more on the codification movement, see Bloomfield, *American Lawyers in a Changing Society*, 59–90; and Cook, *The American Codification Movement*. See also Haar, *The Golden Age of American Law*, 423–25.

4. Chipman, *Reports and Dissertations, in Two Parts;* Boorstin, *The Mysterious Science of the Law;* Miller, *The Life of the Mind in America*, 156–65.

5. Hoffman, *A Course of Legal Study.*

6. Gould, "The Law School at Litchfield" (italics in original).

7. "University Notes," August 5, 1829, 124–25.

8. Grigsby, *Discourse on the Life and Character of Hon. Littleton Waller Tazewell*, 30; Shepard, "Lawyers Look at Themselves," 12, 14. See also Ferguson, *Law and Letters in American Culture*, 29.

9. Sampson, *Anniversary* (1824), in *Sampson's, Discourse, and Correspondence with Various Learned Jurists upon the History of the Law*, 35–37. See also Bloomfield, *American Lawyers in a Changing Society*, 59–90; Chroust, *The Rise of the Legal Profession in America*, 2:54–61; Cook, *The American Codification Movement;* Miller, *The Life of the Mind in America*, 239–54.

10. Bloomfield, *American Lawyers in a Changing Society*, 87.

11. Hulsebosch, *Constituting Empire*, 17–41.

12. St. George Tucker, *Blackstone's Commentaries;* Swift, *A System of the Laws of the State of Connecticut.*

13. Dane, *A General Abridgement and Digest of American Law;* Livingston, *A Civil Code of the State of Louisiana*. Livingston also compiled U.S. penal laws (Livingston, *A System of Penal Law for the United States of America*). For a list of legal works published in the 1820s, see Cohen, *Bibliography of Early American Law.*

14. Reeve, *The Law of Baron and Femme*, preface.

15. Ibid.

16. In 1825 there were twenty-four states in the union. Reeve addressed the law of descent in the states of New Hampshire, Vermont, Massachusetts, Rhode Island, Connecticut, New York, New Jersey, Pennsylvania, Delaware, Maryland, Ohio, Virginia, North Carolina, South Carolina, and Georgia.

17. Kin of the whole blood were descended from the same father and mother. Kin of the half blood were descended from one common parent, but not both (*Black's Law Dictionary*, 173). "Collateral relatives" refers to next of kin who are not in the direct line of inheritance, such as cousins (ibid., 262). "Seisin" refers to possession of real property under the claim of a freehold estate (ibid., 1358).

18. Kent, *Commentaries on American Law,* 4:373–422 (quote on p. 374).

19. Ibid., 4:346.

20. Ibid., 1:442.

21. Ibid., 1:515.

22. Ibid., 1:546–47.

23. Ibid., 1:439; 2:326; Raack, "'To Preserve the Best Fruits'," 336; Stychin, "The Commentaries of Chancellor James Kent," 448.

24. Blackstone, *Commentaries on the Laws of England,* 1:75.

25. Timothy Follett, Litchfield Law School student notebook (1812–13), YLS; Seth Staples, Litchfield Law School student notebook (1798), LHS.

26. Kent, *Commentaries on American Law,* 1:443.

27. Ibid., 3:169–170. Kent referred to Lord Tenterden's treatise as "*Lord Chancellor Abbott on Shipping.*" Among his recommendations for maritime treatises were Reeves, *History of the Law of Shipping and Navigation;* Tenterden, *Treatise of the Law Relative to Merchant Ships and Seamen;* and Francis Ludlow Holt, *System of the Shipping and Navigation Laws of Great Britain,* which contained all British shipping and navigation laws up to 1820.

28. Leeuwen, *Commentaries on the Roman Dutch Law;* Bouly-Paty, *Cours de Droit Commercial Maritime.*

29. Kent, *Commentaries on American Law,* 3:141.

30. Ibid., 1:443.

31. Ibid., 1:444.

32. Ibid., 1:445.

33. Ibid., 1:445.

34. Ibid., 1:444–46.

35. Bryson, *Legal Education in Virginia,* 609; Charles Campbell to Mildred W. Campbell, December 1826, Charles Campbell Papers, UVA; Campbell to Elizabeth M. Campbell, Petersburg, January 29, 1827, ibid.; Henry St. George Tucker to St. George Tucker, October 5, 1816, Tucker-Coleman Papers, EGS. For more on Henry St. George Tucker's political life, see Hamilton, *The Making and Unmaking of a Revolutionary Family,* 143–47, 180–81.

36. Morton Horwitz and William Nelson, among others, have provided generalized interpretations of changes in early nineteenth-century American law that do not take into account these regional differences; see Horwitz, *The Transformation of American Law;* and Nelson, *Americanization of the Common Law.*

37. Although he perhaps exaggerates the agrarian character of Virginia in the early nineteenth century—Virginia tobacco planters and other farmers were, after all, members of a wider commercial community—F. Thornton Miller has produced a convincing portrait of early national Virginia as a place that was less oriented toward capitalistic progress and thus does not fit Horwitz's mold (Miller, *Juries and Judges versus the Law*).

38. Ibid., 105–6; Henry St. George Tucker, *Notes on Blackstone's Commentaries, for the Use of Students,* v.

39. Henry St. George Tucker, *Commentaries on the Laws of Virginia,* 1:v.

40. Henry St. George Tucker, *Notes on Blackstone's Commentaries;* Henry St. George Tucker, *Commentaries on the Laws of Virginia.*

41. Henry St. George Tucker, *Commentaries on the Laws of Virginia,* 1:ii (italics in original).

42. Ibid., 1:ii.

43. Ibid., 1:v–vi.

44. Ibid., 1:1.

45. Ibid., 1:23–24.

46. Ibid., 1:79 (italics in original).

47. Ibid., 1:23.

48. Henry St. George Tucker cites 2 *Wilson's Reports* 348, 350, to support his argument that the common law had its roots in lost statute law. *Wilson's Reports* refer to cases heard at the English King's Bench and Court of Common Pleas. Although Henry Tucker did not cite Blackstone, these references to *Wilson's Reports* can also be found in Blackstone, *Commentaries on the Laws of England,* 1:50n, in a discussion of the nature and origins of the common law. He cites St. George Tucker, *Blackstone's Commentaries,* 1:53n, for the passage with which he disagreed. Pennsylvanian James Wilson discussed the nature and origins of the common law in "Of the Common Law," in *The Works of James Wilson,* 336.

49. Henry St. George Tucker, *Commentaries on the Laws of Virginia,* 1:23 (italics in original).

Conclusion

1. Charles James Faulkner, "Winchester Law School Notes," Faulkner Law Practice/Winchester Law School Materials, 1825–26, Faulkner Family Papers, VHS.

2. Pole, "Reflections on American Law and the American Revolution," 142–43.

3. For discussions on local and national identities and their places in post-Revolutionary American expansion, see Greene, "Colonial History and National History"; Greene, "Elaborations"; and Zuckerman, "Exceptionalism After All," 259–62. See also Hendrickson, *Peace Pact,* 26–27, 178–79.

Bibliography

Archival Sources

Alderman Library Special Collections, University of Virginia, Charlottesville, Virginia (UVA)
Charles Campbell Papers
Earl Gregg Swem Library Special Collections, College of William and Mary, Williamsburg, Virginia (EGS)
Litchfield Law School Student Notebooks
Tucker-Coleman Papers
Ingraham Memorial Library, Litchfield Historical Society, Litchfield, Conn. (LHS)
James Gould Papers
Litchfield Law School Papers
Litchfield Law School Student Notebooks
John Cotton Smith Correspondence
Library of Congress, Washington, D.C. (LOC)
James Kent Papers
Kent Family Papers
University of Connecticut Special Collections, Storrs, Conn. (UCSC)
Litchfield Law School Notebooks (photocopies)
Virginia Historical Society, Richmond, Virginia (VHS)
Faulkner Family Papers
Grinnan Family Papers
Grigsby Papers
Litchfield Law School Student Notebook (1794)
Lillian Goldman Library, Yale Law School (YLS)
Litchfield Law School Student Notebooks

Case Law

American Insurance Company and the Ocean Insurance Company (of New York) v. 356 Bales of Cotton, David Canter, 26 U.S. 511 (1828)

Butt v. Rachel and others, 4 Munford (Va.) 213 (1813)

Davis's Executors v. Fulton et. als., 2 Tenn. 111 (1805)
Fairfax's Devisee v. Hunter's Lessee, 11 U.S. 603 (1813); *Glasgow's Lessee v. Smith and Blackwell*, 2 Tenn. 144 (1805)
Goodell v. Jackson, 20 Johnson's Reports [N.Y.] 693 (1823)
Henry Wheaton and Robert Donaldson v. Richard Peters and John Grigg, 33 U.S. 591(1834)
Hudgins v. Wright, 1 Hening & Munford (Va.) 134 (1806)
Hunter v. Fairfax, District Court at Winchester, Va. (1794)
Johnson v. M'Intosh, 21 U.S. 543, 550–51 (1823)
Marguerite v. Choteau, 37 U.S. 507 (1825)
Martin v. Hunter's Lessee, 14 U.S. 304 (1816)
Noland v. Cromwell, 4 Munford (Va.) 161 (1814)
Ogden v. Saunders, 25 U.S. 213 (1828)
William Robinson, Jr. v. William Noble's Administrators, 33 U.S. 88 (1834)
Worcester v. Georgia, 31 U.S. 515 (1832)

Published Sources

Abernethy, Thomas Perkins. *Western Lands and the American Revolution*. New York, 1959.
Adams, James Truslow. *New England in the Republic: 1776–1850*. Gloucester, Mass., 1960.
Adams, John. *A Defense of the Constitutions of Government of the United States*. Philadelphia, 1787.
———. *The Works of John Adams*. Vol. 4. Boston, 1851.
Adams, John, and Daniel Leonard. *The American Colonial Crisis: The Daniel Leonard–John Adams Letters to the Press, 1774–1775*. Edited by B. Mason. New York, 1972.
Adams, Willi Paul. *The First American Constitutions: Republican Ideology and the Making of the State Constitutions in the Revolutionary Era*. Chapel Hill, N.C., 1980.
Alexander, Gregory. *Commodity and Property: Competing Visions of Property in American Legal Thought, 1776–1970*. Chicago, 1997.
Alexander, Jay F. "Legal Careers in Eighteenth Century America." *Duquesne Law Review* 23 (1985): 631–58.
Allen, David Grayson. *In English Ways: The Movement of Societies and the Transferal of English Local Law and Custom to Massachusetts Bay in the Seventeenth Century*. Chapel Hill, N.C., 1981.
Amar, Akhil Reed. *The Bill of Rights: Creation and Reconstruction*. New Haven, Conn., 1998.
Anderson, Benedict. *Imagined Communities*. Rev. ed. London, 1991.
Appleby, Joyce Oldham. *Inheriting the Revolution: The First Generation of Americans*. Cambridge, Mass., 2000.
Bailyn, Bernard. *Ideological Origins of the American Revolution*. Enlarged ed. Cambridge, Mass, 1992.
Baker, J. H. "Criminal Courts and Procedure at Common Law." In *The Legal Profession and the Common Law: Historical Essays*. London, 1986.
Basch, Norma. *In the Eyes of the Law: Marriage and Property in Nineteenth-Century New York*. Ithaca, N.Y., 1982.
Bauer, Elizabeth Kelley. *Commentaries on the Constitution, 1790–1860*. New York, 1952.

Berkhofer, Robert F., Jr. *The White Man's Indian: Images of the American Indian from Columbus to the Present.* New York, 1979.

Berlin, Ira. *Many Thousands Gone: The First Two Centuries of Slavery in North America.* Cambridge, Mass., 1998.

Bilder, Mary Sarah. "English Settlement and Local Governance." In *The Cambridge History of Law in America*, vol. 1, *Early America (1580–1815)*, edited by Michael Grossberg and Christopher Tomlins. Cambridge, 2008.

———. "The Lost Lawyers: Early American Legal Literates and Transatlantic Legal Culture." *Yale Journal of Law and the Humanities* 11 (1999): 47–107.

———. *The Transatlantic Constitution: Colonial Legal Culture and the Empire.* Cambridge, Mass., 2004.

Billings, Warren M. *A Little Parliament: The Virginia General Assembly in the Seventeenth Century.* Richmond, Va., 2004.

———. "The Transfer of English Law to Virginia, 1606–50." In *Westward Enterprise: English Activities in Ireland, the Atlantic, and America, 1480–1650*, edited by K. R. Andrews, N. P. Canny, and P. E. H. Hair. Detroit, 1979.

Billings, Warren M., John E. Selby, and Thad W. Tate. *Colonial Virginia: A History.* White Plains, N.Y., 1986.

Black, Barbara. "The Constitution of Empire: The Case for the Colonists." *University of Pennsylvania Law Review* 124 (1976): 1157–1211.

Black, Henry Campbell, comp. *Black's Law Dictionary: Definitions of the Terms and Phrases of American and English Jurisprudence.* 6th ed., by the publisher's editorial staff. St. Paul, Minn., 1990.

Blackstone, Sir William. *Commentaries on the Laws of England.* Facsimile of the 1st ed. of 1765–69. Edited by Stanley N. Katz. Chicago, 1979.

Bloomfield, Maxwell. *American Lawyers in a Changing Society, 1776–1876.* Cambridge, Mass, 1976.

Bonfield, Lloyd. "Marriage, Property, and the 'Affective Family.'" *Law and History Review* 1 (Autumn 1983): 297–312.

Bonomi, Patricia U. *A Factious People: Politics and Society in Colonial New York.* New York, 1971.

Boorstin, Daniel J. *The Mysterious Science of the Law: An Essay on Blackstone's Commentaries Showing How Blackstone, Employing Eighteenth-Century Ideas of Science, Religion, History, Aesthetics, and Philosophy, Made of the Law at Once a Conservative and a Mysterious Science.* Chicago, 1996. Originally published, Cambridge, Mass, 1941.

Botein, Stephen. "The Legal Profession in Colonial North America." In *Lawyers in Early Modern Europe and America*, edited by Wilfred Prest. New York, 1981.

Bouly-Paty, Pierre-Sebastian. *Cours de droit commercial maritime, d'apres les principes et suivant l'ordre du code de commerce.* Paris, 1821.

Brackenridge, H. H. *Considerations on the Jurisprudence of the State of Pennsylvania.* Philadelphia, 1808.

———. *Gazette Publications.* Carlisle, Pa., 1806.

———. *Law Miscellanies: Containing an Introduction to the Study of the Law, Notes on Blackstone's Commentaries, shewing the Variations of the Law of Pennsylvania from the Law of*

England, and what Acts of Assembly might require to be Repealed or Modified; Observations on Smith's Edition of the Laws of Pennsylvania; Strictures on Decisions of the Supreme Court of the United States, and On Certain Acts of Congress, with Some Law Cases, and a Variety of Other Matters, Chiefly Original. Philadelphia, 1814.

———, ed. *Narratives of a Late Expedition against the Indians with an Account of the Barbarous Execution of Col. Crawford; and the Wonderful Escape of Dr. Knight and John Slover from Captivity, in 1782.* Philadelphia, 1783.

———. "Thoughts on the Present Indian War." In *Gazette Publications.* Carlisle, Pa., 1806.

Brewer, Holly. *By Birth or Consent: Children, Law, and the Anglo-American Revolution in Authority.* Chapel Hill, N.C., 2005.

———. "Entailing Aristocracy in Colonial Virginia: 'Ancient Feudal Restraints' and Revolutionary Reform." *William and Mary Quarterly,* 3rd ser., 54 (April 1997): 307–46.

Brophy, Alfred L. "'*Ingenium est Fateri per quos profeceris*': Francis Daniel Pastorius' *Young Country Clerk's Collection* and Anglo-American Legal Literature, 1682–1716." *University of Chicago Law School Roundtable* 3 (1996): 637–734.

———. "Reason and Sentiment: The Moral Worlds and Modes of Reasoning of Antebellum Jurists." *Boston University Law Review* 79 (1999): 1161–1213.

Brown, Elizabeth Gaspar. *British Statutes in American Law, 1776- 1836.* Ann Arbor, Mich., 1964.

———. "A Jeffersonian's Recommendations for a Lawyer's Education: 1802." *American Journal of Legal History* 13 (April 1969): 139–44.

Brown, Richard D. *The Strength of a People: The Idea of an Informed Citizenry in America, 1650–1870.* Chapel Hill, N.C., 1996.

Brown, Richard Maxwell. *The South Carolina Regulators.* Cambridge, Mass, 1963.

Bryman, Donna Stillman. "St. George Tucker and the Complexities of Antislavery Advocacy in Jeffersonian Virginia." Master's thesis, College of William and Mary, 1972.

Bryson, W. Hamilton. *Legal Education in Virginia, 1779–1979: A Biographical Approach.* Charlottesville, Va., 1982.

Burgh, James. *Political Disquisitions; or, An Enquiry into Public Errors, Defects, and Abuses.* Reprint of 1774 ed. New York, 1971.

Bush, Jonathan. "Free to Enslave: The Foundations of Colonial American Slave Law." *Yale Journal of Law and the Humanities* 5, no. 2 (1993): 417–70.

Bushman, Richard. *The Refinement of America: Persons, Houses, Cities.* New York, 1993.

Cairns, John. "Blackstone, an English Institutist: Legal Literature and the Rise of the Nation State." *Oxford Journal of Legal History* 4, no. 3 (1984): 318–60.

———. "Blackstone, the Ancient Constitution and the Feudal Law." *Historical Journal* 28, no. 3 (1985): 711–17.

Canady, Hoyt P. *Gentlemen of the Bar: Lawyers in Colonial South Carolina.* New York, 1987.

Carr, Lois Green, and Lorena S. Walsh. "The Planter's Wife: The Experience of White Women in Seventeenth-Century Maryland." *William and Mary Quarterly,* 3rd ser., 34 (October 1977): 542–71.

Carrington, Paul D. "The Revolutionary Idea of University Legal Education." *William and Mary Law Review* 31 (1990): 527–74.

Chaplin, Joyce E. "Expansion and Exceptionalism in Early American History." *Journal of American History* 88 (March 2002): 1431–63.

Chipman, Nathaniel. *Reports and Dissertations, in Two Parts. Part 1: Reports of cases determined in the Supreme Court of the State of Vermont, in the years 1789, 1790, and 1791. Part 2: Dissertations on the statute adopting the common law of England, the statute of conveyances, the statute of offsets, and on the negotiability of notes. With an appendix, containing forms of special pleadings in several cases; forms of recognizances; of justices records; and of warrants of commitment.* Rutland, Vt., 1793.

———. *Sketches of the Principles of Government.* Rutland, Vt., 1793.

Christian, Edward, Esq. *Notes to Blackstone's Commentaries, which are calculated to Answer all the Editions.* Boston, 1801.

Christie, Ian R., and Benjamin W. Labaree. *Empire or Independence, 1760–1776.* New York, 1976.

Chroust, Anton-Hermann. *The Rise of the Legal Profession in America.* 2 vols. Norman, Okla., 1965.

Clark, Peter. *English Provincial Society from the Reformation to the Revolution: Religion, Politics, and Society in Kent, 1500–1640.* Sussex, U.K., 1977.

Clinton, Catherine. *The Plantation Mistress: Woman's World in the Old South.* New York, 1982.

Cohen, Morris L. *Bibliography of Early American Law.* Buffalo, N.Y., 1998.

———. "Thomas Jefferson Recommends a Course of Law Study." *University of Pennsylvania Law Review* 119 (1971): 823–44.

Conrad, Stephen A. "Metaphor and Imagination in James Wilson's Theory of the Federal Union." *Law and Social Inquiry* 13 (Winter 1988): 1–70.

———. Review of *Conceptual Change and the Constitution,* edited by Terrence Ball and J. G. A. Pocock. *Constitutional Commentary* 7 (1990): 196–202.

———. "The Rhetorical Constitution of 'Civil Society' at the Founding: One Lawyer's Anxious Vision." *Indiana Law Journal* 72 (1997): 335–73.

Cook, Charles M. *The American Codification Movement: A Study of Antebellum Legal Reform.* Westport, Conn., 1981.

Cooper, J. P. "Ideas of Gentility in Early-Modern England." In *Land, Men, and Beliefs: Studies in Early Modern History,* edited by George E. Aylmer and John S. Morrill. London, 1983.

———. "Patterns of Inheritance and Settlement by Great Landowners from the Fifteenth to the Seventeenth Centuries." In *Family and Inheritance: Rural Society in Western Europe, 1200–1800,* edited by Jack Goody, Joan Thirsk, and E. P. Thompson. Cambridge, 1976.

Cornell, Saul, and Gerald Leonard. "The Consolidation of the Early Federal System, 1791–1812." In *The Cambridge History of Law in America,* vol. 1, *Early America (1580–1815),* edited by Michael Grossberg and Christopher Tomlins. Cambridge, 2008.

Crowley, John E. "Family Relations and Inheritance in Early South Carolina." *Histoire Sociale* 17 (May 1984): 35–57.

Cullen, Charles T. *St. George Tucker and Law in Virginia, 1772- 1804.* New York, 1987.

———. "St. George Tucker and the Discipline of Law in Jeffersonian Virginia." Paper given at the Omohundro Institute for Early American History and Culture Colloquium, Williamsburg, Va., 1979.

Dane, Nathan. *A Civil Code of the State of Louisiana.* New Orleans, 1825.

———. *A General Abridgement and Digest of American Law, with Occasional Notes and Comments.* Boston, 1823–29.

Davis, David Brion. *The Problem of Slavery in the Age of Revolution, 1770–1823*. Ithaca, N.Y., 1975.

Day, Alan F. "Lawyers in Colonial Maryland, 1660–1715." *American Journal of Legal History* 17 (April 1973): 145–65.

Dayton, Cornelia Hughes. "Turning Points and the Relevance of Colonial Legal History." *William and Mary Quarterly*, 3rd ser., 50 (January 1993): 7–17.

———. *Women before the Bar: Gender, Law, and Society in Connecticut, 1639–1789*. Chapel Hill, N.C., 1995.

Deloria, Philip J. *Playing Indian*. New Haven, Conn., 1998.

Dick, Everett. *The Lure of the Land: A Social History of the Public Lands from the Articles of Confederation to the New Deal*. Lincoln, Neb., 1971.

Dickason, Olive P. *The Law of Nations and the New World*. Edmonton, Alberta, Canada, 1989.

Ditz, Toby L. *Property and Kinship: Inheritance in Early Connecticut, 1750–1820*. Princeton, N.J., 1986.

Doolittle, I. G. "Sir William Blackstone and His *Commentaries on the Laws of England*: A Biographical Approach." *Oxford Journal of Legal Studies* 3, no. 1 (1983): 111–35.

Doyle, Christopher Leonard. "Lord, Master, and Patriot: St. George Tucker and Patriarchy in Republican Virginia, 1772–1851." Ph.D. diss., University of Connecticut, 1995.

Dumbauld, Edward. *Thomas Jefferson and the Law*. Norman, Okla., 1978.

DuPonceau, Peter S. *A Discourse on the Early History of Pennsylvania: Being an Annual Oration Delivered before the American Philosophical Society, held at Philadelphia, for Promoting Useful Knowledge; Pursuant to their Appointment, in the Hall of the University of Pennsylvania, on Wednesday, the 6th of June, 1821*. Philadelphia, 1821.

———. *A Dissertation on the Nature and Extent of the Jurisdiction of the Courts of the United States, being a Valedictory address Delivered to the Students of the Law Academy of Philadelphia, at the close of the Academical Year, on the 22d April, 1824. To which are Added, a Brief Sketch of the National Judiciary Powers Exercised in the United States Prior to the Adoption of the Present Federal Constitution, by Thomas Sargeant, Esq., and the Author's Discourse on Legal Education, Delivered at the Opening of the Law Academy, in February, 1821. With an Appendix and Notes*. Philadelphia, 1824.

———. *Grammar of the language of the Lenni Lenape or Delaware Indians translated from the German manuscript of the late Rev. David Zeisberger, for the American Philosophical Society, Transactions of the Historical and Literary Committee of the American Philosophical Society*. Vol. 1. Philadelphia, 1819.

Edgar, Walter. *South Carolina: A History*. Columbia, S.C., 1998.

Ellis, Joseph J. *American Sphinx: The Character of Thomas Jefferson*. New York, 1997.

Elton, G. R. *England under the Tudors*. London, 1955. Reprinted, 1963.

Ely, James. *The Guardian of Every Other Right: A Constitutional History of Property Rights*. 2nd ed. New York, 1998.

Evans, Thomas. *An Address to the People of Virginia, Respecting the Alien & Sedition Laws. By a Citizen of this State*. Richmond, 1798.

Ferguson, Robert A. *Law and Letters in American Culture*. Cambridge, Mass., 1984.

Fernandez, Mark F. "The Appellate Question: A Comparative Analysis of Supreme Courts of Appeal in Virginia and Louisiana, 1776–1840." Ph.D. diss., College of William and Mary, 1991.

———. *From Chaos to Continuity: The Evolution of Louisiana's Judicial System, 1712–1862.* Baton Rouge, La., 2001.

Fields, Barbara. "Slavery, Race, and Ideology in the United States of America." *New Left Review* 181 (May-June 1990): 95–118.

Fisher, Samuel H. "The Litchfield Law School." An address delivered before the Litchfield Historical Society, August 19, 1930. Litchfield, Conn., 1930.

Four Letters on Interesting Subjects. Philadelphia, 1776.

Freehling, William W. *The Road to Disunion: Secessionists at Bay, 1776–1854.* New York, 1990.

Freeman, Joanne. *Affairs of Honor: National Politics in the New Republic.* New Haven, Conn., 2002.

Frey, Sylvia. *Water from the Rock: Black Resistance in a Revolutionary Age.* Princeton, N.J., 1991.

Friedman, Lawrence M. "Heart against Head: Perry Miller and the Legal Mind." Review of *The Life of the Mind in America, from the Revolution to the Civil War,* by Perry Miller. *Yale Law Journal* 77 (May 1968): 1244–59.

———. *A History of American Law.* New York, 1973.

Gawalt, Gerard W. "Massachusetts Legal Education in Transition, 1766–1840." *American Journal of Legal History* 17 (January 1973): 27–50.

Goebel, Julius, Jr. "Constitutional History and Constitutional Law." *Columbia Law Review* 38 (April 1938): 555–77.

Goetsch, Charles C. "The Litchfield Law School: A Modern View." Paper given at the American Society for Legal History Conference, 1979.

Gould, Eliga H. "The Question of Home Rule." *William and Mary Quarterly,* 3rd ser., 64 (April 2007) 255–58.

Gould, James. "The Law School at Litchfield." *United States Law Journal* 3 (1822): 400.

Green, L. C., and Olive P. Dickason. *The Law of Nations and the New World.* Edmonton, Alberta, Canada, 1989.

Greene, Jack P. "Colonial History and National History: Reflections on a Continuing Problem." *William and Mary Quarterly,* 3rd ser., 64 (April 2007): 235–50.

———. "The Colonial Origins of American Constitutionalism." In *The United States Constitution: Roots, Rights, and Responsibilities,* edited by A. E. Dick Howard. Washington, D.C., 1992.

———. "Elaborations." *William and Mary Quarterly,* 3rd ser., 64 (April 2007): 281–86.

———. "From the Perspective of Law: Context and Legitimacy in the Origins of the American Revolution." *South Atlantic Quarterly* 85 (1986): 56–75.

———. *Negotiated Authorities: Essays in Colonial Political and Constitutional History.* Charlottesville, Va., 1994.

———. *Peripheries and Center: Constitutional Development in the Extended Polities of the British Empire and the United States, 1607–1788.* New York, 1990.

———. "Political Mimesis: A Consideration of the Historical and Cultural Roots of Legislative Behavior in the British Colonies in the Eighteenth Century." *American Historical Review* 75 (December 1969): 337–60.

———. *Pursuits of Happiness: The Social Development of Early Modern British Colonies and the Formation of American Culture*. Chapel Hill, N.C., 1988.
———. "Search for Identity: An Interpretation of the Meaning of Selected Patterns of Social Response in Eighteenth-Century America." *Journal of Social History* 3 (Spring 1969–Spring 1970): 189–220.
Greene, Jack P., and J. R. Pole, eds. *The Blackwell Encyclopedia of the American Revolution*. Cambridge, Mass., 1991.
Greene, Lorenzo J. *The Negro in Colonial New England*. New York, 1942.
Greven, Philip J. *Four Generations: Population, Land, and Family in Colonial Andover, Massachusetts*. Ithaca, N.Y., 1970.
Grey, Thomas C. "Origins of the Unwritten Constitution: Fundamental Law in American Revolutionary Thought." *Stanford Law Review* 30 (May 1978): 843–93.
Grigsby, Hugh. *Discourse on the Life and Character of Hon. Littleton Waller Tazewell*. Richmond, Va., 1860.
Grimké, John Faucheraud. *Charge, Delivered to the Grand Juries of Beaufort and Orangeburgh Districts, by the Honorable J. F. Grimke, one of the Associate Judges of the State of South Carolina, November Term*. Charleston, S.C., 1798.
———. *Charges by Hon. Judge Grimke at the Courts of General Sessions of the Peace for Districts of Cheraw & Camden*. Charleston, S.C., 1783.
———. *The Duty of Executors and Administrators: Pointing out, in a plain and familiar manner, how executors are to proceed in the probate of wills, getting in the effects, and paying the debts and legacies of their testator: shewing also who are entitled by law to be the administrators of an intestate person: With full and clear Directions to a Man's Relations how his Estate will be distributed among them, according to the Laws of South Carolina. To which are prefixed, all the Statutes and Acts Relative to these subjects, Mr. Blackstone's Rules for Interpreting Wills and Deeds, and a Table of Inheritance, with a concise and easy explanation thereof. To which is added, A variety of Precedents of Wills, Codicils, & c. With Instructions for every Person to make, alter and republish his will; and likewise, All the Forms made use of in the Court of Ordinary*. New York, 1797.
———. *The Petition and Memorial of the Subscriber, in behalf of the Company incorporated by law, for opening the Navigation of the Catawba and Wateree Rivers*. Charleston, S.C., 1808.
———, ed. *The Public Laws of the State of South Carolina, From its First Establishment as a British Province Down to the Year 1790, Inclusive, in which is comprehended such of the Statutes of Great Britain as were made of Force by the Act of Assembly of 1712, With an Appendix containing such other Statutes as have been enacted or declared to be of force in this State, either virtually or expressly, to which is added the Titles of all the Laws (with their respective dates) which have been passed in South Carolina down to the present time, also The Constitution of the United States with the amendments thereto, and likewise The Newly Adopted Constitution of the State of South Carolina, Together with a Copious Index to the Whole*. Philadelphia, 1790.
———. *The South Carolina Justice of Peace, Containing all the Duties, Powers and Authorities of that office, as regulated by the Laws now of force in this State, and Adapted to the Parish and County Magistrate: to which is added, a great variety of Warrants, Indictments and other*

precedents with several additional ones interspersed under their several Heads, and an addition of several other decisions which have been had in the courts of this state, besides those contained in the first edition. Philadelphia, 1796.

———. *State of South Carolina. At the Courts of General Sessions of the Peace held for the districts of Cheraws and Camden, the 15th and 26th of November, 1783, before the Hon. Judge Grimke, the Grand Juries of the above districts having requested that the Charge delivered by the Court be published, together with their Presentments.* Charleston, S.C., 1783.

Grossberg, Michael. "Social History Update: 'Fighting Faiths' and the Challenges of Legal History." *Journal of Social History* 25 (Autumn 1991): 191–201.

Gutzman, C. Kevin. "Jefferson's Draft Declaration of Independence, Richard Bland, and the Revolutionary Legacy: Giving Credit Where Credit Is Due." *Journal of the Historical Society* 1, no. 2–3 (2001): 137–54.

Haar, Charles M., ed. *The Golden Age of American Law.* New York, 1965.

Hall, Ford W. "The Common Law: An Account of Its Reception in the United States." *Vanderbilt Law Review* 4 (1951): 791–825.

Hall, Kermit L., ed. *Land Law and Real Property in American History: Major Historical Interpretations.* New York, 1987.

———. *The Magic Mirror: Law in American History.* New York, 1989.

———, ed. *The Oxford Companion to the Supreme Court of the United States.* New York, 1992.

Hall, Mark David. *The Political and Legal Philosophy of James Wilson, 1742–1798.* Columbia, Mo., 1997.

Hamilton, Phillip Forrest. *The Making and Unmaking of a Revolutionary Family: The Tuckers of Virginia, 1752–1830.* Charlottesville, Va., 2003.

———. "Revolutionary Principles and Family Loyalties: Slavery's Transformation in the St. George Tucker Household of Early National Virginia." *William and Mary Quarterly,* 3rd ser., 55 (October 1998): 531–56.

———. "The Tucker Family and the Dynamics of Generational Change in Jeffersonian Virginia, 1775–1830." Ph.D. diss., Washington University, St. Louis, 1995.

Hartog, Hendrik. *Public Property and Private Power: The Corporation of the City of New York in American Law, 1730–1870.* Ithaca, N.Y., 1989.

Haskins, George L. "The Beginnings of Partible Inheritance in the American Colonies." *Yale Law Journal* 51 (June 1942): 1280–1315.

Haywood, John. *The Natural and Aboriginal History of Tennessee, Up to the First Settlements therein by the White People in the Year 1768.* Edited by Mary U. Rothrock. 1823. Reprint, Jackson, Tenn., 1959.

Hendrickson, David C. *Peace Pact: The Lost World of the American Founding.* Lawrence, Kans., 2003.

Henretta, James A., and James D. Rice. "Law as Litigation: An Agenda for Research." *William and Mary Quarterly,* 3rd ser., 50 (January 1993): 176–80.

Hill, L. M. "The Two-Witness Rule in English Treason Trials: Some Comments on the Emergence of Procedural Law." *American Journal of Legal History* 12 (April 1968): 95–111.

Hindus, Michael S. *Prison and Plantation: Crime, Justice, and Authority in Massachusetts and South Carolina, 1767–1878.* Chapel Hill, N.C., 1980.

Hoffer, Peter Charles. "Custom as Law: A Comment on J. R. Pole's 'Reflections.'" *William and Mary Quarterly*, 3rd ser., 50 (January 1993): 160–67.

———. *The Law's Conscience: Equitable Constitutionalism in America*. Chapel Hill, N.C., 1990.

Hoffman, David. *An Address to Students of Law in the United States*. Baltimore, 1824.

———. *A Course of Legal Study: Respectfully Addressed to the Students of Law in the United States*. Baltimore, 1817.

———. *A Lecture Being the Second of a Series of Lectures, Introductory to a Course of Lectures now delivering in the University of Maryland*. Baltimore, 1825.

———. *A Lecture Introductory to a Course of Lectures, Now Delivering in the University of Maryland*. Baltimore, 1823.

———. *Syllabus of a Course of Lectures on Law; Proposed to be Delivered in The University of Maryland; Addressed to the Students of Law in the United States*. Baltimore, 1821.

Holt, Francis Ludlow. *System of the Shipping and Navigation Laws of Great Britain*. London, 1820.

Holt, Wythe. "Morton Horwitz and the Transformation of American Legal History." *William and Mary Law Review* 23 (Summer 1982): 663–723.

Horn, James. *Adapting to a New World: English Society in the Seventeenth-Century Chesapeake*. Chapel Hill, N.C., 1997.

Horsman, Reginald. *Race and Manifest Destiny: The Origins of American Racial Anglo-Saxonism*. Cambridge, Mass., 1981.

Horsnell, Margaret E. *Spencer Roane: Judicial Advocate of Jeffersonian Principles*. New York, 1986.

Horton, John Theodore. *James Kent: A Study in Conservatism, 1763–1847*. New York, 1939.

Horwitz, Morton J. "The Transformation in the Conception of Property in American Law, 1780–1860." *University of Chicago Law Review* 40 (Winter 1973): 248–90.

———. *The Transformation of American Law, 1780–1860*. Cambridge, Mass, 1977.

Howard, Ronald W. "From Proprietary Colony to Royal Province." In *The Empire State: A History of New York*, edited by Milton Klein. Ithaca, N.Y., 2001.

Huebner, Timothy S. *The Southern Judicial Tradition: State Judges and Sectional Distinctiveness, 1790–1890*. Athens, Ga., 1999.

Hulsebosch, Daniel J. *Constituting Empire: New York and the Transformation of Constitutionalism in the Atlantic World, 1664–1830*. Chapel Hill, N.C., 2005.

———. "*Imperia in Imperio*: The Multiple Constitutions of Empire in New York, 1750–1777." *Law and History Review* 16 (Summer 1998): 319–79.

Hurst, James Willard. *Law and the Conditions of Freedom*. Madison, Wis., 1956.

Ifft, Richard A. "Treason in the Early Republic: The Federal Courts, Popular Protest, and Federalism during the Whiskey Insurrection." In *The Whiskey Rebellion: Past and Present Perspectives*, edited by Stephen R. Boyd. Westport, Conn., 1985.

Ingersoll, Charles Jared. *A Discourse concerning the Influence of America on the Mind: Being the Annual Oration Delivered before the American Philosophical Society, at the University in Philadelphia, on the 18th October, 1823*. Reprinted in *American Philosophic Addresses, 1700–1900*, edited by Joseph L. Blau. New York, 1946.

Inglis, Charles. *The True Interest of America Impartially Stated*. Philadelphia, 1776.

Iredell, James. *Laws of the State of North Carolina, Published, According to Act of Assembly.* Edenton, N.C., 1791.

———. *The Papers of James Iredell.* Edited by Don Higginbotham. 2 vols. Raleigh, N.C., 1976.

Ireland, Owen. *Religion, Ethnicity, and Politics: Ratifying the Constitution in Pennsylvania.* University Park, Pa., 1995.

Jay, Stewart. "Origins of Federal Common Law: Part One." *University of Pennsylvania Law Review* 133 (June 1985): 1003–1116.

———. "Origins of Federal Common Law: Part Two." *University of Pennsylvania Law Review* 133 (July 1985): 1231–1333.

Jefferson, Thomas. "Autobiography" (1821). In vol. 1 of *Works of Thomas Jefferson,* edited by Paul Leicester Ford. New York, 1904–5.

———. *Notes on the State of Virginia.* Edited by William Peden. New York, 1972.

———. *Writings of Thomas Jefferson.* Vol. 1. Edited by Paul Leicester Ford. New York, 1892.

Jezierski, John V. "Parliament or People: James Wilson and Blackstone on the Nature and Location of Sovereignty." *Journal of the History of Ideas* 32 (January–March 1971): 95–106.

Johnson, Herbert A. *Imported Eighteenth-Century Law Treatises in American Libraries, 1700–1799.* Knoxville, Tenn., 1978.

Jones, Dorothy V. *License for Empire: Colonialism by Treaty in Early America.* Chicago, 1982.

Jones, E. Alfred. *American Members of the Inns of Court.* London, 1924.

Jones, Herbert S. "America's First Law School." *My Country* 2 (1968): 2–7.

Jordan, Winthrop D. *White over Black: American Attitudes toward the Negro, 1550–1812.* Chapel Hill, N.C., 1968.

Karsten, Peter. *Heart versus Head: Judge-Made Law in Nineteenth-Century America.* Chapel Hill, N.C., 1997.

Katz, Stanley N. "Looking Backward: The Early History of American Law" (book review). *University of Chicago Law Review* 33 (Summer 1966): 867–84.

———. "The Problem of a Colonial Legal History." In *Colonial British America: Essays in the New History of the Early Modern Era,* edited by Jack P. Greene and J. R. Pole. Baltimore, 1984.

———. "Republicanism and the Law of Inheritance in the American Revolutionary Era." *Michigan Law Review* 76 (November 1977): 1–29.

Keim, C. Ray. "Primogeniture and Entail in Colonial Virginia." *William and Mary Quarterly,* 3rd ser., 25 (October 1968): 545–86.

Kelly, Alfred, and Winfred A. Harbison. *The American Constitution: Its Origins and Development.* 5th ed. New York, 1976.

Kennedy, Duncan. "The Structure of Blackstone's Commentaries," *Buffalo Law Review* 28 (1979): 205–382.

Kent, James. *Commentaries on American Law.* 1st ed. 4 vols. New York, 1826–30.

———. *Commentaries on American Law.* 2nd ed. 4 vols. New York, 1832.

———. *Commentaries on American Law.* 3rd ed. 4 vols. New York, 1835.

———. *Commentaries on American Law.* 4th ed. 4 vols. New York, 1841.

———. *Dissertations: Being the Preliminary Part of a Course of Law Lectures by James Kent, Professor of Law in Columbia College.* New York, 1795.

———. *An Introductory Lecture to a Course of Law Lectures, Delivered November 17, 1794*. New York, 1794.

Klafter, Craig Evan. "The Americanization of Blackstone's *Commentaries*." In *Essays on English Law and the American Experience*, edited by Elisabeth A. Cawthon and David E. Narrett. College Station, Tex., 1994.

———. "The Influence of Vocational Law Schools on the Origins of American Legal Thought, 1779–1929." *American Journal of Legal History* 37 (1993): 307–31.

———. *Reason over Precedents: Origins of American Legal Thought*. Westport, Conn., 1993.

Klein, Milton M. *The Empire State: A History of New York*. Ithaca, N.Y., 2001.

———. "Prelude to Revolution in New York: Jury Trials and Judicial Tenure." *William and Mary Quarterly*, 3rd ser., 17 (October 1960): 439–62.

Klein, Rachel N. *Unification of a Slave State: The Rise of the Planter Class in the South Carolina Backcountry, 1760–1808*. Chapel Hill, N.C., 1990.

Konefsky, Alfred S., and John H. Schlegel. "Mirror, Mirror on the Wall: Histories of American Law Schools." *Harvard Law Review* 95 (February 1982): 833–51.

Konig, David Thomas. *Law and Society in Puritan Massachusetts: Essex County, 1629–1692*. Chapel Hill, N.C., 1979.

———. "Regionalism in Early American Law." In *The Cambridge History of Law in America*, vol. 1, *Early America (1580–1815)*, edited by Michael Grossberg and Christopher Tomlins. Cambridge, 2008.

———. "A Summary View of the Law of British America." *William and Mary Quarterly*, 3rd ser., 50 (January 1993): 42–50.

Leeuwen, Simon van. *Commentaries on the Roman Dutch Law*. London, 1820.

Lerner, Ralph. *The Thinking Revolutionary: Principle and Practice in the New Republic*. Ithaca, N.Y., 1997.

Levine, Peter. "The Fries Rebellion: Social Violence and the Politics of the New Nation." *Pennsylvania History* 40 (July 1973): 241–58.

Lieberman, David. *The Province of Legislation Determined: Legal Theory in Eighteenth Century Britain*. Cambridge, 1989.

Linklater, Andro. *Measuring America: How the United States was Shaped by the Greatest Land Sale in History*. New York, 2002.

Livingston, Edward. *A Civil Code of the State of Louisiana*. New Orleans, 1825.

———. *A System of Penal Law for the United States of America: Consisting of a Code of Crimes and Punishments, a Code of Procedure in Criminal Cases, a Code of Prison Discipline, and a Book of Definitions*. Washington, D.C., 1828.

Lobban, Michael. "Blackstone and the Science of Law." *Historical Journal* 30 (June 1987): 311–35.

Lockmiller, David. *Sir William Blackstone*. Chapel Hill, N.C., 1938.

Lutz, Donald. *The Origins of American Constitutionalism*. Baton Rouge, La., 1988.

———. *Popular Consent and Popular Control: Whig Political Theory in the Early State Constitutions*. Baton Rouge, La., 1980.

Mann, Bruce H. "The Evolutionary Revolution in American Law: A Comment on J. R. Pole's 'Reflections.'" *William and Mary Quarterly*, 3rd ser., 50 (January 1993): 168–75.

———. "Legal Reform and the Revolution." In *Blackwell Encyclopedia of the American Revolution*, edited by Jack P. Greene and J. R. Pole. Cambridge, Mass., 1991.

———. *Neighbors and Strangers: Law and Community in Early Connecticut.* Chapel Hill, N.C., 1987.

Marder, Daniel. *Hugh Henry Brackenridge.* New York, 1967.

Marshall Wythe Blackstone Commemoration Ceremonies, in Celebration of the Beginning of the John Marshall Bicentennial Year and the 175th Anniversary of the First Chair of Law in the United States and the Creation of a Chair of Taxation at the College of William and Mary. Williamsburg, Va., 1954.

McColley, Robert. *Slavery and Jeffersonian Virginia.* 2nd ed. Urbana, Ill., 1973.

McCoy, Drew. *The Elusive Republic: Political Economy in Jeffersonian America.* Chapel Hill, N.C., 1980.

McDowell, Gary L. "The Language of Law and the Foundations of American Constitutionalism." *William and Mary Quarterly,* 3rd ser., 55 (July 1998): 375–98.

McKenna, Marian C. *Tapping Reeve and the Litchfield Law School.* New York, 1986.

McKirdy, Charles R. "The Lawyer as Apprentice: Legal Education in Eighteenth Century Massachusetts." *Journal of Legal Education* 28 (1976): 124–36.

McLoughlin, William G. "Thomas Jefferson and the Beginning of Cherokee Nationalism, 1806 to 1809." *William and Mary Quarterly,* 3rd ser., 32 (October 1975): 547–80.

McManus, Edgar J. *Black Bondage in the North.* Syracuse, N.Y., 1973.

Melish, Joanne Pope. *Disowning Slavery: Gradual Emancipation and "Race" in New England, 1780–1860.* Ithaca, N.Y., 1998.

Miller, F. Thornton. *Juries and Judges versus the Law: Virginia's Provincial Legal Perspective, 1783–1828.* Charlottesville, Va., 1994.

Miller, Perry. *The Life of the Mind in America from the Revolution to the Civil War.* New York, 1965.

Montesquieu, Charles de Secondat, Baron de. *Spirit of the Laws.* Edited by Robert Maynard Hutchens. Chicago, 1952.

Morgan, Philip D. "Work and Culture: The Task System and the World of Lowcountry Blacks, 1700 to 1880." *William and Mary Quarterly,* 3rd ser., 39 (October 1982): 563–99.

Morris, Richard B. "Primogeniture and Entailed Estates in America." *Columbia Law Review* 27 (January 1927): 24–51.

Morris, Thomas. *Southern Slavery and the Law, 1607–1860.* Chapel Hill, N.C., 1996.

Murrin, John. "The Legal Transformation: The Bench and Bar of Eighteenth-Century Massachusetts." In *Colonial America: Essays in Politics and Social Development,* edited by Stanley Katz and John Murrin. 3rd ed. New York, 1984.

Nash, Gary B., and Jean R. Soderlund. *Freedom by Degrees: Emancipation in Pennsylvania and Its Aftermath.* New York, 1991.

Nedelsky, Jennifer. *Private Property and the Limits of American Constitutionalism: The Madisonian Framework and Its Legacy.* Chicago, 1990.

Nelson, William E. *Americanization of the Common Law: The Impact of Legal Change on Massachusetts Society, 1760–1830.* Cambridge, Mass., 1975.

Newman, Paul Douglas. "The Fries Rebellion of 1799: Pennsylvania Germans, the Federalist Party, and American Political Culture." Ph.D. diss., University of Kentucky, 1996.

———. "Fries's Rebellion and American Political Culture, 1798–1800." *Pennsylvania Magazine of History and Biography* 119 (January–April 1995): 37–73.

Nolan, D. R. "Sir William Blackstone and the New American Republic: A Study of Intellectual Impact." *New York Law Review* 51 (1976): 731–59.

Onuf, Peter. "State Sovereignty and the Making of the Constitution." In *Conceptual Change and the Constitution,* edited by Terence Ball and J. G. A. Pocock. Lawrence, Kans., 1988.

Paine, Thomas. *Common Sense.* In *The Life and Major Writings of Thomas Paine,* edited by Philip Foner. New York, 1961.

———. *Rights of Man.* In *The Life and Major Writings of Thomas Paine,* edited by Philip Foner. New York, 1961.

Patterson, Orlando. *Slavery and Social Death: A Comparative Study.* Cambridge, Mass., 1982.

Pearce, Roy Harvey. *The Savages of America: A Study of the Indian and the Idea of Civilization.* Baltimore, 1965.

Pocock, J. G. A. *The Ancient Constitution and the Feudal Law: A Study of English Historical Thought in the Seventeenth Century.* Rev. ed. Cambridge, 1993.

Pole, J. R. "Property and Law in the American Republic." *Paths to the American Past.* New York, 1979.

———. "Reflections on American Law and the American Revolution." *William and Mary Quarterly,* 3rd ser., 50 (January 1993): 123–59.

Pound, Roscoe. *The Lawyer from Antiquity to Modern Times.* St. Paul, Minn., 1953.

Presser, Stephen B. *The Original Misunderstanding: The English, the Americans, and the Dialectic of Federalist Jurisprudence.* Durham, N.C., 1991.

———. "Revising the Conservative Tradition: Towards a New American Legal History." In *Law in the American Revolution and the Revolution in the Law: A Collection of Review Essays on American Legal History,* edited by Henrik Hartog. New York, 1981.

Preyer, Kathryn. "Jurisdiction to Punish: Federal Authority, Federalism, and the Common Law of Crimes in the Early Republic." *Law and History Review* 4 (Autumn 1986): 223–65.

Raack, David W. "'To Preserve the Best Fruits': The Legal Thought of Chancellor James Kent." *American Journal of Legal History* 33 (October 1989): 320–66.

Rakove, Jack. *Original Meanings: Politics and Ideas in the Making of the Constitution.* New York, 1996.

———. "The Origins of Judicial Review: A Plea for New Contexts." *Stanford Law Review* 49 (May 1997): 1031–64.

Randolph, Edmund. *History of Virginia.* Edited by Arthur H. Shaffer. Charlottesville, Va., 1970.

Reed, Alfred Z. *Training for the Public Profession of the Law.* New York, 1921.

Reeve, Tapping. *The Law of Baron and Femme; of Parent and Child; of Guardian and Ward; of Master and Servant; and of the Powers of Courts of Chancery. With an Essay on the Terms, Heir, Heirs, and Heirs of the Body.* New Haven, Conn., 1816.

———. *A Treatise on the Law of Descents in the Several States of America.* New York, 1825.

Reeves, John. *History of the Law of Shipping and Navigation.* Dublin, 1792.

Reid, John Phillip. *Controlling the Law: Legal Politics in Early National New Hampshire.* DeKalb, Ill., 2004.

———. *In Defiance of the Law: The Standing Army Controversy, the Two Constitutions, and the Coming of the American Revolution.* Chapel Hill, N.C., 1981.

Robertson, Lindsay G. *Conquest by Law: How the Discovery of America Dispossessed Indigenous Peoples of Their Lands.* New York, 2005.

Robson, David W. *Educating Republicans: The College in the Era of the American Revolution, 1750–1800.* Westport, Conn., 1985.

Roeber, A. G. *Faithful Magistrates and Republican Lawyers: Creators of Virginia Legal Culture, 1680–1810.* Chapel Hill, N.C., 1981.

Ross, Richard J. "The Legal Past of Early New England: Notes for the Study of Law, Legal Culture, and Intellectual History." *William and Mary Quarterly,* 3rd ser., 50 (January 1993): 28–41.

Rowe, Gary D. "The Sound of Silence: *United States v. Hudson & Goodwin,* the Jeffersonian Ascendancy, and the Abolition of Federal Common Law Crimes." *Yale Law Journal* 101 (1992): 919–48.

Royster, Charles. *The Fabulous History of the Great Dismal Swamp Company.* New York, 1999.

Ryerson, Richard. *The Revolution Is Now Begun: The Radical Committees of Philadelphia, 1765–1776.* Philadelphia, 1978.

Sack, Saul. "Student Life in the Nineteenth Century." *Pennsylvania Magazine of History and Biography* 85, no. 3 (1961): 255–88.

Sakolski, A. M. *The Great American Land Bubble: The Amazing Story of Land-Grabbing, Speculations, and Booms from Colonial Days to the Present Time.* 1932. Reprint, New York, 1966.

Salmon, Marylynn. *Women and the Law of Property in Early America.* Chapel Hill, N.C., 1986.

Sampson, William. *Sampson's Discourse, and Correspondence with Various Learned Jurists upon the History of the Law, with the Addition of Several Essays, Tracts, and Documents, Relating to the Subject.* Edited and compiled by Pishey Thompson. Washington, D.C., 1826.

Schafer, Judith Kelleher. *Slavery, the Civil Law, and the Supreme Court of Louisiana.* Baton Rouge, La., 1994.

Scheckel, Susan. *The Insistence of the Indian: Race and Nationalism in Nineteenth-Century American Culture.* Princeton, N.J., 1998.

Schultz, David. "Political Theory and Legal History: Conflicting Depictions of Property in the American Political Founding." *American Journal of Legal History* 37 (October 1993): 464–95.

Scott, Robert Morton. "St. George Tucker and the Development of American Culture in Early Federal Virginia, 1790–1824." Ph.D. diss., George Washington University, 1991.

Shammas, Carole. *A History of Household Government in America.* Charlottesville, Va., 2002.

Sheehan, Bernard W. *Seeds of Extinction: Jeffersonian Philanthropy and the American Indian.* New York, 1974.

Shepard, E. Lee. "Breaking into the Profession: Establishing a Law Practice in Antebellum Virginia." *Journal of Southern History* 48 (August 1982): 393–410.

———. "Lawyers Look at Themselves: Professional Consciousness and the Virginia Bar, 1770–1850." *American Journal of Legal History* 25 (January 1981): 1–23.

Shoemaker, Nancy. *A Strange Likeness: Becoming Red and White in Eighteenth-Century North America.* New York, 2004.

Simon, Walter G. "The Evolution of Treason." *Tulane Law Review* 35, no. 4 (1961): 667–704.

Snyder, Terri L. "Legal History of the Colonial South: Assessment and Suggestions." *William and Mary Quarterly*, 3rd ser., 50 (January 1993): 18–27.

Speth, Linda E. "More Than Her 'Thirds': Wives and Widows in Colonial Virginia." *Women and History* 4 (Winter 1982): 5–41.

Stimson, Shannon C. *The American Revolution in the Law: Anglo-American Jurisprudence before John Marshall.* Princeton, N.J., 1990.

Stone, Lawrence. *The Family, Sex, and Marriage in England, 1500–1800.* London, 1977.

Story, Joseph. *Commentaries on Equity Jurisprudence.* 2 vols. Boston, 1836.

———. "Review, *A Course of Legal Study Respectfully Addressed to the Students of Law in the United States,* by David Hoffman, Professor of Law in the University of Maryland." *North American Review* 6 (1817), 45–77.

Stychin, Carl F. "The Commentaries of Chancellor James Kent and the Development of an American Common Law." *American Journal of Legal History* 37 (October 1993): 440–63.

Sullivan, James. *History of Land Titles in Massachusetts.* Boston, 1801.

Swift, Zephaniah. *An Oration on Domestic Slavery, Delivered at the North Meeting-House in Hartford, on the 12th Day of May, A.D. 1791; At the Meeting of the Connecticut Society for the Promotion of Freedom, and the Relief of Persons unlawfully holden in Bondage.* Hartford, Conn., 1791.

———. *A System of the Laws of the State of Connecticut, in Six Books.* Windham, Conn., 1795.

Taylor, Creed. *Journal of the Law School, and of the Moot Court Attached to it; at Needham, in Virginia: with an Appendix, Comprising a Variety of Precedents adapted to the proceedings of the Courts, Agreeably to the Revised Code, of 1819; and of the Pleadings in Law and Equity, with complete Records thereof.* Richmond, Va., 1822.

Tenterden, Lord Charles Abbott. *Treatise of the Law Relative to Merchant Ships and Seamen.* London, 1802.

Thompson, E. P. *Customs in Common.* New York, 1993.

Tucker, Henry St. George. *Commentaries on the Laws of Virginia, Comprising the Substance of A Course of Lectures delivered to The Winchester Law School.* 2 vols. Winchester, Va., 1831.

———. *Notes on Blackstone's Commentaries, for the Use of Students.* Winchester, Va., 1826.

Tucker, St. George. *Blackstone's Commentaries: With Notes of Reference to the Constitution and Laws of the United States and of the Commonwealth of Virginia: With an Appendix to Each Volume, Containing Short Tracts upon Such Subjects as Appeared Necessary to Form a Connected View of the Laws of Virginia as a Member of the Federal Union.* 5 vols. Philadelphia, 1803. Reprint, Chicago, 1986.

———. *Reflections on the Cession of Louisiana to the United States.* Washington, D.C., 1803.

Tucker, St. George, and Jeremy Belknap. "Queries Respecting the Slavery and Emancipation of Negroes in Massachusetts, Proposed by the Hon. Judge Tucker of Virginia, and Answered by the Rev. Dr. Belknap." In *Collections of the Massachusetts Historical Society,* 1st ser., vol. 4, 1795. Reprint, Boston, 1835.

"University Notes," August 5, 1829. In *The Virginia Literary Museum and Journal of Belles Lettres, Arts, Sciences, &c.,* edited at the University of Virginia. Charlottesville, Va., 1830.

VanBurkleo, Sandra Frances, "That Our Pure Republican Principles Might Not Wither": Kentucky's Relief Crisis and the Pursuit of 'Moral Justice,' 1818–1826." Ph.D. diss., University of Minnesota, 1988.

Vattel, Emmerich de. *Droits des gens.* Translated by Charles G. Fenwick. Washington, D.C., 1916.

Waldstreicher, David. *In the Midst of Perpetual Fetes: The Making of American Nationalism, 1776–1820.* Chapel Hill, N.C., 1997.

Walsh, Lorena S. "'Till Death Us Do Part': Marriage and Family in Seventeenth-Century Maryland, 1658–1705." In *The Chesapeake in the Seventeenth Century: Essays on Anglo-American Society and Politics,* edited by Thad Tate and David Ammerman. New York, 1979.

Walsh, Lorena S., and Russell Menard. "Death in the Chesapeake: Two Life Tables for Men in Early Colonial Maryland." *Maryland Historical Magazine* 69 (Summer 1974): 211–27.

Warden, Lewis C. *The Life of Blackstone.* Charlottesville, Va., 1938.

Waterman, Julius S. "Thomas Jefferson and Blackstone's *Commentaries.*" *Illinois Law Review* 27 (1933): 629–55.

Watson, Alan. *The Evolution of the Law.* Baltimore, 1985.

———. *Slave Law in the Americas.* Athens, Ga., 1989.

———. "The Structure of Blackstone's Commentaries." *Yale Law Review* 97 (1988): 795–821.

Weir, Robert M. *Colonial South Carolina: A History.* Millwood, N.Y., 1983.

———. "Conservation, Class, and Controversy in Early America." In *Cultures and Identities in Colonial American Society,* edited by Alan Tully and Robert Olwell. Baltimore, 2005.

White, G. Edward. "Symposium: The Chancellor's Ghost." *Chicago-Kent Law Review* 74 (1988): 254–62.

Wiebe, Robert H. *The Opening of American Society: From the Adoption of the Constitution to the Eve of Disunion.* New York, 1984.

Wiecek, William M. *Liberty under Law: The Supreme Court in American Life.* Baltimore, 1998.

———. "*Somerset*: Lord Mansfield and the Legitimacy of Slavery in the Anglo-American World." *University of Chicago Law Review* 42 (Autumn 1974): 86–146.

Wilkinson, Charles F. *American Indians, Time, and the Law: Native Societies in a Modern Constitutional Democracy.* New Haven, Conn., 1987.

Williams, Penry. *The Tudor Regime.* Oxford, 1979.

Williams, Robert A., Jr. *The American Indian in Western Legal Thought: The Discourses of Conquest.* New York, 1990.

Willman, Robert. "Blackstone and the 'Theoretical Perfection' of English Law in the Reign of Charles II." *Historical Journal* 26 (March 1983): 39–70.

Wills, Garry. "James Wilson's New Meaning for Sovereignty." In *Conceptual Change and the Constitution,* edited by Terence Ball and J. G. A Pocock. Lawrence, Kans., 1988.

Wilson, James. *The Works of James Wilson.* Edited by Robert Green McCloskey. 2 vols. Cambridge, Mass., 1967.

Wolfe, Christopher. *The Rise of Modern Judicial Review: From Constitutional Interpretation to Judge-Made Law.* New York, 1986.

Wood, Gordon. *The Creation of the American Republic, 1776–1787.* New York, 1969.

———. *The Radicalism of the American Revolution.* New York, 1993.

Zagarri, Rosemarie. "The Rights of Man and Woman in Post-Revolutionary America." *William and Mary Quarterly,* 3rd ser., 55 (April 1998): 203–30.

Zilversmit, Arthur. *The First Emancipation: The Abolition of Slavery in the North.* Chicago, 1967.

———. "Quok Walker, Mumbet, and the Abolition of Slavery in Massachusetts." *William and Mary Quarterly,* 3rd ser., 25 (October 1968): 614–24.

Zuckerman, Michael. "Exceptionalism After All: Or, The Perils of Postcolonialism." *William and Mary Quarterly,* 3rd ser., 64 (April 2007): 259–62.

Index

Jeffersonian America

Jan Ellen Lewis and Peter S. Onuf, editors
Sally Hemings and Thomas Jefferson: History, Memory, and Civic Culture

Peter S. Onuf
Jefferson's Empire: The Language of American Nationhood

Catherine Allgor
Parlor Politics: In Which the Ladies of Washington Help Build a City and a Government

Jeffrey L. Pasley
"The Tyranny of Printers": Newspaper Politics in the Early American Republic

Herbert E. Sloan
Principle and Interest: Thomas Jefferson and the Problem of Debt (reprint)

James Horn, Jan Ellen Lewis, and Peter S. Onuf, editors
The Revolution of 1800: Democracy, Race, and the New Republic

Phillip Hamilton
The Making and Unmaking of a Revolutionary Family: The Tuckers of Virginia, 1752–1830

Robert M. S. McDonald, editor
Thomas Jefferson's Military Academy: Founding West Point

Martha Tomhave Blauvelt
The Work of the Heart: Young Women and Emotion, 1780–1830

Francis D. Cogliano
Thomas Jefferson: Reputation and Legacy

Albrecht Koschnik
"Let a Common Interest Bind Us Together": Associations, Partisanship, and Culture in Philadelphia, 1775–1840

John Craig Hammond
Slavery, Freedom, and Expansion in the Early American West, 1787–1820

David Andrew Nichols
Red Gentlemen and White Savages: Indians, Federalists, and the Search for Order on the American Frontier

Douglas Bradburn
The Citizenship Revolution: Politics and the Creation of the American Union, 1774–1804

Clarence E. Walker
Mongrel Nation: The America Begotten by Thomas Jefferson and Sally Hemings

Timothy Mason Roberts
Distant Revolutions: 1848 and the Challenge to American Exceptionalism

Peter J. Kastor and François Weil, editors
Empires of the Imagination: Transatlantic Histories of the Louisiana Purchase

Eran Shalev
Rome Reborn on Western Shores: Historical Imagination and the Creation of the American Republic

Leonard J. Sadosky
Revolutionary Negotiations: Indians, Empires, and Diplomats in the Founding of America

Philipp Ziesche
Cosmopolitan Patriots: Americans in Paris in the Age of Revolution

Leonard J. Sadosky, Peter Nicolaisen, Peter S. Onuf, and Andrew J. O'Shaughnessy, editors
Old World, New World: America and Europe in the Age of Jefferson

Sam W. Haynes
Unfinished Revolution: The American Republic in a British World, 1815–1850

Michal Jan Rozbicki
Culture and Liberty in the Age of the American Revolution

Ellen Holmes Pearson
Remaking Custom: Law and Identity in the Early American Republic